AMERICAN

BREAD

AMERICAN BREAD

A CALENDAR OF AMERICAN
HEROES AND VILLAINS,
BIOGRAPHIES FOR EACH DAY OF THE YEAR
along with
CHANTS, PRAYERS, SONGS
AND CELEBRATIONS

written and otherwise assembled by
DON BROPHY

PAULIST PRESS
Paramus, N.J. / New York / Toronto

INTRODUCTION

Stated simply, this book is a way of reflecting on the American experience in the light of religion and myth. It is a celebration of the people who gave character to our country, arranged so that each day marks an anniversary in some person's life.

Readers who don't come from a liturgical religious tradition may find this presentation puzzling. They may accept the biographical part of it but feel uncomfortable with the scripture readings and prayers that follow. They may even feel the "religious" side of it is forced and unconvincing. If any of you feel that way, I would urge you simply to accept the prayers as a literary form in much the same way you might accept a sonnet or an epic poem as a literary form. Don't let the conventions of the form disturb you. In the long run you will find that the prayer form opens up more doors than it closes. It gives us a different way of speaking and thinking about our experience.

Those readers who do come from a liturgical tradition will recognize the style of this book immediately. It is modeled after the "calendar of the saints" for the Christian liturgical year—in which each saint was given his or her own feast day, with some special prayers that could be inserted into the mass for that day. It is a device Christians have used to keep their history close at hand.

Mircea Eliade points out that religious man tends to use two kinds of time: historical time and sacred time. Historical time moves in a linear pattern toward the future, in the process of which past events recede farther and farther into the past. Sacred time, on the other hand, is circular, reversible, and recoverable. Like the liturgical calendar, it can repeat itself. The point of contact between these two time-modes is found in ritual. "By means of rites," says Eliade, "religious man can pass without danger from ordinary temporal duration to sacred time." In other words, ritual can make the past become present without loosening the worshiper's grip on his own world. To the believing Christian Jesus is not just "remembered" in the eucharist, he is "present." In a similar way the saint or past hero becomes more "present" in a ritual (for instance on his feast day) than he does simply by our reading about him in a book. In ritual prayer the past and the present are rolled together in one ball, enabling us—the people of the present time—to break bread with the heroes of old.

This goes to explain why this book has taken the form it has. The idea was to create a sense of myth and mystery so the past could be brought within our reach once more. The calendar of American people and the use of prayer formulas from the Christian eucharistic service help to reinforce the feeling of sacred time. It is not a parody. It is a way of taking history seriously.

However, there may be some people—different from the group noted previously—who believe this book *is* a parody. They may object to the fact that many people celebrated on these pages are clearly not saints. And they may object to the larger idea of taking prayer forms long reserved for hallowed occasions and applying them to "secular" history.

To this second group of people I can only speak of my personal belief which lies at the foundation of this book. The belief holds that we, as a people, are good. And because we are good the past—all the past—is holy, because the past has made us into what we are. Belief in our own goodness frees us to look at history without blinking, facing up to our weaknesses with a sense of joy. The past is holy because it is our womb.

Once we believe in ourselves it becomes possible to look at history in a nonjudgmental way. Of course we can still have opinions about people and events. We can disapprove of past actions, but we no longer disapprove as persons who stand outside the process. Like it or not, we Americans have been shaped by Al Capone just as we have been shaped by Abraham Lincoln. Al and Abe are coursing through our blood. We cannot rid ourselves of one and keep the other. We can exorcise our evil spirits only by placing our own existence and our identity in peril.

It is precisely at this point that the religious vision provides relief for the time-traveler. Because most religions have an eschatological thrust—a promise of future reconciliation that presupposes history is evolving in a positive direction. We believe we are good because we believe we are part of this process. History has been lifted up in us. The patchwork of the past is reconciled and harmonized in our "now"; even those evil strains that are a part of our heritage have lost their virulence in our bloodstream.

This is not a utopian ideal. It doesn't claim that the present moment is perfect. If anything, it says that the present moment is imperfect, because we are only midway on our journey. If today is an improvement over yesterday, the future promises to see an even greater rising and converging of human history.

In closing, a few words should be said about the way names were selected for this calendar. All the persons included are deceased Americans, except for a few explorers and early missionaries who were not American. A few native-born Americans who chose to work outside the United States (such as Whistler, Henry James, and T.S. Eliot) were omitted, as were naturalized Americans like Einstein and Stravinsky whose greatest accomplishments were realized before they came to this country. There was a conscious effort to include people who had a broad impact on popular culture and to exclude those who spoke for a small elite. This explains why Horatio Alger and Zane Grey got in and William Dean Howells did not. Finally, there are many names that belong on this list but which could not be included because of space limitations or conflicts over dates.

JANUARY

January 1

PAUL REVERE

"Listen, my children, and you shall hear of the midnight ride of Paul Revere." Paul Revere was a gold- and silversmith in Boston, born there on New Year's Day in 1735. He was a pioneer in the copper plating industry. He was also a propagandist, a patriot, a soldier, and a civic leader. But mostly Revere is remembered for that ride in April of '75, immortalized by Longfellow, to warn the citizens of Lexington and Concord that British troops were marching. "To every Middlesex village and farm—a cry of defiance, and not of fear, a voice in the darkness, a knock at the door, and a word that shall echo for evermore!"

PROCESSIONAL: *Is 52, 1-2* Awake, awake, put on your strength, O Zion . . . Shake yourself from the dust, arise, O captive Jerusalem; loose the bonds from your neck, O captive daughter of Zion. *Ps 44, 23-24* Rouse thyself! Why sleepest thou, O Lord? Awake! Do not cast us off forever! Why dost thou hide thy face? Why dost thou forget our affliction and oppression?

COMMUNION: In haste have we been summoned to this place, not daring to sit as the bread is broken in our midst. Overhead a shadow gallops in the night, leaving in its passing death, and perhaps, beyond that, freedom.

January 2

PHILIP FRENEAU

Philip Freneau was probably America's first national poet, the first writer to identify himself with national rather than sectional or denominational loyalties. During the Revolutionary War Freneau's satirical pieces aimed at the British did much to maintain the spirit of the patriot cause. He spent most of his time at sea as a privateer and merchant captain, or farming at his New Jersey estate. Freneau was born on Jan. 2, 1752, and he died in 1832.

OFFERTORY: Receive, Lord God, in this day of chaos, with the world turned upside down, these fragile gifts, these fragile words. To us they seem inadequate when confronted by such need. But in your keeping may our words still live, may our gestures offer healing, long after more solid gifts have been consumed.

RECESSIONAL: An age employed in edging steel/Can no poetic raptures feel;/No solitude's attracting power,/No leisure of the noon day hour,/No shaded stream, no quiet grove/Can this fantastic century move.*

January 3

LUCRETIA MOTT

Lucretia Mott was born Jan. 3, 1973, in Massachusetts and studied at a school run by the Society of Friends. In time she was accepted as a Quaker minister, and she traveled the country preaching religion and social reform. She received two rebuffs that changed her life: First she was shunned by the Quakers because she championed the abolition of slaves; then she was shunned by the world antislavery conference in London because she was a woman. In 1848 with Elizabeth Cady Stanton she helped found the women's rights movement at Seneca Falls, N.Y. and was the movement's most effective spokesperson for the next 30 years until her death.

PROCESSIONAL: *Gen 24, 60* "Our sister, be the mother of thousands of ten thousands; and may your descendents possess the gate of those who hate them." *Wis 7, 11-12* All good things came to me along with her, and in her hands uncounted wealth. I rejoiced in them all, because wisdom leads them.

PETITION: If you would take us, Lord, take all of us; don't take just our virtues or just our souls. Embrace our accidents as well: the timbre of our voices, the contours of our hair, our color, and our sex. What has caused us so much anguish putting all together we will not let you casually divide.

January 4

ELIZABETH BAYLEY SETON

Elizabeth Seton was born in 1774 to a wealthy New York family. After

*From "To An Author" by Philip Freneau.

the death of her husband she resolved to enter the Roman Catholic Church, even though it meant abandoning her friends and relatives and the comfortable life of her youth. Moving to Baltimore, she established a school for girls and gathered a group of helpers who organized themselves into a community of nuns under her direction. Mother Seton and her Sisters of Charity were instrumental in laying the foundation of the parochial school system in the United States. She died on Jan. 4, 1821 and was declared a saint by Pope Paul VI in 1975.

OFFERTORY: This gift, Lord God, is made without condition; everything is risked, nothing held back. We do not disavow our history, but we are no longer able to return, and do not wish to anyhow. See, the cup of our days is totally poured out, leaving only faith that you will fill it up again.

COMMUNION: *Sir 1, 19* He saw her and apportioned her; he rained down knowledge and discerning comprehension, and he exalted the glory of those who held her fast.

January 5

CALVIN COOLIDGE

Calvin Coolidge was the only American President to have a policy of dynamic idleness. As Irving Stone said of him: "He was an incorruptible man; all his sins were sins of omission." Coolidge became President after several undistinguished years as a Massachusetts legislator, lieutenant governor, and governor, capped by two undistinguished years as vice president under Harding. His chief occupation at the White House was taking a nap each afternoon, and his most trenchant political observation was that "the business of America is business." Coolidge was born in 1872; he died on Jan. 5, 1933.

PETITION: God watch over Calvin as he sleeps in glory, because we watched him while he slept on earth. And yet preserve him too—as we might keep a teddy bear cherished from our youth; once he gave us comfort when what we needed was prodding. For those familiarities we honor him; for his failures we have long since paid the price.

RECESSIONAL: *Eccles 5, 2* Be not rash with your mouth, nor let your heart be hasty to utter a word before God, for God is in heaven, and you upon earth; therefore let your words be few.

January 6

CARL SANDBURG

Carl Sandburg was born in Galesburg, Ill. on Jan. 6, 1878, the son of a blacksmith who had emigrated from Sweden. Sandburg worked his way through college, accepting many different jobs that taught him what hard work was like. For a time he dabbled in socialist politics, and later he took a job as an editor of the Chicago *Daily News*. Sandburg's *Chicago Poems* were published in 1916, establishing him as a forceful and skillful user of the American idiom. Like Whitman, Sandburg believed in the intuitive rightness of the common man and the vitality of simple labor. Sandburg won two Pulitzer Prizes, one for his six-volume biography of Lincoln. He died in North Carolina in 1967.

PROCESSIONAL: The people will live on./The learning and blundering people will live on./They will be tricked and sold and again sold/And go back to the nourishing earth for rootholds . . .* *Ps 33, 12* Blessed is the nation whose God is the Lord, the people whom he has chosen as his heritage!

COMMUNION: I asked professors who teach the meaning of life to tell me what is happiness./And I went to famous executives who boss the work of thousands of men./They all shook their heads and gave me a smile as though I was trying to fool with them./And then one Sunday afternoon I wandered out along the Desplaines river/And I saw a crowd of Hungarians under the trees with their women and children and a keg of beer and an accordion.*

January 7

NIKOLA TESLA

Nikola Tesla was second only to Edison among the inventive wizards of electronics in the 19th and 20th centuries. Working mostly by himself, Tesla claimed more than 700 patents for devices such as the telephone repeater, synchronous and split-phase motors, several kinds of oscillators, and the Tesla coil. In 1893, three years before Marconi's patent, Tesla designed a wireless telegraph system. Tesla came to the United States from his native Yugoslavia in 1883 and lived most of his life on Long Island. He died on Jan. 7, 1943.

PETITION: From the moment of creation you, God, poured invisible powers upon the earth. Now give us sense and ingenuity like that of your

*Excerpt from "The People Will Live On" taken from *The People, Yes* by Carl Sandburg, © 1936 by Harcourt Brace Jovanovich, Inc.; © 1964 by Carl Sandburg. The poem "Happiness" is taken from *Chicago Poems* by Carl Sandburg © 1916 by Holt, Rinehart and Winston, Inc.; © 1944 by Carl Sandburg. Both reprinted by permission of Harcourt Brace Jovanovich, Inc.

son Nikola that we may search them out in their hidden places and use them for the welfare of all your people.

RECESSIONAL: *1 Cor 12, 4-6* There are varieties of gifts, but the same Spirit; and there are varieties of service, but the same Lord; and there are varieties of working, but it is the same God who inspires them all in every one.

January 8

JOHN CARROLL

John Carroll, the first American bishop of the Catholic Church, came from a well-known Maryland family (his brother was a signer of the Declaration of Independence). Carroll took his education in Europe. Ordained, he found himself thrown into the American revolution, accompanying Benjamin Franklin on a diplomatic mission to Canada and working to rally Catholics to the patriot cause. Carroll became bishop of Baltimore in 1789, the same year in which he founded a college later called Georgetown. He did much in his remaining years to build up his small communion and to dispel the residue of suspicion still directed toward it. He was born this day in 1735; he died in 1815.

PROCESSIONAL: *Sir 45, 24* A covenant of peace was established with him, that he should be leader of the sanctuary and of his people, that he and his descendants should have the dignity of the priesthood for ever. *Ps 89, 29* I will establish his line for ever and his throne as the days of the heavens.

OFFERTORY: Because we give you presents, God, it doesn't mean that we will hold back gifts from others. We have loyalties on several levels; you can't expect us to ignore the rest of them for you. Receive these gifts; we give them to you gladly. But grant us leave to share what we have left with other friends. And yet be with us on that day when offerings are few, and we must choose between our friends and you.

January 9

EDWARD BOK

Edward Bok was one of America's best known and most successful editors —the man who pioneered the modern women's magazine. After starting with the Scribner's Publishing Co., Bok in 1887 became editor of the faltering *Ladies' Home Journal* and quickly swept it clean of the pristine narrowmindedness which people of the day thought beneficial to women. Bok hired first-rate authors like Twain and Kipling, and offered his readers articles on such scandalous subjects as venereal disease and women's sufferage. His autobiography, *The Americanization of Edward Bok,* won the Pulitzer Prize in 1921. He died on Jan. 9, 1930.

PETITION: Don't look down your fine semitic nose at us, Lord God, or couch your word in euphemisms for our ears. Be our Father if you must, but leave machismo to the likes of Baal or Odin. Your son Edward spoke to men and women with equal dignity. Treat us with the same respect. If not, we'll come to think that our position requires us to spare you frankness in return.

January 10

ISAAC JOGUES

Isaac Jogues was born in Orleans, France, on Jan. 10, 1607, and he died 39 years later in what is now New York state, tortured and finally murdered by Mohawk indians. Jogues came to the new world as a Jesuit missionary, a job which in those days required him to be also a woodsman and explorer. He was the first missionary to reach Michigan, and the first European to see Lake George. At one time he was captured by the Iroquois and tortured, but was ransomed by the Dutch at Albany. He returned to Canada and to martyrdom in 1646. Jogues was formally declared a saint of the Roman Catholic Church in 1930.

PROCESSIONAL: *Is 58, 10* If you pour yourself out for the hungry and satisfy the desire of the afflicted, then shall your light rise in the darkness and your gloom be as the noonday. *Ps 36, 7-9* How precious is thy steadfast love, O God! The children of men take refuge in the shadow of thy wings . . . Thou givest them drink from the river of thy delights. For with thee is the fountain of life; in thy light do we see light.

OFFERTORY: Our gift have been poured out upon the barren earth. We have nothing to show for all our efforts. Only in faith can we perceive roots twining in the soil. Even your greatest gifts, Lord God, you keep hidden from our eyes.

January 11

FRANCIS SCOTT KEY

Francis Scott Key was a Washington lawyer in 1814 when James Madison asked him to arrange for the release of a friend captured by British troops. During the mission Key was himself detained on an enemy ship while the British bombarded Fort McHenry in Baltimore. Through the night of Sept. 13-14 he watched anxiously to see whether the American fort would haul down its colors, and rejoiced the next morning to see the flag still there. The poem he wrote to mark that occasion was later set to music and became his country's national anthem. Key died on Jan. 11, 1843.

PROCESSIONAL: *Is 26, 9* My soul yearns for thee in the night, my spirit within me earnestly seeks thee. For when thy judgments are in the earth, the inhabitants of the world learn righteousness. *Response:* What is that which the breeze, o'er the towering steep,/As it fitfully blows, half conceals, half discloses?/Now it catches the gleam of the morning's first beam./In full glory reflected now shines in the stream:/'Tis the star-spangled banner! O long may it wave/O'er the land of the free and the home of the brave!*

COMMUNION: In darkness we wait for you, Lord. With dread and longing we wait for the coming of your light.

January 12

JACK LONDON

Jack London was born in San Francisco on Jan. 12, 1876, grew up in poverty, and quit school to go to sea. For a number of years he knocked around, did odd jobs, lived as a hobo, went to Alaska for the gold rush, and dipped into philosophy. In 1900 he published the first of his stories that were to make him rich and famous. With novels such as *Call of the Wild* and *The Sea Wolf*, he helped to glorify the rugged individualism of his age. In his head London was a socialist, but in his gut a raw primitive, and his primitive instincts won out in the struggle. London died of an overdose of morphine at his California ranch in 1916.

PETITION: Father keep us in touch with all of our parts. We are not simply constructs of mind and will, pretty two-layered people all balanced and ordered. We are earth and fire and water and air. Inside us we have subterranean courses, unseen but felt, plunging and leaping, neither evil nor good—pure energy only. Teach us to utilize all these resources. Keep us in touch with all of our forces.

*From "The Star Spangled Banner" by Francis Scott Key.

RECESSIONAL: *Is 11, 6, 9* The wolf shall dwell with the lamb, and the leopard shall lie down with the kid, and the calf and the lion and the fatling together . . . They shall not hurt or destroy in all my holy mountain; for the earth shall be full of the knowledge of the Lord as the waters cover the sea.

January 13

STEPHEN FOSTER

Stephen Foster was born in Pittsburgh and lived most of his life there. That probably explains why the songs he wrote about the old south were so unreal. They were sentimental ballads that described serene plantations and obedient, kindly negroes who, if they did wander far from their place of slavery, always longed to go back there. Taken purely as music, however, Foster's songs had a universal appeal that persists to this day. Pete Seeger points out that Foster had a genius for fitting syllables to tunes. Surely no American who has heard them can ever really forget "My Old Kentucky Home," "Swanee River," or "Old Black Joe." Foster died on this day in 1864 at the age of 38.

OFFERTORY: Our hearts long for your sunlight, O Lord. Our memories reach back to the warmth of sunlight when our hearts were young. Take this sad world into your transforming fire; send your sun into our world, and make our hearts verdant and bountiful.

COMMUNION: *Ps 84, 10-11* A day in thy courts is better than a thousand elsewhere. I would rather be a doorkeeper in the house of my God than dwell in the tents of wickedness. For the Lord God is a sun and a shield; he bestows favor and honor.

January 14

HUMPHREY BOGART

Humphrey Bogart was the ultimate movie tough guy. No one else could match him. No one else could capture as well as Bogart the vulnerability that lies beneath strength, the secret softness, like a faint lisp, that gives human dimension to the man of action. His greatest films, *The Maltese Falcon*, *Key Largo*, *Casablanca*, and *The Treasure of Sierra Madre*, made Bogart into a folk hero—the man every American male would like to be: strong, quick, worldly-wise, mildly cynical, yet compassionate in spite of himself. Bogart died of cancer on this day in 1957.

15

PROCESSIONAL: *Wis 5, 18-20* He will put on righteousness as a breast-plate, and wear impartial justice as a helmet; he will take holiness as an invincible shield, and sharpen stern wrath for a sword, and creation will join with him to fight against the madmen. *Response* It's still the same old story, a fight for love and glory,/A case of do or die!/The world will always welcome lovers,/As time goes by.*

RECESSIONAL: It was nice while it lasted. We'll never forget these moments we've had. But it doesn't take much to see that the problems of a few people don't amount to a hill of beans in this crazy world. So we part, each in a different direction. We won't be ruled by yesterday. But neither will we forget it.

January 15

MATTHEW BRADY

Matthew Brady was born in New York and got involved in photography as a young man through a meeting with Samuel F. B. Morse. For a period of time in the 1840s he was in demand as a society photographer, winning several art awards and amassing considerable wealth. With the advent of the Civil War Brady invested his time and fortune into a photographic record of the war, training himself and his assistants to follow troops onto the battlefield as combat cameramen. After the war Brady grew ill, sold all his plates to pay off his debts, and died penniless in New York on Jan. 15, 1896.

OFFERTORY: You, God, are the one who gives meaning to images; receive these gifts pulled from the storehouse of memory. Our past is in disarray, picture marching after picture in no order and without direction. Take these offerings, these shadows, and give them shape; give body to them, so that we can see more clearly where we've been, and therefore be more certain who we are.

COMMUNION: *Sir 12, 7-8* He filled them with knowledge and understanding, and showed them good and evil. He set his eye upon their hearts to show them the majesty of his works.

January 16

MARSHALL FIELD

Marshall Field is the man who transformed the department-store business. Born in Massachusetts, Field was a traveling salesman in Chicago in 1861 when he opened the retail store that still bears his name. Field's store was the first to have a restaurant for customers, the first to display prices on all merchandise, and one of the first to offer credit. In addition, it had the good fortune to survive the Chicago fires of 1871 and 1877. Marshall Field died on Jan. 16, 1906 after founding a family that would provide commercial and social leadership in Chicago for three generations.

PETITION: Franchisers have been living off you for generations, God. Isn't it time you made them stop? Your problem isn't too little marketing, it's too much—and misrepresentation, and mislabeling. Come to us again as you were when you started out in life: honest goods, with no pretense, and absolutely free. We, in turn, will try to stop overcharging people for ourselves.

January 17

BENJAMIN FRANKLIN

Benjamin Franklin was born Jan. 17, 1706, in Boston, the place where he became a printer's apprentice and learned the value of hard work and success. For the remainder of his life Franklin would be the apostle of frugality and wealth as much as he was the apostle of liberty. Indeed he was much too canny to take the lead on a subject as volatile as independence, but once committed to the cause he was the indispensible cog, a Machiavelli in broadcloth, who for most Europeans represented the happy mixture of reason and simplicity that typified the American revolution. Vying for the world's respect, he was second only to Washington; in the world's affections he was second to none.

PROCESSIONAL: *Wis 7, 7-8* I prayed, and understanding was given me; I called upon God, and the spirit of wisdom came to me. I preferred her to scepters and thrones. *Ps 49, 1-3* Hear this, all peoples! Give ear, all inhabitants of the world, both low and high, rich and poor together! My mouth shall speak wisdom; the meditation of my heart shall be understanding.

RECESSIONAL: Like glistening branches stacked upon the altar the people waited, drenched in their own tears. Without expectation they waited. Then the Lord called down fire from the skies and they burst forth in flame, they burst forth in light.

January 18

TOM DOOLEY

Tom Dooley could have lived a comfortable life. He came from a well-to-do family, went to a fine college and to medical school. Given his charm and energy, he could have become a wealthy pediatrician in some residential suburb. Instead he forgot all that (or perhaps he remembered it) and went off to the mountain jungles of Laos to serve as a simple doctor for people with no medical care. He also began an international agency to bring doctors to other people in other remote areas. He established seven hospitals, wrote four books, and raised $2 million on speaking tours. Tom Dooley died of cancer on Jan. 18, 1961, one day after his 34th birthday.

OFFERTORY: Reassured by the accouterments of the sacrifice, and comforted by ritual, we ask you to bless these public presents, Lord. Indeed, do bless them. Receive this civilized routine with equanimity. But if you do, join it with offerings made this day in blood and pain, by people shorn of beauty and of grace, by people trapped in darkness, and alone. Take our gift and theirs together. Make them one, so that we will taste the bitterness of sacrifice and be nourished by what we find in it.

COMMUNION: *Eccles 11, 1-2* Cast your bread upon the waters, for you will find it after many days. Give a portion to seven, or even to eight, for you know not what evil may happen on earth.

January 19

ROBERT E. LEE

Robert E. Lee was born Jan. 19, 1807, the son of a landed Virginia family that was related by marriage to George Washington. Lee attended West Point and built an impressive army career in the west and in Mexico. Offered command of the Union army in 1860, Lee instead chose to fight with the Confederacy. In the ensuing struggle he proved himself to be a brilliant and audacious field commander, loved by his own soldiers and respected by his foes. Noble in defeat as in victory, Lee in 1865 became a college president in Virginia, remaining there until his death in 1870.

PROCESSIONAL: *Dan 11, 11-12* The king of the south shall come out and fight with the king of the north; and he shall raise a great multitude, but it shall be given into his hand. And when the multitude is taken, his heart shall be exalted, and he shall cast down tens of thousands, but he shall not prevail. *Ps 122, 6, 8-9* Pray for the peace of Jerusalem! For my brethren and companions' sake I will say, "Peace be within you!" For the sake of the house of the Lord our God, I will seek your good.

OFFERTORY: Young men shining in the brilliant sun were offered to the god of battles. He, the priest with the gentle eyes, sent them forth (marching row-on-row beneath the snapping banners) bravely to the place of slaughter. There is something beautiful in sacrifice, he said, that men must fear. The time for real weeping comes when death becomes delight.

January 20

JOHN MARSHALL

On this day in 1801, John Marshall, a Virginia patriot and legislator, was appointed Chief Justice of the United States. He served in that capacity for 34 years, elevating the court from the weakest link in the federal system to the supreme arbiter of American law. In the celebrated decision of *Marbury vs. Madison* Marshall decreed that the court could overturn the act of any other branch on the grounds of unconstitutionality. He also presided over the celebrated trial of Aaron Burr, preserving peace when that issue threatened to divide the nation. Marshall died in 1835.

PETITION: Come Lord God and rescue us who are victimized by our own handiwork. For the laws we made to illuminate our path have blinded our eyes and cause our feet to stumble. Come, bring soothing darkness. The stars that were fixed in the sky at the time of our fathers will be sufficient to keep us on our course.

COMMUNION: *Ps 72, 2, 4* May he judge thy people with righteousness, and thy poor with justice! May he defend the cause of the poor of the people, give deliverance to the needy, and crush the oppressor!

January 21

STONEWALL JACKSON

By all accounts Gen. Thomas J. Jackson was a moody, scrupulous, God-fearing man. He believed in obedience to such a degree that once when a superior officer asked Jackson to wait in his office, and then forgot about him, Jackson sat at attention all night until the officer returned. One would not expect a man like Jackson to be a creative leader. Yet he was one of the few military geniuses in American history: inflexible in defense, rapid and fierce in attack. Jackson was born on Jan. 21, 1824. In 1863 he won his greatest victory at Chancellorsville. Toward the end of the battle he rode ahead of his lines to examine the field and some of his own soldiers fired by mistake, wounding him fatally.

PROCESSIONAL: *Is 8, 14* He will become a sanctuary, and a stone of offense, and a rock of stumbling to both houses of Israel, a trap and a snare to the inhabitants of Jerusalem. *Ps 66, 3-4* "How terrible are thy deeds! So great is thy power that thy enemies cringe before thee. All the earth worships thee; they sing praises to thee, sing praises to thy name."

RECESSIONAL: We go forth not knowing if victory will follow from the struggle, or whether the way we go will take us to the sought-for destination. There is no other goal than the journey itself. Someday, unexpectedly, our path will simply halt upon a nameless river, and we shall be called across to sleep among the trees.

January 22

D. W. GRIFFITH

David W. Griffith was a pioneer in the art of making motion pictures, being the first director to use such film techniques as the fade-in and fade-out, soft focus, back lighting, rapid cutting, and the moving camera. He also helped to create the first generation of movie stars, including Douglas Fairbanks, Mary Pickford, Lillian and Dorothy Gish, and Mack Sennett. Griffith was born in La Grange, Ky. on Jan. 22, 1875. His great films like *Birth of a Nation* (produced in 1914) and *Intolerance* (1916) had a mythical quality that went beyond history to reveal the deeper currents of humanity. Griffith died in Hollywood in 1948.

OFFERTORY: You take our days at face value, unadorned by heroism, the routine of years as hard as crusts, and inside them you see freshness, life, and hope. Accept these presents one more time and change them according to your vision. And as you do, teach us, too, to see beneath appearances. Like children we shall learn to walk again, and our eyes shall learn again to see.

January 23

JOHN HANCOCK

John Hancock was one of those people who enter public life for personal advantage, but once engaged remain to serve the general good. Born Jan. 23, 1737, Hancock was a wealthy shipowner in Boston whose fortune was menaced by British taxes. He rapidly became a leader in the revolutionary movement, was chosen president of the Continental Congress, and was the first signer of the Declaration of Independence. After the war he served nine terms as governor of Massachusetts, dying in office in 1793.

PROCESSIONAL: *Is 42, 6, 9* I have given you as a covenant to the people, a light to the nations . . . Behold, the former things have come to pass, and new things I now declare. *Lev 25, 10* Proclaim liberty throughout the land to all its inhabitants.

PETITION: May it always come to pass, Lord God, that what satisfies your will serves to better our position too. Frankly we'd rather be on top than on the bottom; there's nothing particularly sacred about failure. Our only plea is this: if our best interests do diverge from yours, give us warning in advance. Then we'll have time to accept our fate with dignity, and cut our losses as we do.

January 24

JOHN A. SUTTER

John Sutter lived like a feudal lord in California in the 1840s. A Swiss soldier of fortune, Sutter established himself in an abandoned Russian castle along the Sacramento River where he raised wheat and cattle on vast acres obtained through a Spanish land grant. Then on Jan. 24, 1848 one of Sutter's foremen cleaning out the race of a sawmill found shiny particles among the gravel. It was gold. Sutter tried to keep the discovery secret, but the news leaked out. In the next year 80,000 prospectors came to California, and Sutter, unable to clear the title to his property, lost the gold, the land, the castle, and everything else.

COMMUNION: The Lord disappears as we approach him in his secret place, hidden from our sight. He touches us like a running stream, but like water he escapes our grasp.

RECESSIONAL: *Lam 4, 1-2* How the gold has grown dim, how the pure gold is changed! The holy stones lie scattered at the head of every street. The precious sons of Zion, worth their weight in fine gold, how they are reckoned as earthen pots, the work of a potter's hands!

AL CAPONE

No one ever pretended Al Capone was a nice guy. It has been estimated that 300 people died by his hand or by his orders. Capone was born in Naples in 1899, emigrated to Brooklyn as a child and moved to Chicago as a young man already involved in the rackets. He took over the Torrio mob in 1925, and he eliminated his chief competitors, the Bugs Moran gang, in a memorable massacre on St. Valentine's day four years later. Federal agents finally got him for income tax evasion in 1931. Released from jail in 1939 he moved to Miami Beach where on Jan. 25, 1946, he died of a heart attack, complicated by syphillis, a millionaire.

PROCESSIONAL: *Job 24, 14, 17* The murderer rises in the dark, that he may kill the poor and needy; and in the night he is as a thief. For deep darkness is morning to all of them; for they are friends with the terrors of deep darkness. *Ps 71, 4-5* Rescue me, O my God, from the hand of the wicked, from the grasp of the unjust and cruel man. For thou, O Lord, art my hope.

OFFERTORY: Receive these presents, God, as payment of protection against the terrors that creep through the alleys of the night seeking to overthrow our hearts. We are, each of us, gardens harboring vipers. Just as our parents partook of good and evil, may we by this food discover if not innocence once more, then safety, and a sleep that is free of demons.

DOUGLAS MACARTHUR

His friends considered him a god. His detractors said he was vain and self-serving. He was Douglas MacArthur, born Jan. 26, 1845, the highest-ranking student ever to graduate from West Point, the youngest chief of staff in Army history, and one of its ablest leaders. MacArthur had a contempt for politics that is endemic to men who achieve their ends by force. And yet his greatest triumph may have been political: when he introduced western-style democracy to Japan after World War II. MacArthur was an enigma in his time: a proud, posturing, and arrogant man who had moments of real compassion. He is an enigma still today.

PROCESSIONAL: *Is 13, 11* I will punish the world for its evil, and the wicked for their iniquity; I will put an end to the pride of the arrogant, and lay low the haughtiness of the ruthless. *Ps 144, 1-2* Blessed be the

Lord, my rock, who trains my hands for war, and my fingers for battle; my rock and my fortress, my stronghold and my deliverer, my shield and he in whom I take refuge, who subdues the peoples under him.

RECESSIONAL: Today the guns are silent. A great tragedy has ended. A great victory has been won. The skies no longer rain death—the seas bear only commerce—men everywhere walk upright in the sunlight. The entire world lies quietly at peace. The holy mission has been completed.*

January 27

JAMES G. BLAINE

James G. Blaine was one of the most powerful and enduring politicians of his era, serving as a Member of Congress from Maine, as a United States Senator, as secretary of state under Garfield and Benjamin Harrison, and as an unsuccessful candidate for the presidency in 1884. Blaine was largely responsible for casting the shadow of American power over the Caribbean, and the shadow of the Republican party over Maine—conditions from which neither the Caribbean nor Maine has completely recovered to this day. Blaine was born in 1830, and he died on Jan. 27, 1893.

PETITION: Enlighten us, Lord God, whose job it is to counsel, who are expected to be wise but who know too well our failing. We are like parents rocking children in the night, frightened of the darkness in our own hearts. Your people are fragile crutches for each other. Come to our support, we pray, so that if weakness is to be our nature, then weakness shall also be our glory.

January 28

JACKSON POLLACK

Jackson Pollack was born Jan. 28, 1912 in Cody, Wyo. but spent most of his adult life in New York where he went to study at the Art Students' League. He was steered toward representational painting. Rejecting that, Pollack developed his own style of abstract art, laying large canvases on the floor and pouring, dripping, and spattering paint on them, sometimes adding sand and other materials. Pollack's highly personalized and emo-

---

*Douglas MacArthur, address of Sept. 2, 1945, after the signing of the Japanese surrender.

tional style was one of the most significant turns in 20th century art and inspired many followers in the school of abstract expressionism. Pollack died in an automobile accident in 1956.

OFFERTORY: Out of our deepest reservoirs we bring forth gifts into the daylight. Don't ask us in advance what they will be, for giving in its purest form is by necessity astonishment for you and us alike. Instead receive them simply, so that spread upon your altar they will arrange themselves in meaning—a pattern that reveals worth in them, and in ourselves.

COMMUNION: *Ps 139, 13-14* Thou didst form my inward parts, thou didst knit me together in my mother's womb. I praise thee, for thou art fearful and wonderful. Wonderful are thy works!

January 29

ROBERT FROST

Robert Frost was born in San Francisco in 1874 but lived most of his life in New England, mainly in rural Vermont. To his public he was a genial sage who wrote folksy poetry in language easy to understand. This was a façade manufactured by Frost whose family life was marred by suicide and madness and whose personality could also embrace deliberate cruelty and anguished self-doubt. His poetry, apparently so simple on the surface, had depths that transcended their homely surroundings and earned for Frost recognition as one of the great poets of the English language. He died on Jan. 29, 1963.

COMMUNION: I have been one acquainted with the night./I have walked out in rain—and back in rain./I have outwalked the furthest city light./I have looked down the saddest city lane./I have passed the watchman on his beat/And dropped my eyes, unwilling to explain./I have stood still and stopped the sound of feet/When far away an interrupted cry/Came over houses from another street,/But not to call me back or say good-bye;/And further still at un unearthly height,/One luminary clock against the sky/Proclaimed the time was neither wrong nor right./I have been one acquainted with the night.*

*"Acquainted With the Night" from *The Poetry of Robert Frost* edited by Edward Connery Lathem. Copyright 1928, © 1969 by Holt, Rinehart and Winston, Inc.,© 1956 by Robert Frost. Reprinted by permission of Holt, Rinehart and Winston, Publishers.

January 30

Betsy Ross

Betsy Ross was a seamstress living on Arch Street in Philadelphia in 1777 when, according to legend, a delegation from Congress asked her to make a flag with stars and stripes for the Continental army. It is said she so impressed George Washington by showing how to make a five-pointed star with a single cut of her scissors that he discarded plans for a six-pointed star. The Betsy Ross legend is largely discredited today. However the fact of her existence is not. She did make flags for the government, and she lived to the ripe old age of 84, dying on Jan. 30, 1836.

PETITION: Give honor to your daughter Betsy, honor more than ever. Even if she didn't make the flag, she provided garments to keep her people warm. There will always be those who say banners are important and clothes are not, but your design, Lord God, puts people's welfare above the good of any cause. So give honor to your daughter Betsy. Her work was holy.

COMMUNION: *Is 49, 22* Behold I will lift up my hand to the nations, and raise my signal to the peoples; and they shall bring your sons in their bosom, and your daughters shall be carried on their shoulders.

January 31

Thomas Merton

Thomas Merton's life opened out like a series of connected rooms, each one brighter and more spacious than the one before it. Merton was born Jan. 31, 1915 of American parents in southern France, and was educated in France, England, and the United States. He was a sensitive and aimless youth; he wrote poetry, novels, and joined the Communist party. In 1939 he became a Catholic and two years later entered the contemplative order of Trappists. An autobiographical account of his conversion was published as *The Seven Storey Mountain* in 1948. Over the next 20 years he emerged as a popular and profound spiritual writer who was able to combine ancient religious values with a frank awareness of the condition of 20th-century man. He wrote about racial justice as easily as he wrote about meditation. In his later years he became interested in eastern spirituality. While on a trip to Bangkok in 1968 to confer with Buddhist monks he met with an accident and was killed.

OFFERTORY: What we keep for ourselves will never be new again. In surrender we discover change. Receive these gifts, God; we treasure them too much to hide them. In your fire they will become transformed, and we who touch their newness will find power in ourselves to change as well.

RECESSIONAL: The whole/World is secretely on fire. The stones/Burn, even the stones/They burn me. How can a man be still or/Listen to all things burning? How can he dare/To sit with them when/All their silence/Is on fire?*

*Excerpt from "In Silence" from *The Strange Islands* by Thomas Merton, © 1957 by the Abbey of Gethsemani, Inc. Reprinted by permission of New Directions Publishing Corporation.

FEBRUARY

February 1

MATTHEW MAURY

Matthew Maury is considered to be the founder of the modern science of oceanography. A Virginian by birth, he was an employee of the U.S. Navy in 1855 when his pioneering work *The Physical Geography of the Sea* was published. He subsequently represented the United States at the first international conference on the oceans. During the Civil War Maury was an agent for the Confederate States in England, but he returned to Virginia in 1868 to accept a chair of science at V.M.I. He died on Feb. 1, 1873.

COMMUNION: *Ps 46, 2-3* We will not fear though the earth should change, though the mountains shake in the heart of the sea; though its waters roar and foam, though the mountains tremble with its tumult.

RECESSIONAL: Your food, Lord, is like purest air that engulfs our chambers and lets us go deep—lets us go deep, past the mountains of memory and into the darkness, to grapple there with the slithery beast, to wallow in the primal mud where the answer and the mystery are bound together. Your food, Lord, is like purest air.

February 2

JOHN L. SULLIVAN

John L. Sullivan was born in Boston in 1859 and became a prizefighter at the age of 19. In 1882 he knocked out Paddy Ryan to become heavyweight champion of the world, a title he held with great visibility for ten years during the golden closing decade of the 19th century. A bareknuckle fighter, Sullivan once went 75 rounds in defense of his championship. Finally dethroned by "Gentleman Jim" Corbett, Sullivan spent his remaining years as a vaudeville performer, bar owner, and (after his conversion) as a temperance lecturer. He died on this day in 1918.

PETITION: Father, you who give strength to arms and strength to nations, help us to use our present strength wisely, so that in the reign of the new victor we may not be hated for our deeds, or be the butt of jokes, a laughingstock in public places. Give us the kind of strength that lives in the spirit, even when it ebbs from the body.

COMMUNION: *Ps 29, 11* May the Lord give strength to his people! May the Lord bless his people with peace!

February 3

HORACE GREELEY

Born of a poor New Hampshire family on Feb. 3, 1811, and having little formal education, Horace Greeley grew to be one of the great opinion-shapers of his time, being the founder of the New York *Tribune* and one of the founders of the Republican party. Greeley was a staunch abolitionist before the Civil War, but an equally strong advocate of clemency for Southern leaders after the war. Critical of the Grant administration, he was nominated by the Democrats to oppose Grant in the election of 1872. Greeley lost. Exhausted by the campaign, he died a few weeks later.

PROCESSIONAL: *Sir 16, 11-12* Mercy and wrath are with the Lord; he is mighty to forgive, and he pours out wrath. As great as his mercy, so great is also his reproof; he judges a man according to his deeds. *Ps 103, 8* The Lord is merciful and gracious, slow to anger and abounding in steadfast love.

February 4

BILL HAYWOOD

"Big Bill" Haywood was born Feb. 4, 1869 in Salt Lake City and was working as a miner by the age of 9. Joining the Western Federation of Miners during the bloodiest era of labor unionism, Haywood quickly became the hard-nosed advocate of confrontation and violence. Clarence Darrow helped him beat a murder rap in Idaho stemming from the death of an anti-union politician. Fired from the W.F.M., Haywood continued as leader of the International Workers of the World, a socialist precursor of industrial unionism. He was jailed in 1917 for his opposition to the World War; out on bail, he fled to the Soviet Union where he died in 1928.

COMMUNION: *Job 19, 7-8* Behold I cry out, "Violence!" but I am not answered; I call aloud, but there is no justice. He has walled up my way, so that I cannot pass, and he has set darkness upon my paths.

RECESSIONAL: A litany to anger: Let anger rise up, let it swell, let it burst forth in retribution. A curse on him who, forced to swallow injustice for a generation, accepts his fate with serenity. Let him choke!

February 5

ADLAI E. STEVENSON

Adlai Stevenson was the nearest thing to an intellectual cult hero America ever knew. Witty and articulate, with courtly (sometimes impish) manners, his style was a pole apart from Dwight Eisenhower whose rapport with the people was more secure and who twice overwhelmed Stevenson in presidential balloting. In a sense, Stevenson represented the epitome of *noblesse oblige* liberalism that began with the New Deal and fell to pieces in the 1960s. He was born Feb. 5, 1900 in Los Angeles; he died of a heart attack in London in 1965 while serving as John Kennedy's ambassador to the United Nations.

PROCESSIONAL: *Eccles 4, 1* I saw all the oppressions that are practiced under the sun. And behold, the tears of the oppressed, and they had no one to comfort them! On the side of their oppressors there was power, and there was no one to comfort them. *Ps 71, 2* In thy righteousness deliver me and rescue me; incline thy ear to me, and save me!

OFFERTORY: We offer you, Father, our idealism; give it back toughened by the fire. We offer you our wit; give it back emptied clean of arrogance. We offer you our skills; give them back tempered by compassion. Father we offer you our dreams; give them back refashioned by your will.

February 6

BABE RUTH

He was born George Herman Ruth on Feb. 6, 1895 in Baltimore, but all his life he was called Babe, the Bambino. He was a larger-than-life figure, a loveable, carousing, unreformable, grown-up kid whose career was a series of grand gestures. As a pitcher for the Boston Red Sox, and later as an outfielder for the New York Yankees, he was the epic sports hero of his day. Even long after he retired, during World War II, the ultimate insult hurled by Japanese soldiers at Americans facing them in the jungle darkness was the cry: "Babe Ruth stinks!" Had he heard it, the Babe would have roared with delight.

PETITION: Grant us, Lord God, each in our own way, the courage to live life to its depths. Like your servant Babe, free us to exploit our talents to their fullest, to laugh loudly, and to accept joy and sorrow, life and death, with the same open-armed embrace.

COMMUNION: *1 Mac 3, 3-4* He extended the glory of his people. Like a giant he put on his breastplate; he girded on his armor of war and waged battles, protecting the host by his sword. He was like a lion in his deeds, like a lion's cub roaring for prey.

February 7

SINCLAIR LEWIS

Sinclair Lewis was born Feb. 7, 1885 in Sauk Center, Minn., a prairie town like those he so brilliantly caricatured in a series of novels that appeared from 1920 onward: *Main Street*, *Babbitt*, *Arrowsmith*, and *Elmer Gantry*. He had an unerring knack of capturing the language, the mores, and the shallowness of American small-town life, a fact that both amused and scandalized his readers. Lewis declined the Pulitzer Prize in 1925. Five years later he became the first American to be awarded the Nobel Prize for literature. He died in 1951.

PETITION: God give me unclouded eyes and freedom from haste. God give me quiet and relentless anger against all pretense and all pretentious work and all work left slack and unfinished. God give me a restlessness whereby I may neither sleep nor accept praise until my observed results equal my calculated results, or in pious glee I discover and assault my error. God give me strength not to trust in God.*

February 8

CONNIE MACK

He was born Cornelius McGillicuddy in East Brookfield, Mass., but since

*Martin Arrowsmith's prayer, from *Arrowsmith*.

that name wouldn't fit on the baseball scoreboard he shortened it to Connie Mack. Mack was a pretty fair catcher before the turn of the century. Eventually he became a manager, then part owner of the Philadelphia Athletics in the newly formed American League. He managed the A's from 1901 to 1951, winning nine league championships, five world series, and developing such stars as Rube Wadell, Lefty Grove, and Jimmy Foxx. His bust at the Cooperstown Hall of Fame is inscribed simply "Mr. Baseball." Connie Mack died on this day in 1956.

PROCESSIONAL: Take me out to the ball game,/Take me out to the crowd. *Is 17, 12* Ah, the thunder of many peoples, they thunder like the thundering of the sea! Ah, the roar of nations, they roar like the roaring of mighty waters!

OFFERTORY: The acclaim does not last, O Lord; the tumult and the shouting die away. So before they disappear we give them back: the cheers, the strength, the beauty. Only in your care will they echo down the corridor of years, long after the game is finished.

February 9

AMY LOWELL

Amy Lowell was a relative of James Russell Lowell, the Brahmin poet and literary critic. Amy was made of different stuff: eccentric, cigar smoking, she was an imposing woman with a sharp tongue and a relish for controversy. She was the acknowledged leader of the imagist poets that included Hilda Dolittle and Marianne Moore. Her own verse, while longwinded, was surprisingly spare and delicate, and devoted to the glories of her native New England. Amy Lowell was born on Feb. 9, 1874, and she died in 1925.

COMMUNION: Because my roots are in it,/Because my leaves are of it,/Because my flowers are for it,/Because it is my country/And I speak to it of itself/And sing of it with my own voice/ . . . Certainly it is mine.*

February 10

BILL TILDEN

Bill Tilden was probably the finest tennis player America ever produced: a

---

*Excerpt from "Lilacs" by Amy Lowell, from *The Complete Poetical Works of Amy Lowell*. Reprinted by permission of Houghton Mifflin Co.

big man with a booming service for his day and an all-round court game. He won the American national championship from 1920 to 1925 and in 1930. He led the U.S. Davis Cup team to victory seven straight years. Even as late as 1945, when Tilden was 52, he was the professional doubles champion. Tilden was born Feb. 10, 1893 in Pennsylvania; he died in 1953.

COMMUNION: Praise God who made the sun and grass, who made the bright sun, the hot sun of summer. Praise God who made the grass, cool and green, who made the sharp, white chalk in the sun. Praise God who made all bodies, all muscles, straining, reaching, coming together in a flash of white. Praise God.

February 11

THOMAS ALVA EDISON

A compulsive, humorless man given to working at odd hours of the day or night, Thomas Alva Edison was earning his own living at 15 and had his first patent by the age of 21. He was a tinkerer more than a scientist, a man who fiddled around with ways to utilize the newly harnessed power of electricity. Among his greatest inventions were the incandescent lamp, the phonograph, and the motion-picture camera—devices that filled the lives of his countrymen with light, music, and laughter. Edison was born on Feb. 11, 1847 in Ohio. He died in 1931, honored in all parts of the world.

PROCESSIONAL: *Is 65, 17-18* Behold, I create new heavens and a new earth; and the former things shall not be remembered or come into mind. But be glad and rejoice for ever in that which I create. *Sir 36, 6* Show signs anew, and work further wonders; make thy hand and thy right arm glorious.

RECESSIONAL: Because he gave us records, we no longer need to sing. Because he gave us films, we forgot the words to stories. Because he gave us bulbs, we snuffed out the candle flame. O Lord, think twice about Thomas who gave us ease and took our mysteries.

February 12

ABRAHAM LINCOLN

Abraham Lincoln, the 16th President of the United States, was born in

Kentucky Feb. 12, 1809 and was raised in Indiana and Illinois. He was, in turn, a country lawyer, state legislator, U.S. Representative, and a well-known trial lawyer before becoming President. By nature he was a deeply humanitarian, nondogmatic and simple person, but with a tendency toward moodiness and superstition. In the chaos that prevailed during his lifetime, Lincoln's moral vision enabled him to act when others were snared in details, and to forgive when others were obsessed with action.

OFFERTORY: God, our Father, all of us in our time are carried by fate toward some dark and forbidding shore. Accept this gift as you accepted the gift of our father Abraham, so that the final sacrifice, when it comes, will serve the cause of justice, and that the distant shore, when we reach it, will be filled with light.

COMMUNION: *Is 9, 2, 4* The people who walked in darkness have seen a great light; those who dwelt in the land of deep darkness, on them has light shined. For the yoke of his burden, and the staff for his shoulder, the rod of his oppressor, thou hast broken as on the day of Midian.

RECESSIONAL: With malace toward none; with charity for all; with firmness in the right, as God gives us to see the right, let us strive on to finish the work we are in; to bind up the nation's wounds; to care for him who shall have borne the battle, and for his widow and his orphan—to do all which may achieve and cherish a just and a lasting peace, among ourselves and with all nations.*

February 13

COTTON MATHER

Cotton Mather is probably best known for his connection with the Salem witchcraft trials which he helped inspire (but disapproved of). He should be remembered for other things. He was a formidable scholar and scientist, being one of the first Americans elected to the Royal Society. As a political leader he championed increased liberties for the colonies. His history of New England was acclaimed on both sides of the Atlantic, and he was an early advocate of innoculation against smallpox. To us today Mather may be the most famous of American Puritans. But on the day of his death, Feb. 13, 1728, he was, quite simply, the most famous American.

PROCESSIONAL: *Is 1, 24-25* "I will vent my wrath on my enemies, and avenge myself on my foes. I will turn my hand against you and will smelt

*From Lincoln's Second Inaugural Address.

away your dross as with lye and remove all your alloy." *Prov 4, 4* He taught me, and said to me, "Let your heart hold fast my words; keep my commandments, and live; do not forget, and do not turn away from the words of my mouth."

COMMUNION: Austere as the winter snow you come, Lord, burning with an icy fire. Ah, destructive purity—we are caught, cauterized in your gaze. Proud and cold you reach your hand to us: We are used to living on your crumbs.

February 14

WILLIAM TECUMSEH SHERMAN

William Tecumseh Sherman has been called the first general of the modern era; certainly he was the ablest general of the Civil War. He was a master of maneuver and a keen psychologist. His dramatic march through Georgia in 1864 was, more than any battlefield defeat, a vivid demonstration of the Confederacy's helplessness. Unsparing in battle (it was Sherman who said "War is hell"), he was compassionate and generous as a victor. After retiring as chief of staff of the army he spurned an opportunity to become President in 1884 and died peaceably on Feb. 14, 1891.

PROCESSIONAL: The tribes assembled at Shiloh; they gathered on the banks of the Savannah where trees hung rich with fruit; they met in the valley of the Chattahoochee. *Is 63, 3-4* "I have trodden the wine press alone . . . I trod them in my anger and trampled them in my wrath . . . For the day of vengence was in my heart, and my year of redemption has come."

COMMUNION: Spare me, Lord God; grant me one refuge that is mine alone; do not beat down my landscape. Come, Lord God; invade this secret garden; you alone shall be my protector and my strength.

February 15

SUSAN B. ANTHONY

Susan B. Anthony was born to a Quaker family in Adams, Mass. on Feb. 15, 1820. She was a strong-willed woman, well educated for her day, and she used her talents as a schoolteacher, antislavery crusader, and from 1854 onwards as the foremost champion of women's rights in the United

States. For more than a half-century she was a visible and controversial standard-bearer of votes for women, suffering abuse and ridicule, and being arrested twice for voting illegally. She died in 1906, 14 years before the Ninteenth Amendment was ratified and women were finally enfranchised.

OFFERTORY: We offer you bread, wine, Lord, not one better than the other: both equal. We offer you men, women, Lord, not one better than the other: both equal. These all are simple gifts, grown from the good earth. Consecrate them. Comingle them in your sight. All these gifts shall be made one.

RECESSIONAL: Give to us, Lord God, the same strength to endure trials and scorn as you gave to your holy woman Susan, so that we, nourished by these mysteries, may persevere in the struggle for justice, even for those goals which will not be realized in our lifetime.

February 16

STEPHEN DECATUR

Lord Nelson called it "the most bold and daring act of the age" when young Lieutenant Decatur took a small band of American sailors at night into the harbor of Tripoli on Feb. 16, 1804 to burn the frigate *Philadelphia*, previously captured by the Barbary pirates. Handsome and dashing, Decatur was an instant hero. Subsequently he commanded the frigates *Constitution* and *United States*, fighting bravely against the British in the War of 1812. It was Decatur who, upon returning from that war, made the famous toast to "Our country, may she ever be right, but our country, right or wrong."

PETITION: Your mercy attends in a white cloud, Lord God, just as your servant Stephen rode on billowing sails. Shelter your people, we beg you; march off our coasts in readiness, so that—even if we forget to serve your cause—you will not forget to serve ours.

COMMUNION: *Ps 107, 23-24* Some went down to the sea in ships, doing business on the great waters; they saw the deeds of the Lord, his wondrous works in the deep.

February 17

GERONIMO

For more than 30 years a small band of Chiricahua Apaches led by their chief Geronimo raided settlements in Texas, Arizona, and New Mexico, repeatedly eluding attempts by the American and Mexican armies to capture them, or to hold them once captured. The final campaign in 1887 lasted for 18 months and saw 5000 troopers engaged in an attempt to capture only 35 Apache men with 110 dependents. Geronimo's hostility toward whites is understandable: his mother, wife, and children had been killed by them many years before. Finally captured, he spent his last years under armed guard at Fort Sill, Okla. He died on Feb. 17, 1909.

PROCESSIONAL: *Is 59, 17-18* He put on garments of vengence for clothing, and wrapped himself in fury as a mantle. According to their deeds, so will he repay, wrath to his adversaries, requital to his enemies. *Ps 71, 11* "God has forsaken him; pursue and seize him, for there is none to deliver him."

RECESSIONAL: Go, you are sent forth into exile. No longer will you ride the hills of your youth. Did you think that time would last forever? Go now, life is waiting for you.

February 18

WENDELL WILLKIE

Born Feb. 18, 1892, Wendell Willkie grew up in Elwood, Ind., drinking deeply of populist politics and the religion of Big Business. Harold Ickes called him "a simple, barefoot Wall Street lawyer." Impressed with his energy and boyish good looks, Republicans in 1940 nominated him for the presidency, not fully realizing that Willkie was no less progressive than FDR. Losing in a close race, Willkie became, during the darkest days of World War II, a worldwide spokesman for American democracy and a prophet for a new era of global cooperation which he predicted would follow the war. He died in 1944.

OFFERTORY: One world we seek, O Lord: one people, one humanity. The cynic says it is a dream, but we shall not dilute our hope. Come, take this bread, divided and broken; take our hearts which we have walled off from each other. Come, mender of broken worlds, broken hearts, and make them whole.

COMMUNION: *Ps 96, 10* Say among the nations, "The Lord reigns! Yea, the world is established, it shall never be moved; he will judge the peoples with equity."

February 19

BILLY MITCHELL

In July 1921 Brig. Gen. Billy Mitchell astonished American military leaders and the watching world by sinking two derelict warships with bombs dropped from airplanes. The age of air power had arrived. His military superiors, however, failed to seize on the fact. Mitchell's continued and sometimes shrill advocacy of the airplane won for him first a demotion and then a court martial with suspension from service. He died on Feb. 19, 1936, nearly six years before the Japanese, as Mitchell had predicted they would, made a surprise air attack on Pearl Harbor.

OFFERTORY: With this silver machine we carry glory to the Lord; with silver wings we crown his glory. The silent gifts are fused and stowed; slowly they are lifted to the sky. The Lord cannot refuse our cleverness, our generosity.

COMMUNION: *Ps 18, 12-13* Out of the brightness before him there broke through his clouds hailstones and coals of fire. The Lord also thundered in the heavens, and the Most High uttered his voice, hailstones and coals of fire.

February 20

FREDERICK DOUGLASS

Born as a slave in Maryland around 1817, Frederick Douglass escaped to the north when he was 21 years old. The knowledge of reading and writing he acquired clandestinely as a slave helped to make him, within a few years, a leading figure in the abolitionist movement. His forte was public speaking. In an age when oratory was a highly regarded art, Douglass was the champion of the lecture stage in Europe and America. When the war was over he held several minor posts in the Grant administration. He died Feb. 20, 1895.

COMMUNION: *Prov 8, 6-8* Hear, for I will speak noble things, and from my lips will come what is right; for my mouth will utter truth; wickedness is an abomination to my lips. All the words of my mouth are righteous; there is nothing twisted or crooked in them.

RECESSIONAL: Your words have nourished me, O Lord, as did the words of your servant Frederick. Let all our words be food, we pray—food healthy and beneficial for each other. Let us speak no longer in empty calories.

MALCOLM X

He was born Malcolm Little in Omaha, Neb. and was raised in Wisconsin and Michigan, partly in foster homes and reform schools. In Boston and Harlem he was a robber, dope pusher, and pimp. But while serving a jail term in 1946 his life changed abruptly. He became Malcolm X, "national minister" of the Nation of Islam, an eloquent spokesman and effective organizer in the black liberation movement. Eventually he broke with the Black Muslims over their insistence on racial separatism and formed his own organization with a socialistic bent. On Feb. 21, 1965, while addressing a gathering of supporters in Harlem, he was shot to death by an assassin.

PROCESSIONAL: I've had enough of someone else's propaganda. I'm for truth, no matter who tells it. I'm for justice, no matter who is for or against it. I'm a human being first and foremost, and as such I'm for whoever and whatever benefits humanity as a whole. *Response* Only when mankind would submit to the One God who created all—only then would mankind even approach the "peace" of which so much *talk* could be heard. . . . but toward which so little *action* was seen.*

PETITION: Be with us God, Father, as you were with brother Malcolm on the road to justice, on the road to Mecca. Be with us, Almighty One, as you were with brother Malcolm on the road to gentleness, on the road to peace. Be with us as you were with brother Malcolm, God, Father, Yahweh, Allah.

February 22

GEORGE WASHINGTON

He was an imposing man for his era, standing six feet tall and with a body hardened by outdoor labor. His manner was reserved, even diffident. His voice was strangely high-pitched. His face was scarred by smallpox. He told anyone who listened that he was unfit for leadership. Everyone followed him just the same, even New Englanders who normally scorned Virginia aristocrats such as he. They followed him from New York to Trenton and Princeton, to Valley Forge, to Yorktown, and then on a perilous journey as a new nation called the United States. He led, they followed.

*Reprinted by permission of Grove Press. From *The Autobiography of Malcolm X,* © 1965 by Alex Haley and Betty Shabazz.

PROCESSIONAL: *Prov 2, 20-22* You will walk in the way of good men and keep to the paths of the righteous. For the upright will inhabit the land, and men of integrity will remain in it; but the wicked will be cut off from the land, and the treacherous will be rooted out of it. *Ps 31, 3-4* Yea, thou art my rock and my fortress; for thy name's sake lead me and guide me, take me out of the net which is hidden for me, for thou art my refuge.

PETITION: Lord God you did give your son George strength to respond again and again when his people called on him. Give us strength also who follow in his footsteps. Even more, make us alert to the newer calls of his people, so that his response, so glorified in his day, will not be wasted in ours.

RECESSIONAL: The name of American, which belongs to you in your national capacity, must always exalt the just pride of patriotism more than any apellation derived from local discriminations . . . You have in a common cause fought and triumphed together . . . Your union ought to be considered as a main prop of your liberty, and that the love of the one ought to endear to you the preservation of the other.*

February 23

W. E. B. Du Bois

William E. B. Du Bois was the first black American in the 20th century to repudiate the policy of accommodation with whites and agitate actively for racial equality. Born Feb. 23, 1868, Du Bois was teaching economics and history at Atlanta University when his manifesto was issued in 1903. He joined the newly-formed N.A.A.C.P. as editor of its journal and later as director of research. Long interested in African independence, Du Bois moved there permanently in 1962, a short time after revealing his conversion to Marxism and his membership in the Communist party. He died in Accra, Ghana, in 1963.

COMMUNION: *Job 3, 23-24* Why is light given to a man whose way is hid, whom God has hedged in? For my sighing comes as my bread, and my groanings are poured out like water.

RECESSIONAL: Our suffering will nourish us; this is what we believe. We will dine on bitter weeds, consuming our anger until it becomes a force to open the fountains of the desert and roll back the walls of the sea.

*From Washington's Farewell Address, 1796.

February 24

GEORGE ROGERS CLARK

George Rogers Clark was more responsible than any man for the inclusion of Illinois in the original boundaries of the United States. His feats of generalship during the Revolutionary War won him the title of the "Washington of the West." A Virginian, Clark led an expedition that captured the settlements of Kaskaskia and Vincennes from the British and indians in 1778. When the British retook the latter, Clark led an epic trek through 200 miles of wilderness in midwinter. Despite incredible hardships he and his band of 170 men appeared before the British fort on Feb. 24, 1779, attacked it, and won a quick victory. With that one small battle, America stepped westward from the Appalachians to the Mississippi.

OFFERTORY: Smile on these gifts, Lord God, as you smiled on the offerings of those men, our forebears, on their sufferings, their hunger, their tears. In our day we have become used to giving you pretty presents when what you really want is sacrifice.

February 25

JOHN FOSTER DULLES

John Foster Dulles was born Feb. 25, 1888 in Washington, D.C. and was educated at Princeton and the Sorbonne. His entire life was given to diplomacy, both as a private lawyer and government official. He figured prominently in the formation of the United Nations. From 1952 onward he was Secretary of State under Eisenhower, helping to bring the "cold war" into a new phase based on active opposition rather than containment. His intensely moral outlook, coupled with policies of "massive retaliation" and "brinksmanship" characterized American foreign policy in the 1950s. Dulles died in 1959.

PROCESSIONAL: *Ex 15, 2-3* The Lord is my strength and my song, and he has become my salvation. . . . The Lord is a man of war; the Lord is his name. *Rev 19, 15* From his mouth issues a sharp sword with which to smite the nations, and he will rule them with a rod of iron; he will tread the wine press of the fury of the wrath of God the Almighty.

PETITION: Our lives are balanced precariously, O Lord, between life and death, between freedom and slavery. These scales we constructed by ourselves. Help us to live calmly, we pray, lest we bring about our own destruction. And give us faith so that in time we can throw away our scales and be content with your measuring alone.

February 26

BUFFALO BILL CODY

William F. Cody was born Feb. 26, 1846 in Scott County, Iowa. He worked as a prospector, a Pony Express rider, as an army scout during the Civil War, and as a professional hunter for the Kansas Pacific Railroad. By his own count he shot more than 4000 buffalo for construction crews. Made popular in the dime novels (where he was dubbed "Buffalo Bill"), his fame reached new heights after he killed a Cheyenne chief in hand-to-hand combat. For many years thereafter he toured the U.S. and Europe with his own Wild West Show. He died, a wealthy man, in Denver, Colo. in 1917.

OFFERTORY: Once we offered you the slaughtered bullock. Yes, and all the bullocks until the pasture was swept clean, until creation was undone. And when all the gifts were gone, we were left to ape the ancient ritual, turning slaughter into show biz. Father we beg you: take these empty gestures and make of them a new creation; bring life upon the earth once more so that we again can have food for living, and gifts for giving.

RECESSIONAL:
Buffalo Bill's
defunct
       who used to
       ride a watersmooth-silver
                      stallion
and break onetwothreefourfive pigeonsjustlikethat
                              Jesus
he was a handsome man
                 and what i want to know is
how do you like your blueeyed boy
Mister Death*

February 27

HENRY WADSWORTH LONGFELLOW

Henry Wadsworth Longfellow was born Feb. 27, 1807 in Portland, Me., graduated from Bowdoin College in the same class with Hawthorne, and

---

for 24 years was professor of literature at Bowdoin and Harvard. His first book of poetry appeared before he was 30, and they poured off his pen thereafter: *The Village Blacksmith, Evangeline, The Song of Hiawatha, The Courtship of Miles Standish*, and *Paul Revere's Ride*—works inspired by American themes and colored by German romanticism. He was a kind, gentle man, much loved and widely read in his day but increasingly neglected after his death in 1882.

RECESSIONAL: Lives of great men all remind us/We can make our lives sublime,/And, departing, leave behind us/Footprints on the sands of time;/Footprints, that perhaps another,/Sailing o'er life's solemn main,/A forlorn and shipwrecked brother,/Seeing, shall take heart again.*

February 28

HENRY LUCE

Born in Tengchow, China, Henry Luce first came to the United States when he was 15. He seemed never to forget his Presbyterian missionary upbringing which gave him an overflowing measure of apostolic zeal. After Yale and Oxford he worked on newspapers, then in 1923 brought out the first issue of *Time*, the pungent weekly newsmagazine that peddled Luce's GOPolitics and verbal gamesmanship. With other magazines *Life, Fortune*, and *Sports Illustrated*, Luce built a journalistic empire financially strong and politically powerful. He died on Feb. 28, 1967.

PROCESSIONAL: Arise, O Lord, and look with favor upon this nation, for her cause and yours is the same. *Ps 102, 13* Thou wilt arise and have pity on Zion; it is the time to favor her; the appointed time has come.

PETITION: For everything we have a category, everything has a label: what is good, what is bad, who is a villain, who heroic—Art, Religion, National Affairs, People. This, O Lord, is the work of your servant Henry. But we do it too. Teach us again and again to pay attention to those mysteries that are left when all the pigeonholes are filled. For only in mystery will we find perhaps ourselves, and probably you.

February 29

JOHN PHILIP HOLLAND

John Philip Holland was born in Ireland on Feb. 29, 1840 and became a schoolteacher in New Jersey while in his 20s. The battle of the *Monitor* and the *Merrimac* got Holland thinking about ironclad submarines. For

*From "A Psalm of Life" by H.W. Longfellow.

20 years he experimented with various ideas. At last in 1898 he launched the first practical undersea craft that used a gasoline engine while surfaced and an electric motor while submerged. Holland died in 1914, not in time to see German U-boats based on his design wreck havoc with allied shipping during World War I.

PETITION: Father, you whose servant John did find a way to hide a war machine under the bright waters, protect us who ride in peace along the surface. Protect also those heedless ones who cross the boundaries of our days while we watch secretly, destruction lurking in our hands. Protect us all, we pray, and forgive us.

Communion: *Ps 69, 13-14* With thy faithful help rescue me from sinking in the mire; let me be delivered from my enemies and from the deep waters.

MARCH

March 1

GLEN MILLER

Glen Miller was born March 1, 1909 in Iowa and grew up in Grant City, Okla., milking cows to pay for lessons on the trombone. For many years after college he played and arranged for dance bands, mostly in New York. In 1937 he organized his own band, and after a long period of trial and error it evolved an individual sound using tight harmony among the horns and a clarinet lead—a "sweet" dance band that for five years ruled casinos and juke boxes with its arrangements of "Moonlight Serenade," "Little Brown Jug," "American Patrol" and others. In December 1944 Miller died when his airplane was lost over the English Channel.

PROCESSIONAL: *Is 23, 16* "Make sweet melody, sing many songs, that you may be remembered." *Ps 89, 36-37* "His line shall endure for ever, his throne as long as the sun before me. Like the moon it shall be established for ever; it shall stand firm while the skies endure."

PETITION: We are each one of us, Lord God, not a single instrument but an ensemble; without your hand our parts are discordant. Grant to each of us the gift of harmony and integrity so that we can sing with joy your song and our own.

March 2

SAM HOUSTON

Among other things, Sam Houston was a friend of the indians, an adopted son of the Cherokee, and was once rebuked by John C. Calhoun for appearing before him in indian garb. After serving as governor and U.S. Representative from Tennessee, Houston was sent to Texas to negotiate with the Cherokees for the safety of white settlers. He stayed to become commander in chief of the Texas armies, first president of the Lone Star Republic, and U.S. Senator from Texas. Houston, who was born this day in 1793, died at the age of 80, deposed by Texans when he refused to back the Confederacy in the Civil War.

PROCESSIONAL: *Is 48, 13* My hand laid the foundation of the earth, and my right hand spread out the heavens; when I call to them, they stand forth together. *Ps 78, 72* With upright heart he tended them, and guided them with skillful hand.

RECESSIONAL: I wish no prouder epitaph to mark the board or slab that may lie on my tomb than this: "He loved his country, he was a patriot; he was devoted to the Union." If it is not for this that I have suffered martyrdom, it is sufficient that I stand at quits with those who have wielded the sacrificial knife.*

March 3

ALEXANDER GRAHAM BELL

Born in Edinburgh, Scotland on March 3, 1847, Alexander Graham Bell moved to Canada when he was 23, and thence to Boston where he opened a school for training teachers of the deaf. It was in this connection that he began experimenting with methods of transmitting the voice by electricity, resulting in the creation of the first telephone in 1876. In his later years Bell was a popular lecturer, president of the National Geographic Society, and a regent of the Smithsonian Institution.

COMMUNION: *Ps 50, 3* Our God comes, he does not keep silence, before him is a devouring fire, round about him a mighty tempest.

RECESSIONAL: We speak, are still. We speak, are still. Speak, are still. You have spoken to us, are still. Are still.

March 4

KNUTE ROCKNE

Knute Rockne was a pure leader. He possessed leadership in its most concentrated form. In retrospect we can see only his inspirational qualities, but Rockne teams were also meticulously drilled and prepared. Each was an intricate, graceful machine, bursting with energy. During his tenure as head coach at Notre Dame between 1918 and 1930 his teams won 105 games, lost only 12, and tied five. To many Americans, this genial Norwegian-American was the transcendent symbol of amateur athletics. He

*Sam Houston, after being dismissed as a U.S. Senator from Texas, 1857.

was born March 4, 1888; he died in an airplane accident on March 31, 1931.

PETITION: God our Father, give our country leaders with the talents, the humor, and the pure zest for life as your servant Knute. Let them see clearly, as he did, that the struggle exists for the betterment of the people, that the people are not simply grist for the struggle.

COMMUNION: Notre Dame, our mother, tender, strong and true./Proudly in the heavens, gleams the gold and blue,/Glory's mantle cloaks thee, golden is thy fame,/And our hearts forever praise thee, Notre Dame,/And our hearts forever love thee, Notre Dame.*

March 5

CRISPUS ATTUCKS

Not much is known about Crispus Attucks except that he was black, probably a runaway slave, and that he was among a crowd of people harassing some British soldiers in Boston on March 5, 1770. The soldiers became frightened and fired into the crowd. Whether it was a "massacre" as the Americans claimed is questionable. But that issue made little difference to Crispus Attucks, the black man who wanted to be free, whose life ended that day on the Boston cobblestones.

PROCESSIONAL: I knew from my youth what slavery was like; I knew the oppressor when I saw him on the street. *Ps 17, 10-11* They close their hearts to pity; with their mouths they speak arrogantly. They track me down; now they surround me; they set their eyes to cast me to the ground.

COMMUNION: *1 Cor 7, 22-23* He who was called in the Lord as a slave is a freedman of the Lord. Likewise he who was free when called is a slave of Christ. You were bought with a price; do not become slaves of men.

March 6

OLIVER WENDELL HOLMES

For more than 30 years he could be seen on the streets of Washington: a

---

*"Notre Dame, Our Mother" by Charles L. O'Donnell, C.S.C. and Joseph J. Casasanta, copyright © 1931 & 1932 by Melrose Music Corp. Copyright renewed. All rights reserved. Assigned to Edwin H. Morris & Co., Inc. Used by permission of Chappell & Co., Inc.

distinguished man with a white moustache, an associate justice of the Supreme Court, the most famous jurist of his age and perhaps in American history. He was Oliver Wendell Holmes, son of the famous poet. In the span of his lifetime he knew both John Quincy Adams and Alger Hiss. His career was a confluence of law, common sense, and high literary style. By the time of his death on March 6, 1935 he was, in the words of Walter Lippmann, "a sage with the bearing of a cavalier, [who wore] wisdom like a gorgeous plume."

PROCESSIONAL: *Deut 25, 13-15* "You shall not have in your bag two kinds of weights, a large and a small. You shall not have in your house two kinds of measures, a large and a small. A full and just weight you shall have, a full and just measure you shall have; that your days may be prolonged in the land which the Lord your God gives you." *Ps 37, 30-31* The mouth of the righteous utters wisdom, and his tongue speaks justice. The law of his God is in his heart; his steps do not slip.

RECESSIONAL: We thank you, Lord God, for the full measure of your justice, for nourishing us in body and spirit. Give us also compassion and selflessness that we may share with others as freely as you have shared with us.

March 7

LUTHER BURBANK

Luther Burbank was born March 7, 1849 in Lancaster, Mass. Having read Darwin at the age of 19, he set out to create new and better species of plants, establishing a nursery in Santa Rosa, Calif. for that purpose. Through the process of grafting he developed nearly a hundred new varieties of vegetables, more than a hundred fruits, and numerous new forms of flowers. He died in 1926.

PETITION: With tender care and patience your servant Luther did bring upon this earth a multitude of plants and flowers. Grant to us, O Lord, the foresight to protect these and other living things that our way of life threatens to destroy.

COMMUNION: *Song 4, 13-15* Your shoots are an orchard of pomegranates with all choicest fruits, henna with nard, nard and saffron, calamus and cinnamon, with all trees of frankincense, myrrh and aloes, with all chief spices—a garden fountain, a well of living water, and flowing streams from Lebanon.

March 8

WILLIAM HOWARD TAFT

William Howard Taft had a distinguished career as a lawyer, Federal judge, law school dean, governor of the Philippines, secretary of war, 27th President of the United States, and Chief Justice of the Supreme Court. He was a corpulent and good-humored man. Although sometimes taken for granted, even by his friends, he was a dogged worker and a skilled negotiator. Taft was born in 1857; he died on March 8, 1930.

PETITION: Remember, Lord, your servant William who dutifully did everything asked of him and thereby rose to the places of honor. Remember, too, your servants without names who refused to do what was asked of them and likewise found honor in your eyes. Give us, when our time comes, the wisdom to choose our own path.

March 9

JOHN ERICSSON

On March 9, 1862 a pair of odd-looking ships fought a battle in the water of Hampton Roads, near Norfolk, Va. The fight between the *Monitor* and the *Merrimack* was indecisive, but when it was over, all the warships in the world were suddenly out of date. The age of ironclads had arrived. The *Monitor* was a truly revolutionary design, being the work of 61-year-old John Ericsson, a Swedish-born engineer who came to the U.S. in 1839. Like an iceburg, most of the *Monitor* was under the water; it had a revolving turret and a screw propeller. Ericsson built other monitors during the course of the war, and his model became the prototype of all modern naval vessels.

COMMUNION: *Ps 29, 3* The voice of the Lord is upon the waters; the God of glory thunders, the Lord, upon many waters.

RECESSIONAL: Did you smile, Lord, God of Battles, when the iron monsters first collided? Did you smile when crashing split the air at Guadalcanal, or on that Sunday in Oahu? With your hand you make crabs scuttle from hulks that sleep on muddy floors. Are you the God of Thunder, or do you reveal yourself only in the silence when the thunder dies away? And do you smile?

March 10

Harriet Tubman was the most famous of the "conductors" of the Underground Railroad. She made 19 separate trips into the south, leading more than 300 slaves to safety, despite the fact that she herself was an escaped slave whose capture would have brought an immense reward. She was a woman of strength and intelligence, and in her day honored as "the Moses of her people." She died at the age of 93 on March 10, 1913.

PETITION: Grant, O Lord, that we who walk the path of freedom with faltering steps may learn from this holy woman Harriet, who, having fled the chains of slavery, turned back to help others make the same journey.

OFFERTORY: *Deut 23, 15-16* "You shall not give up to his master a slave who has escaped from his master to you; he shall dwell with you, in your midst, in the place which he shall choose within one of your towns, where it pleases him best; you shall not oppress him."

March 11

RICHARD E. BYRD

Son of a distinguished Virginia family, Richard E. Byrd was an aviation pioneer and polar explorer. He was the first man to fly an airplane over the North Pole (for which he won the Congressional Medal of Honor) and over the South Pole. He led five separate expeditions to Antarctica, discovering vast new areas in that region, and at one time nearly dying while spending five months alone in a weather-observation shack. He died as a retired rear admiral in the U.S. Navy on March 11, 1957.

OFFERTORY: Alone we come before you, God Father, our hearts in the grip of winter. Do not turn away from us. Take that which is all we can give: our loneliness, our solitude.

RECESSIONAL: May this mystery be for us who took part in it a new dawn after winter darkness. May it freshen our souls with the taste of spring and the expectation of growth and life.

March 12

JOHN PETER ALTGELD

John Peter Altgeld was the Adlai Stevenson of his day—a liberal governor of Illinois who took positions of conscience that were contrary to popular taste. Altgeld grew up in poverty in Ohio, studied law on his own, became a judge in Chicago, and finally governor. One of his first acts was the pardoning of three persons jailed following the Haymarket riots six years earlier (when a bomb exploded during a labor rally). Two years later Altgeld asked President Cleveland to withdraw federal troops sent to Chicago during the Pullman strike. Both actions created storms of criticism but made Altgeld a legendary figure among midwest reformers. Altgeld died on March 12, 1902.

PROCESSIONAL: *Mt 10, 21-22* Brother will deliver up brother to death, and the father his child, and children will rise against parents and have them put to death; and you will be hated by all for my name's sake. But he who endures to the end will be saved. *Ps 112, 6-7* For the righteous will never be moved; he will be remembered for ever. He is not afraid of evil tidings; his heart is firm, trusting in the Lord.

RECESSIONAL: Sleep   softly, . . . eagle   forgotten, . . . under   the stone,/Time has its way with you there and the clay has its own./Sleep on, O brave-hearted, O wise-man, that kindled the flame—/To live in mankind is far more than to live in a name,/To live in mankind, far, far, more . . . than to live in a name.*

March 13

CLARENCE DARROW

Clarence Darrow, who died this day in 1938, was a sagatious courtroom lawyer with an inbuilt sympathy for the underdog. In his lifetime he defended many clients low in the public esteem, including Eugene V. Debs and "Big Bill" Haywood. His two most famous cases were the Leopold-Loeb murder trial in 1924 and the Scopes "monkey trial" the following year. Both of which he lost. Both of which he won.

PETITION: I know the future is with me, and what I stand for here; not merely for the lives of these two unfortunate lads, but for all boys and all

---

*From "The Eagle That Is Forgotten," a memorial to John P. Altgeld from *Collected Poems* by Vachel Lindsay. Copyright 1923 by Macmillan Publishing Co., Inc., renewed 1951 by Elizabeth C. Lindsay. Used by permission.

girls; for all of the young, and as far as possible, for all of the old. I am pleading for life, understanding, charity, kindness, and the infinite mercy that considers all. I am pleading that we overcome cruelty with kindness and hatred with love.*

COMMUNION: *Sir 35, 13-14, 16* He will not show partiality in the case of a poor man; and he will listen to the prayer of one who is wronged. He will not ignore the supplication of the fatherless, nor the widow when she pours out her story. He whose service is pleasing to the Lord will be accepted, and his prayer will reach to the clouds.

March 14

GEORGE EASTMAN

Everyone's life changed in 1888 when George Eastman brought out the "Kodak," an inexpensive camera designed to utilize his newly invented roll-film. The average man now had a language for recording what was true, and sometimes what was beautiful. Thirteen years after the Kodak appeared, the Eastman-Kodak Company in Rochester built the world's largest industrial plant. George Eastman made a lot of money, and he also gave a great deal of it away. He lived simply. He never had a family. On March 14, 1932 at the age of 77 he scrawled out a note that said "My work is done, why wait?" and then he took his own life.

COMMUNION: *Ps 36, 7-9* The children of men take refuge in the shadow of thy wings. They feast on the abundance of thy house, and thou givest them drink from the river of thy delights. For with thee is the fountain of life; in thy light do we see light.

RECESSIONAL: Lord, God of time, with the help of your servant George we have a means of freezing the present moment and keeping it always. Grant that this moment may nourish us on the road ahead and comfort us with the memory of love.

March 15

ANDREW JACKSON

He personally disliked George Washington, was a friend of Aaron Burr,

*From Darrow's final argument in the Leopold-Loeb trial.

and was shot at and wounded by Thomas Hart Benton. Andy Jackson was a tough man. He was born March 15, 1767 of Irish immigrants in South Carolina. He spent his young years at soldering, practicing law, dueling, drinking, and racing horses. Made famous by his victory over the British at New Orleans, he became the sixth President of the United States in 1828 —the first man who was not from the eastern aristocracy to hold that office. He served two terms, always embroiled in conflict, and was more popular at the end than at the beginning.

COMMUNION: *Deut 33, 3* Yea, he loved his people; all those consecrated to him were in his hand; so they followed in thy steps, receiving direction from thee.

RECESSIONAL: May the Great Ruler of Nations grant that the signal blessings with which He has favored ours may not, by the madness of party or personal ambition be disregarded and lost; and may His wise providence . . . inspire a returning veneration for that union which . . . He has chosen as the only means of attaining the high destinies to which we may reasonably aspire.*

March 16

JAMES MADISON

James Madison was one of those politicians, like Eugene McCarthy, with acute minds but with a disinclination to leadership. Madison was a shaping force at the Constitutional Convention of 1786, giving form to the federal system we know today. He was an effective secretary of state under Jefferson. His own two terms as President, beginning in 1809, were marked by national disharmony and a disasterous war with Britain from which Madison and his country barely escaped. He was born on March 16 in 1751; he died in Virginia in 1836.

PROCESSIONAL: *Jer 30, 21* Their prince shall be one of themselves, their ruler shall come forth from their midst; I will make him draw near, and he shall approach me. *Ps 119, 102-104* I do not turn aside from thy ordinances, for thou hast taught me. How sweet are thy words to my taste, sweeter than honey to my mouth! Through thy precepts I get understanding.

OFFERTORY: Father we have been obedient to the law written down for us; we have been faithful to its purpose. Now we offer this law to you that it

*From Jackson's proclamation against Nullification, 1832.

may disappear, that it may be devoured and written on our spirits, that it may transform our hearts even more than our minds. We do this, Father, in order to form a more perfect union with you and with one another.

March 17

BOBBY JONES

More than any other man Bobby Jones was responsible for the popularity of the game of golf in America and around the world. Born March 17, 1902 in Atlanta, Ga., he learned to control a fierce temper and in time came to be regarded as the ultimate sportsman—"the finest competitor ever produced in the United States, or anywhere else" said Paul Gallico. In 1930, after winning the British Open, the British Amateur, the U.S. Open, and the U.S. Amateur, he retired, all worlds conquered.

PETITION: Teach us, Lord, the value of finding excellence in one act, the goodness of doing one thing well. And in the mastery of this one small action, may we gain new respect for our own humanity, and tolerance for others'.

March 18

JOHN C. CALHOUN

John C. Calhoun of South Carolina was born March 18, 1782. He served his state and country as a member of the House of Representatives, of the Senate, as secretary of war, secretary of state, and as vice president under John Quincy Adams and Andrew Jackson. He was an imposing man with a white mane of hair, a temper to match it, and a mind like a steel trap. Increasingly, as the years went on, he upheld the absolute sovereignty of the states, thereby providing the south with an argument for secession and a legal pretext for the Civil War. Calhoun died in 1850 and was buried overlooking the harbor where 10 years later the first shots would be fired at Fort Sumpter.

PROCESSIONAL: Hear my voice: The people are supreme in their own land; foreign powers shall not rule them. *Ps 56, 1-2* Be gracious to me, O God, for men trample upon me; all day long foemen oppress me; my enemies trample upon me all day long, for many fight against me proudly.

OFFERTORY: Is it possible, Lord, that the words we use now will be swords among our children? Is it possible that the bread we share now will be poison for our children? Protect us from the unknown and the unforseen, we beg you. Take these gifts and keep them safe, now and forevermore.

March 19

WILLIAM JENNINGS BRYAN

They called him "the boy orator of the West" in 1896 when William Jennings Bryan came out of Nebraska to win the Democratic nomination for the presidency. He was the champion of the little man, the farmer and the westerner against the powerful banking interests of the east. Three times he ran for President, and three times he lost. Bryan was born on March 19, 1860. He died in 1925, after resigning as Wilson's secretary of state and after being humiliated by Darrow at the Scopes trial in Tennessee. His silver clarion at last was silent.

PROCESSIONAL: *Sir 31, 8-9* Blessed is the rich man who is found blameless, and who does not go after gold. Who is he? And we will call him blessed, for he has done wonderful things among his people. *Ps 99, 6-7* They cried to the Lord, and he answered them. He spoke to them in the pillar of cloud; they kept his testimonies, and the statutes that he gave them.

RECESSIONAL: Where is that boy, that Heaven-born Bryan,/That Homer Bryan, who sang from the West?/Gone to join the shadows with Altgeld the Eagle,/Where the kings and the slaves and the troubadours rest.*

March 20

CHARLES W. ELIOT

Charles W. Eliot shaped American universities into the form we know today. During his 40 years as president of Harvard University he introduced such innovations as elective courses, the graduate school, separate schools of law and medicine, and stringent entrance requirements for the undergraduate college. Eliot was an aristocrat who shrank from the blustery jingoism of Theodore Roosevelt and whose intelligence earned

*From "Bryan, Bryan, Bryan, Bryan: The Campaign of Eighteen Ninety-six, as Viewed at the Time by a Sixteen-Year-Old, etc." from *Collected Poems* by Vachel Lindsay. Copyright 1923 by Macmillan Publishing Co., Inc., renewed 1948 by Elizabeth C. Lindsay. Used by permission.

him a position of moral leadership in American life prior to World War I. He was born this day in 1834. He died in 1926.

PROCESSIONAL: *Prov 3, 13-14* Happy is the man who finds wisdom, and the man who gets understanding, for the gain from it is better than gain from silver and its profit better than gold. *Ps 78, 1* Give ear, O my people, to my teaching; incline your ears to the words of my mouth!

RECESSIONAL: Thou wert our parent, the nurse of our souls,/We were moulded to manhood by thee,/Till freighted with treasure-thoughts, friendships and hopes,/Thou didst launch us on Destiny's sea.*

March 21

FLO ZIEGFELD

Florenz Ziegfeld was twenty-three when he began managing Sandow the Strongman at the Chicago World's Fair. Moving to New York City, he found his true element. In 1907 his first "Follies" appeared, an opulent revue featuring chorus girls, music, and comedians. New productions followed nearly every year until 1931, stocked with performers such as Eddie Cantor, Will Rogers, W.C. Fields, and Fannie Brice. To appear in his elegant stage shows was the goal of every vaudevillian. Ziegfeld was born on March 21, 1869; he died in Hollywood in 1932.

PETITION: Give us a taste for simple truths, Lord God. There is honesty in rhinestones. A pie in the face is good news. Your servant Flo was an evangelist, and once more we acknowledge his creed: A pretty girl is like a melody.

March 22

JONATHAN EDWARDS

Jonathan Edwards was one of early America's most influential theologians and preachers. A stern Calvinist, he was deeply influenced by the revival movements rampant in the mid-18th century; so, while confessing on one hand that salvation came only through faith, he declared that this required a personal regenerative experience as well as a credal assertion. He was dismissed from his pulpit in Northampton, Mass. because of his

*Harvard Bicentennial Ode by Samuel Gilman, 1836.

"enthusiastic" tendencies. He became president of Princeton College before his death on March 22, 1758.

COMMUNION: *Ps 40, 9-10* I have told the glad news of deliverance in the great congregation; lo, I have not restrained my lips, as thou knowest, O Lord. I have not hid thy saving help within my heart, I have spoken of thy faithfulness and thy salvation; I have not concealed thy steadfast love and thy faithfulness from the great congregation.

RECESSIONAL: Cool your anger, God; Father of the Universe; we, your sinners, implore you. We are in your hands, it is true, but you are also in ours. Calm your wrath, we beg you. Let there be peace between us. Or at least a truce.

March 23

FANNIE FARMER

Fannie Farmer, the woman who produced the first modern cookbook, was a quiet, reserved person. As a teenager she had suffered a stroke that ended her formal education and relegated her to the kitchen. She liked it so much that she attended the Boston Cooking School, became a teacher there, and eventually its director. The cookbook she published in 1896 was the first to use standard measures, and it showed an intuitive feeling for diet planning and nutrition. Having gone through many editions, it is still a best seller. Fannie Farmer was born on this day in 1857. She died in 1915.

PETITION: O God hold back your largesse from your people. We must watch our intake. There's nothing more annoying that a surfeit of inspiration, or of wisdom, or even still of goodness. Overflowing charity can leave us just as jaded as a banquet of rich desserts. We look forward to your nourishment, but in moderation please. Give us just one portion and make us hope for more.

RECESSIONAL: *Wis 16, 20-21* Thou didst give thy people the food of angels, and without their toil thou didst supply them from heaven with bread ready to eat, providing every pleasure and suited to every taste. For thy sustenance manifested thy sweetness toward thy children; and the bread . . . was changed to suit every one's liking.

March 24

ANDREW W. MELLON

Andrew Mellon served as secretary of the treasury from 1921 to 1932 under Presidents Harding, Coolidge, and Hoover. As a Pittsburgh banker and one of the richest men in America, he naturally supported fiscal policies favorable to industry and the wealthy classes, thereby contributing to the greatest business boom and the worst depression the nation ever experienced. He was born on March 24, 1855; shortly before his death in 1937 he donated his vast art collection to the nation, forming the basis for the National Gallery of Art in Washington, D.C.

PROCESSIONAL: *Is 2, 7* Their land is filled with silver and gold, and there is no end to their treasures; their land is filled with horses, and there is no end to their chariots. *Eccles 10, 19* Bread is made for laughter, and wine gladdens life, and money answers everything.

OFFERTORY: These gifts we have are not expensive: plain bread and simple wine. We would prefer to give you gold, but this is the bread line, Father, and this is all we have. Come to our bread line, we pray, and eat with us.

COMMUNION: *Dan 11, 43, 45* He shall become ruler of the treasures of gold and silver, and all the precious things of Egypt; yet he shall come to his end, with none to help him.

March 25

GUTZON BORGLUM

Gutzon Borglum was born of Danish-American parents in Idaho on March 25, 1871. While a young man he studied art in San Francisco and in Europe. He was influenced as a sculptor by the free-flowing lines of Rodin and by heroic themes. His colossal head of Lincoln is in the Capitol building in Washington. In 1927 he conceived and began carving the monumental heads of Washington, Jefferson, Lincoln, and Theodore Roosevelt from the living granite of Mount Rushmore, So. Dakota. The largest piece of sculpture in the world, it required 15 years to complete. Borglum died in 1941.

PROCESSIONAL: *Sir 44, 1-3* Let us now praise famous men, and our fathers in their generations. The Lord apportioned to them great glory, his majesty from the beginning. There were those who ruled in their kingdoms, and were men renowned for their power. *Ps 98, 8* Let the floods clap their hands; let the hills sing for joy together.

PETITION: Grant us, Lord God, a new respect for heroes, as you did inspire your servant Gutzon. Help us discover heroes in our day, lest their very absence reveal our own defect: our belief that there is no goal worth great striving.

March 26

ISAAC MEYER WISE

Born in Bohemia, Isaac Wise came to the United States in 1846, four years after he had become a rabbi. Distressed by the lack of unity among American Jews, and convinced that Judaism should embrace what is best in American life, he initiated a reform movement which in his lifetime became a major branch of his religion. He wrote hymns, novels, plays, histories, edited two newspapers, created the Union of Hebrew Congregations, and was founder and first president of Hebrew Union College. Rabbi Wise died in Cincinnati on March 26, 1900.

PETITION: Give to us your followers, Lord God, as you gave to your servant Isaac, a deep love for our fathers so that we might always honor the covenent you made with them, and love for ourselves so that we might always have the courage to read your ancient words with fresh eyes.

COMMUNION: *Is 2, 3* "Come, let us go up to the mountain of the Lord, to the house of the God of Jacob; that he may teach us his ways and that we may walk in his paths."

March 27

HENRY ADAMS

Henry Adams belonged to what has been described as the most gifted family in American history: Both his grandfather and great-grandfather were Presidents of the United States and his father was ambassador to England during the Civil War. Henry was a novelist, a political analyst, and a historian. His most famous book *The Education of Henry Adams* was an acute and profoundly pessimistic vision of the United States and its destiny, arguing that the values of America's founding fathers were all but destroyed by technology and mindless democracy. Adams died on March 27, 1918.

PROCESSIONAL: *Eccles 7, 25* I turned my mind to know and to search out and to seek wisdom and the sum of things, and to know the wickedness of folly and the foolishness which is madness. *Ps 77, 5-6* I consider the days of old, I remember the years long ago. I commune with my heart in the night; I meditate and search my spirit.

OFFERTORY: The world is running down; each moment the vital source diminishes. Our lives are running out; each moment their vital source diminishes. Take our lives, we pray; lift them up, change them, make them yours.

March 28

JIM THORPE

Jim Thorpe could do almost anything on an athletic field. As a football player he made tiny Carlisle College in Pennsylvania into a national power, scoring 25 touchdowns and 198 points in 1912. That same year, at the Stockholm Olympic Games, he achieved an unprecedented feat by winning gold medals in both the pentathlon and the decathlon. However his prizes were taken back when it was discovered he once accepted money for performing. Later, as a professional baseball and football player, his skills rapidly declined. He died in near poverty on March 28, 1953.

PROCESSIONAL: *1 Sam 16, 18* "Behold, I have seen a son of Jesse the Bethlehemite, who is skilful in playing, a man of valor, a man of war, prudent in speech, and a man of good presence; and the Lord is with him." *Hab 3, 19* God, the Lord is my strength; he makes my feet like hinds' feet, he makes me tread upon my high places.

OFFERTORY: See, he runs and leaps. His body is a gift, poured out upon the green grass. How can we reimburse him for something so gladly offered? And what do we do with the skin, now empty, so recently filled with sweet wine?

March 29

JOHN JACOB ASTOR

John Jacob Astor came to America from Germany in 1783 and got into the fur-trading business. Forty years later he was the richest man in the country. His American Fur Trading Company spanned the continent, and he augmented this income through vast real-estate holdings and by loaning money to the U.S. government during the War of 1812 at enormous rates of interest. The family he founded dominated America's social elite for a century after his death, which occurred on March 29, 1848.

COMMUNION: *Gen 33, 18-19* And Jacob came safely to the city of Shechem, which is in the land of Canaan, on his way from Paddanaram; and he camped before the city. And from the sons of Hamor, Shechem's father, he bought for a hundred pieces of money the piece of land on which he had pitched his tent.

RECESSIONAL: His house was built upon the rocks of Oregon, of Alaska, and his domain reached even to the mountains; from the war he took his spoils, and his tribe endured for generations.

March 30

ROGER WILLIAMS

Founder of Rhode Island and an early exponent of religious liberty, Roger Williams was born in 1604 in London and was educated at Cambridge. Emigrating to America, he made enemies in Salem for maintaining, among other heresies, that civil power has no jurisdiction over private conscience, and that the land in the New World belonged to the indians. Banished from Massachusetts, he and a few followers settled in Providence. Williams is generally acknowledged to be the founder of the American Baptist Church. He died sometime in March 1684.

PROCESSIONAL: In the name of God he was cast out; in the name of God he found shelter. *Ps 122, 2-4* Our feet have been standing within your gates, O Jerusalem! Jerusalem, built as a city which is bound firmly together, to which the tribes go up, the tribes of the Lord.

COMMUNION: *1 Cor 10, 29-31* Why should my liberty be determined by another man's scruples? If I partake with thankfulness, why am I denounced because of that for which I give thanks? So, whether you eat or drink, or whatever you do, do all to the glory of God.

March 31

JACK JOHNSON

Jack Johnson was born March 31, 1878 in Galveston, Tex. He was a black man, strong and graceful, a boxer in an era when the professional ring was closed to blacks. Finally winning a shot at the heavyweight title, he knocked out Tommy Burns on Christmas Day 1908 in Sydney, Australia. To the dismay of those who sought a "white hope" to dethrone him, Johnson held the title for eight years, living in opulent fashion and marrying a white woman. He was beaten at last by Jess Willard in 1915, although Johnson later claimed he gave the fight away. Johnson died after an automobile accident in 1946.

COMMUNION: *Ps 89, 13-14* Thou hast a mighty arm; strong is thy hand, high thy right hand. Righteousness and justice are the foundation of thy throne.

RECESSIONAL: The gift long sought after and finally found is richly savored. Let us stop and enjoy its taste. Let us pause and enjoy this moment, enjoy its flavor.

APRIL

April 1

WHITTAKER CHAMBERS

Whittaker Chambers' life was clouded by a sense of doom. He was a brooding, humorless man, intensely righteous but without zest for battle. Chambers was born April 1, 1901. His early family life was neurotic to the point of violence (one brother committed suicide). In 1948 Chambers, by then a defector from the Communist party, accused State Department official Alger Hiss of being a onetime fellow spy. In a series of highly charged congressional hearings and criminal trials that electrified the 1950s, Chambers stuck to his story. Hiss was convicted. Chambers retired to the seclusion of his Maryland farm, his heart assuaged by justice, but not by joy.

PROCESSIONAL: *Acts 22, 14-15* "The God of our fathers appointed you to know his will, to see the Just One and to hear a voice from his mouth; for you will be a witness for him to all men of what you have seen and heard." *Ps 81, 8-9* Hear, O my people, while I admonish you! O Israel, if you would but listen to me! There shall be no strange god among you; you shall not bow down to a foreign god.

RECESSIONAL: Let us give testimony to the truth that orthodoxy might be saved. But guide our actions, God, lest we discover that truth, elusive to the end, has fled our definitions, leaving us, your chosen ones, prostrate before the idol.

April 2

SAMUEL F. B. MORSE

Samuel F. B. Morse was a man with three careers. He started out in life to be a painter, graduated from Yale, studied in Europe, and opened a studio in Boston. He was the founder and longtime president of the National Academy of Design in New York City. In addition to this, Morse was involved in politics, especially during the "nativist" movement of the 1830s and 1840s. In 1836 he ran for mayor of New York on a nativist ticket, but lost. At the age of 41 he began to devote himself to the study of electromagnetism. Although the American Joseph Henry had previously invented the telegraph, Morse was the one who perfected it and who developed the code that bears his name. In 1844 he established the first telegraph line anywhere in the world, joining Baltimore and Washington. Morse was born in 1791, and he died on April 2, 1872.

OFFERTORY: Like opposing forces do the Father and his people await the confrontation, the space between them narrowing. We are twin poles, Lord and laity, who must cautiously and with deference approach each other, gifts in hand, until the right configuration is achieved. And then, when all our power's focused, across that final gap leaps light and understanding.

COMMUNION: *Ps 68, 28* Summon thy might, O God; show thy strength, O God, thou who hast wrought for us.

April 3

"BOSS" TWEED

Born April 3, 1823, William Marcy Tweed grew up on the streets of New York and got into politics though a job in the fire department. Tweed had only a minimal education, but that didn't matter much since he had no intention of actually working. While climbing through a series of city jobs, he simultaneously gained control of Tammany Hall, New York's Democratic stronghold. By 1868 Tweed owned the city and state governments, and with a coterie of friends he systematically looted them of something between $45 and $200 million. Tweed and the Tweed Ring were finally exposed by the press. Tweed was jailed, escaped and fled to Spain, was caught and again put in jail where he died in 1878.

PETITION: God, raise up among your people on diverse occasions figures like big-bellied William, clanking and strutting for our amusement and indignation. Unceasing virtue is boring to the point of tears; misconduct, on the other hand, has knowledge to impart. Show some concern for our development, we beg you, and give us men like Bill who make us poorer with their one hand and with the other make us wiser still.

RECESSIONAL: *Prov 8, 10-11* Take my instruction instead of silver, and knowledge rather than choice gold; for wisdom is better than jewels, and all that you may desire cannot compare with her.

April 4

MARTIN LUTHER KING, JR.

People who see injustice more clearly than those around them tend to be lonely people. Martin Luther King was no exception. On one hand he was a gregarious, funloving person. Yet the mountaintop that offered him a vision of the future also lifted him above the rest of us. He was such a simple man that the public frequently misread him: he was accused of inciting violence when in fact he supported nonviolence; white liberals attacked him for his antiwar stance, black militants for his "passivity." On April 4, 1968 he was shot down by a sniper in Memphis, Tenn. Given the circumstances, it was not unexpected. But why, when this lone man was killed, did the whole nation suddenly feel lonely?

PROCESSIONAL: *Is 49, 6* "It is too light a thing that you should be my servant to raise up the tribes of Jacob and to restore the preserved of Israel; I will give you as a light to the nations, that my salvation may reach to the end of the earth." *Ps 118, 5-6* Out of my distress I called on the Lord; the Lord answered me and set me free. With the Lord on my side I do not fear. What can man do to me?

COMMUNION: I have a dream that one day every valley shall be exalted, every hill and mountain shall be made low, the rough places will be made plain, and the crooked places will be made straight, and the glory of the Lord shall be revealed, and all flesh shall see it together . . .*

April 5

BOOKER T. WASHINGTON

Booker T. Washington was born a slave on April 5, 1856 in Virginia. Moving to West Virginia after the Civil War, he took menial jobs in a coal mine, in a salt factory, and as a janitor, all the while scratching an education out of books and schools for the poor. By 1881, now with college training, he was named to head the newly formed Tuskegee Institute, composed of two decaying buildings in Alabama, where he was supposed to produce black teachers. By his death 34 years later the institute had over 100 buildings, 1500 students, and an endowment of $2 million, and Washington, although denounced by some blacks for his posture of docility, was the best known and most respected black man in America.

OFFERTORY: We offer what we have to give, in the time we have to give it.

*Martin Luther King, Jr., speech at the Lincoln Memorial, Aug. 28, 1963.

We are a people of our age, using what our age provides. Were we blessed with future vision, Lord, able to anticipate the dangers to our children, we might rush to rectify them in advance. We surely would not squander time making gifts to you. But we do not see—nor did our parents before us, nor will our children coming after. This blindness is what makes your children precious, and what makes each generation golden.

RECESSIONAL: We are coming. We are crawling up, working up, yea, bursting up. Often through oppression, unjust discrimination, and prejudice, but through them we are coming up . . . There is no power on earth that can permanently stay our progress.*

April 6

ROBERT E. PEARY

On April 6, 1909 Robert E. Peary, accompanied by Matt Henson, a black American, arrived at a point on the arctic icecap which calculations proved to be the North Pole. They were the first men ever to reach the pole, and they made it after two fruitless tries and after suffering many privations in the icy wilderness. Peary, a naval officer from Pennsylvania, had an overflowing measure of self-confidence and a dogged determination to succeed—traits that served him well in the artic, and also back home when he had to defend his claim to be first at the pole against disbelievers. His deed inflated the pride of expansionist America, and Peary lived his remaining years in the glow of worldwide acclaim.

PROCESSIONAL: *Deut 2, 7* For the Lord your God has blessed you in all the work of your hands; he knows your going through this great wilderness; . . . the Lord your God has been with you; you have lacked nothing. *Ps 148, 7-8* Praise the Lord from the earth, you sea monsters and all deeps, fire and hail, snow and frost, stormy wind fulfilling his command!

PETITION: Be our guide, Lord God, when our horizon has no past or future, or day or darkness, or any nourishment for us in passing. Progress has no meaning in this landscape: the same mile is traversed again and again. Your saints extoll emptiness as suitable for contemplation, but we do not. We require movement clearly marked. Shake us out of this dread languor. Be our guide, and our destination.

*Booker T. Washington, from a speech at Harvard University, 1896.

April 7

BILLIE HOLLIDAY

Billie Holliday was born April 7, 1915 in Baltimore, the daughter of a professional guitarist. She began singing in New York in 1931 without formal training but with an instinctive feel for the line and structure of music. Within four years she was the leading jazz singer of her time. Nicknamed "Lady Day," she was the star of cabaret and concert. In the 1940s she became addicted to heroin which increasingly disrupted her life and eroded her voice, and which eventually hastened her death at the age of 44.

COMMUNION: *Ps 27, 6* And now my head shall be lifted up above my enemies round about me; and I will offer in his tent sacrifices with shouts of joy; I will sing and make melody to the Lord.

RECESSIONAL: The music dwindles in a lazy arc, spiraling into silence. O Lord, save us. Sing our song back to us when we can sing no longer.

April 8

F. W. WOOLWORTH

Frank Woolworth's first attempt at merchandising was a store in Utica, N.Y. where all items were sold for five cents. When that didn't work he tried again with a five-and-ten-cent store in Lancaster, Pa. That seemed to be the right formula. In fact it succeeded so well that by 1912 the F. W. Woolworth Co. was rich enough to build the tallest office building in the world for its New York headquarters. Woolworth was a frugal man who was able to keep low prices by paying low salaries to his clerks. He liked to appear in stores unannounced and try shoplifting to see if the employees were alert. By the time he died on April 8, 1919 he was a millionaire many times over with a thousand stores in the United States, Canada, and England.

PETITION: Almighty Father, you who showered manna on our pilgrim fathers, behold your followers today inundated by low-calorie manna, electric manna—even artificial manna—and none of it any longer free. We have a knack for stretching your beneficence to absurdity. Get us out of this predicament, we beg you. Restore in us the sense of simple things, even if it means taking us again into the wilderness.

April 9

FRANK LLOYD WRIGHT

A pupil of Louis Sullivan in Chicago, Frank Lloyd Wright developed early in his career a unique style of architecture based on the balancing of cubic forms and the harmonizing of structures with their surroundings. Wright was born in 1869 in Wisconsin. The flat plains of the midwest nourished his spirit as well as his body, inspiring him to fashion long, low buildings, in contrast to the vertical thrust of Victorian designs. As a man he was opinionated, dictatorial, delightful with friends, and considered a genius even by his critics. He died on this day in 1959.

PROCESSIONAL: *1 Kings 9, 3* "I have heard your prayer and your supplication, which you have made before me; I have consecrated this house which you have built, and put my name there forever." *Ps 132, 3-5* "I will not enter my house or get into my bed; I will not give sleep to my eyes or slumber to my eyelids, until I find a place for the Lord, a dwelling place for the mighty One of Jacob."

OFFERTORY: Behold, we have designed theologies to capture the transcendent Lord; we have left a place for him around our table; we have constructed a temple for his dwelling. Yet our works are powerless to call you forth, Lord God. Come, manifest yourself: Fill these voids that we have built, so that our past works will be justified and our future reassured.

April 10

THOMAS HART BENTON

For 30 years in the U.S. Senate Thomas Hart Benton spoke for the American west. He represented everything it stood for: hard money, expansion, the union, and the limitation of slavery. Benton had a booming voice, a hot temper, and a formidable ego. Once he put a bullet into Andrew Jackson, even though the two men became allies in later years. It was Benton's opposition to slavery that finally undercut him—representing as he did the slave state of Missouri. Dropped from the Senate, he returned to serve in the House, but by then things had gone too far to be salvaged by one man's magnetism. He was defeated for reelection in 1856, and he died two years later on April 10th.

PETITION: We don't want infallibility, Lord God—just the courage to stay with our personal judgment when the hard choice is at hand. Guide us as you did your servant Thomas down that path we estimate is best, even if it leads to our destruction. In a landscape of unrelenting shadow merely the memory of the light, reinforced with honor, will suffice.

COMMUNION: *Is 43, 4-5* You are precious in my eyes, and honored, and I love you, I give men in return for you, peoples in exchange for your life. Fear not, for I am with you: I will bring your offspring from the east, and from the west I will gather you.

April 11

CHARLES EVANS HUGHES

Charles Evans Hughes was born April 11, 1862 in upstate New York and studied law at Columbia. He had a distinguished career in government service spanning 35 years as governor of New York, secretary of state under Harding, as an associate justice and finally Chief Justice of the United States. A Republican, Hughes was nominated for the presidency in 1916, but lost the election to Wilson. The high-water marks of his career were the arms-limitation treaties he engineered before the First World War and, with the other "nine old men" of the Supreme Court, the blocking of several New Deal programs of Franklin Roosevelt. Hughes retired from the court in 1941 and died in 1948.

OFFERTORY: Our gifts anticipated every need—bread, wine, water, cup, candle, and serving plate. We knew precisely what was wanted. The rubrics specified our gestures; our syllables were measured out in type. And when those gifts were laid in splendor on the table, you, God, chose as usual one we never noticed, or had forgotten, or were ashamed of, for your special keeping. We are chagrined, and forced to the admission that our relationship is fixed not by what we have to give, but by what you wish to take.

April 12

FRANKLIN D. ROOSEVELT

No American President has been more admired and more heartily disliked in his day than Franklin Delano Roosevelt. He combined devious politics with great zest for life. He was a humanitarian who didn't shrink from using other humans for his ends. He was a complex, wily idealist who, elected to lead his country out of an economic depression, led it also through the greatest war the world has seen. On April 12, 1945 he died suddenly of a stroke. In the House of Commons the next day Winston Churchill called him "the greatest champion of freedom who has ever brought help and comfort from the new world to the old."

PROCESSIONAL: *Sir 10, 1* A wise magistrate will educate his people, and the rule of an understanding man will be well ordered. *Ps 145, 4, 7* One generation shall laud thy works to another, and shall declare thy mighty acts. They shall pour forth the fame of thy abundant goodness, and shall sing aloud of thy righteousness.

COMMUNION: The moneychangers have fled from their high seats in the temple of our civilization. We may now restore that temple to the ancient truths.*

April 13

THOMAS JEFFERSON

Thomas Jefferson probably contributed more to the American system of government, and indirectly to the American character, than any other citizen. Not only was he the principal author of the Declaration of Independence and the nation's third President, he also helped establish the principle of religious liberty, the theory of states' rights, the decimal currency system, the idea of free public education, and the orderly absorption of western territories. In addition, he was greatly interested in, and made important contributions to, the fields of philosophy, agriculture, architecture, and natural science. Jefferson was a gentle, even-tempered man: a Virginia aristocrat to the bone. He was not an effective speaker, but he was a brilliant and eloquent writer whose words precisely captured the spirit of American liberty. Jefferson was born on April 13, 1743; he died in 1826.

PROCESSIONAL: We hold these truths to be self-evident, that all men are created equal, that they are endowed by their creator with certain unalienable rights, that among these are life, liberty, and pursuit of happiness.** *Jer 34, 15* You recently repented and did what was right in my eyes by proclaiming liberty, each to his neighbor, and you made a covenant before me in the house which is called by my name.

COMMUNION: The God that gave us life, gave us liberty at the same time: the hand of force may destroy but cannot disjoin them.†

*From Franklin D. Roosevelt's first inaugural address, March 4, 1933.

**From the Declaration of Independence.

†From Summary View of the Rights of British America, by Thomas Jefferson, 1774.

RECESSIONAL: Strengthened by these mysteries, let us once renew our covenant, mutually pledging to each other our lives, our fortunes and our sacred honor.

April 14

RACHEL CARSON

Rachel Carson was born in Pennsylvania in 1907 and for many years was a biologist for the U.S. Bureau of Fisheries. Both as a scientist and as a lover of nature she was fascinated by the interrelations and evolution of living things, whether they were small creatures along the edge of the sea or songbirds in the trees. She wrote four books that were read throughout the world. Her final book, *The Silent Spring*, published in 1962, was a forthright attack on the use of chemical pesticides and proved to be the first shot in the environmental battle that was joined in the second half of the 20th century. Rachel Carson died on April 14, 1964.

OFFERTORY: When the light was newly born, you, creator of the world, made your children guardians of lakes and soil and living things, bidding us be gentle with your gifts. But we have left them smudged and fouled, their purposes demeaned. Roses are chewed up by machines. Refuse clogs your wells. From what is left, these offerings of bread and wine return from our dominion into yours. Handle them with care, we pray. Transform them tenderly, that we might learn from watching, and overcome our heedless ways.

RECESSIONAL: *Ps 8, 3-6, 8* When I look at thy heavens, the work of thy fingers, the moon and the stars which thou hast established; what is man that thou art mindful of him, and the son of man that thou dost care for him? Yet thou hast made him little less than God, and dost crown him with glory and honor. Thou hast given him dominion over the works of thy hands; thou hast put all things under his feet . . . the birds of the air, and the fish of the sea.

April 15

SACCO AND VANZETTI

On April 15, 1920 two men are killed during a payroll robbery in Massachusetts. Three weeks later police arrest Nicola Sacco and Bartolomeo Vanzetti, immigrant laborers. Both men protest their innocence, and the evidence against them is highly circumstantial, but their foreign birth and the fact that they admit to being anarchists weighs against them. Their conviction in 1921 arouses worldwide indignation and appeals for a new trial, especially after another convict confesses to the killings. A new trial is nevertheless not allowed. In April of 1927 Sacco and Vanzetti are sentenced to die, and on August 23rd of that year they are executed.

PROCESSIONAL: *Dan 3, 17* "Our God whom we serve is able to deliver us from the burning fiery furnace; and he will deliver us out of your hand, O king." *Ps 79, 10-11* Why should the nations say, "Where is their God?" Let the avenging of the outpoured blood of thy servants be known among the nations . . . Let the groans of the prisoners come before thee; according to thy great power preserve those doomed to die!

RECESSIONAL: Not only have I struggled all my life to eliminate crimes, the crimes that the official law and the official moral condemns, but also the crimes that the official moral and the official law sanctions and sanctifies—the exploitation and the oppression of the man by the man; and if there is a reason why I am here as a guilty man, if there is a reason why you . . . can doom me, it is this reason and none else . . .*

April 16

JACOB COXEY

One of America's oldest political tactics—the march on Washington—reached a nadir of sorts in 1893 when an "army" of 500 persons led by "General" Jacob Coxey entered the capitol during a financial slump. Coxey was an utterly respectible businessman from Massillon, O. who wanted the government to finance public works programs for the unemployed (an idea that anticipated the New Deal). The march degenerated into a carnival, yet Washington officials panicked, threw Coxey into jail, and effectively broke up his followers. Unruffled, Coxey went back to Massillon where he served one term as mayor and ran for President in 1936 on the Farm-Labor ticket. Coxey was born this day in 1854; he died in 1951.

PETITION: Don't think you can sit there in your holy city and ignore our pilgrimage, Lord God. We've been on the road too long to accept massive silence at your end. Let's have some recognition of the trials we've gone through, the pain and mocking laughter. Receive our delegation. Con-

---

*Bartolomeo Vanzetti, final statement in court, April 9, 1927.

found those stay-at-homes whose hearts have never felt the fire of holy discontent.

April 17

J. P. Morgan

Whenever J. P. Morgan went downtown all the bankers on the pavement looked at him. He was a short, ruddy man with a bulbous nose that made him look more like a brewer than an elder of the Episcopal Church (which he was). He was also a banker so rich and powerful that on one occasion he was able to shore up the United States government with a little loan of $63 million in gold. Morgan could stop financial panics almost by fiat. He bought out Andrew Carnegie with a flip of his checkbook, thereby creating the giant U.S. Steel Corporation. He was also present at the creation of General Electric and International Harvester. Morgan was born April 17, 1837. When he died in 1913 he was the most powerful financial leader in the nation, perhaps in the world.

Processional: *2 Chron. 1, 12* "Wisdom and knowledge are granted to you. I will also give you riches, possessions, and honor, such as none of the kings had who were before you, and none after you shall have the like." *Ps 112, 2-3* His descendants will be mighty in the land; the generation of the upright will be blessed. Wealth and riches are in his house; and his righteousness endures for ever.

Recessional: Riches and power are found in the Lord, and the strength of his house protects us. He has nourished us from out of his storehouse, and in return expects only his due.

April 18

Ernie Pyle

Ernie Pyle had a down-home quality about him. Nothing he ever wrote was hailed as great literature, and he never stood out in a crowd. He was just a common journalist with an eye for human qualities that the high-powered reporters skipped over. Pyle was born in Indiana. He covered the London blitz in 1940. When the U.S. was pulled into the war Pyle wrote about it from the foxholes. He followed American soldiers through North Africa, Italy, Sicily, France, and to the Pacific. His columns appeared in 200 stateside papers and were filled with the names and hometowns of other ordinary men like himself. On April 18, 1945 he was on a small island near Okinawa, close to the front lines as usual, when machine-gun bullets found him and killed him. Millions of Americans who never met him wept as if a friend had died.

OFFERTORY: Out of ordinary gifts your people, God, have fabricated greatness. In the test of fire only the plainest goods will serve; commonness and purity are virtues you ordain. Feed us simply, that simplicity might be ingrained in us. Then, if sacrifice is needed once again, we will be bonded as a stronger people still, and shall not bend.

COMMUNION: *Is 40, 1-2* Comfort, comfort my people, says your God. Speak tenderly to Jerusalem, and cry to her that her warfare is ended, that her iniquity is pardoned.

April 19

BENJAMIN RUSH

Next to Ben Franklin, Benjamin Rush was probably the most versatile man in colonial America. He was a doctor by profession. He established the nation's first free dispensery in 1786 and lectured on medicine at the University of Pennsylvania. Rush was also involved in politics. He was a signer of the Declaration of Independence, was surgeon general of the Continental army, and was treasurer of the United States from 1797 until his death on April 19, 1813. With all these activities Rush found time to champion the abolition of slavery, lobby for the mentally ill, and work to improve public education in his home state of Pennsylvania.

PETITION: Break down the walls of our endeavors, God. Bring confusion to those who would restrict doctors to their medicines and clergy to their prayers. Narrow men are defined by their skills while creative men are opened. Give us breadth of vision and breadth of caring. Every human molecule is a mirror of the whole and must immerse itself therein.

April 20

DANIEL CHESTER FRENCH

Daniel Chester French, one of America's most popular and most prolific sculptors, was born April 20, 1850 in New Hampshire and studied art in Boston, New York, and Italy. French was only 25 when his first major work was unveiled by Emerson—the famous statue of the minuteman that stands in Concord, Mass. Among his other works are the seated statue of John Harvard in Cambridge, the equestrian statue of Grant in Philadelphia, the standing Lincoln in Lincoln, Neb., and—best known of all—the seated statue of Lincoln in the Lincoln Memorial in Washington.

PROCESSIONAL: *Is 51, 1-2* "Hearken to me, you who pursue deliverance, you who seek the Lord; look to the rock from which you were hewn, and to the quarry from which you were digged. Look to Abraham your father and to Sarah who bore you." *Prov 12, 14* From the fruit of his words a man is satisfied with good, and the work of a man's hand comes back to him.

COMMUNION: We asked for life and were given a stone; we fed upon it, and we were nourished.

April 21

JOHN MUIR

John Muir was born April 21, 1838 in Scotland and spent his boyhood in the Wisconsin backwoods. He was planning to become a mechanic, but when an eye injury forced him to give that up he became a naturalist instead. Muir never acquired academic credentials. He went to college but couldn't abide a formal curriculum, and so he never graduated. The bulk of his knowledge he gained firsthand by tramping through thousands of miles of virgin forests in North America, describing them in his journals and in magazine articles. The enthusiasm he generated for the continent's unspoiled lands inspired the U.S. government to set aside vast areas of wilderness, comprising today most of Yosemite National Park and the California sequoia groves. Muir died in 1914.

OFFERTORY: Receive these offerings and preserve them—not from time and decay but from the desecration of the faithless who do not recognize the things they trample on. Lord God we give you what is yours already, and you renew them for our wonderment.

RECESSIONAL: *Ps 96, 11-12* Let the heavens be glad, and let the earth rejoice; let the sea roar and all that fills it; let the field exult, and everything in it! Then shall all the trees of the wood sing for joy.

April 22

J. ROBERT OPPENHEIMER

Both as a physicist and as the administrator of the Los Alamos project in

New Mexico, Robert Oppenheimer is credited with being the "father" of the atomic bomb. Oppenheimer was a sensitive, intensely moral man for whom that title had no glamour and who frequently objected to the way governments used scientific discoveries. Because of these reservations, and because he flirted with socialism as a youth, he came under a cloud of suspicion during the McCarthy era, was tried and had his security clearance taken away. Only toward the end of his life were honors and acclaim restored to him. Oppenheimer was born April 22, 1904. He died in 1967.

PROCESSIONAL: *1 Kings 19, 11-12* A great and strong wind rent the mountains, and broke in pieces the rocks before the Lord, but the Lord was not in the wind; and after the wind an earthquake, but the Lord was not in the earthquake; and after the earthquake a fire, but the Lord was not in the fire. *Response* If the radiance of a thousand suns/were to burst at once into the sky,/That would be like the splendor of the Mighty One . . . /I am become death,/the shatter of worlds.*

PETITION: God you are not a thoughtless parent who puts killing toys into the hands of children. From the beginning of time you dressed the world in mystery; only gradually did we discern its hidden keys. Now with our new-found prize we bless you, and beg your guidance too. For in maturity we have found smallness. Now that the secret is in our hands we are again frightened children.

April 23

STEPHEN A. DOUGLAS

Stephen A. Douglas was born April 23, 1813 in Vermont and moved to Illinois in the 1830s. He went to Congress in 1843 and became a Senator in 1847, rapidly making a name for himself as an able legislator and loyal Democrat. Douglas might have been President, and almost was, but he waffled on the slavery issue, losing friends first in the north and then in the south. Abe Lincoln challenged his Senate seat in 1858 and lost, but not until the two men had engaged in a celebrated series of debates. Two years later Lincoln ran for President as a Republican and Douglas as a Democrat. This time Lincoln won easily. Defeated and cast aside, Douglas died in 1861.

COMMUNION: We strove for peace, but peace was not within our power. Now, Lord God, you come among us with a sword.

*From the *Bhagavad-Gita.*

my strong refuge. My mouth is filled with thy praise, and with thy glory all the day. Do not cast me off in the time of old age; forsake me not when my strength is spent.

April 24

WILLA CATHER

Willa Cather was born in Virginia but moved when she was nine to a farm in Nebraska. It was a region that would have a powerful influence on her life and her writing. Cather was moved by the hard, simple beauty of life on the plains. She absorbed the laconic speech and pared-down expressions of plains people and reproduced them in her novels which were straightforward and unadorned by elaborate rhetoric. Among her best-known works are *O Pioneers!*, *My Antonia*, and *Death Comes for the Archbishop*. Cather herself died on April 24, 1947.

OFFERTORY: Out of the dark soil comes life, green and pliant, responding to your breath, O Lord. Sweet grass carpets the earth as far as the eye can see, to where a solitary house rides the horizon. Receive a gift from out of this bounty—not for our glory, or necessarily for yours, but for the nameless shadows who broke this soil, breaking themselves, and who disappeared. Out of their shadow grows a nation, green and pliant, responding to your breath.

COMMUNION: *Deut 8, 7-8, 10* The Lord your God is bringing you into a good land, a land of brooks of water, of fountains and springs, flowing forth in valleys and hills, a land of wheat and barley . . . And you shall eat and be full, and you shall bless the Lord your God for the good land he has given you.

April 25

EDWARD R. MURROW

Edward R. Murrow was pioneer of electronic journalism, both as a radio reporter from war-torn London during World War II and as a fearless television commentator after the war. His special television reports in the 1950s dramatizing the plight of migrant workers and the methods of Sen. Joseph McCarthy made Murrow a controversial figure without diminishing his popularity with the mass of Americans. Murrow was born April

25, 1908 in North Carolina; he served briefly as an information specialist in the Kennedy administration before his death of cancer in 1965.

PROCESSIONAL: *Jer 11, 6* "Proclaim all these words in the cities of Judah, and in the streets of Jerusalem: Hear the words of this covenant and do them." *Ps 95, 7* O that today you would hearken to his voice! Harden not your hearts.

RECESSIONAL: Strengthened by the example of your servant Edward, may our steps be guided by the light, and when the light is hidden, then by a distant star that is beyond the power of men to move.

April 26

JOHN AUDUBON

John James Audubon was something of a showman. In the salons of London he enjoyed dressing as an American frontiersman, but in the American backwoods he was liable to show up as a European dandy. Actually he was both, being born the illegitimate son of a French officer and a native woman in the West Indies on April 26, 1785. Audubon came to America to make his fortune. He was a failure as a storekeeper in Kentucky, mainly because he spent most of his time making pictures of wild birds. In 1826 he took his drawings to England where they created a sensation. They were scientifically accurate yet lovely works of art. The publication of *Birds of America* in 1827 enabled him to spend the rest of his life doing what he loved best—tramping through fields and swamps sketching wildlife. He died in 1851.

PETITION: Lord God you have preserved us in days of failure and defeat. Teach us the secret of your saving power so that we, too, might have skill in staving off time's descent. May the effect of our passing serve to maintain beauty for all generations. Let our lives be translucent rooms where winter eyes can see the radiance of a hundred Junes.

COMMUNION: *Mt 6, 26* "Look at the birds of the air: they neither sow nor reap nor gather into barns, and yet your heavenly Father feeds them."

April 27

ULYSSES S. GRANT

If you believe the popular myth, Ulysses S. Grant was an unimaginative general and an incompetent President. In truth, Grant was neither of these. He was a bold and innovative field commander, and he was a moderately able President whose terms in office were scarred by the actions of subordinates. Grant was born April 27, 1822 in Ohio, went to West Point, and served in the Mexican War. He resigned from the army and lived for several years on the edge of poverty before the Civil War called him back to service. Grant was a simple and trusting person—perhaps too trusting as a politician—but with a singleness of purpose that served him well when he was confronted by clear-cut issues.

PROCESSIONAL: *Jer 51, 20, 23* "You are my hammer and weapon of war; with you I break nations in pieces; with you I destroy kingdoms" . . . "with you I break in pieces the shepherd and his flock; with you I break in pieces the farmer and his team; with you I break in pieces governors and commanders." *Ps 44, 2* Thou with thy own hand didst drive out the nations, but them thou didst plant; thou didst afflict the peoples, but them thou didst set free.

OFFERTORY: Again and again the nation offered gifts, but somehow they did not suffice: in the Wilderness, at Spottsylvania, Gaines Mill, Cold Harbor—place names like bells tolling. For a hundred miles the ground was drenched with blood; corpses were stacked like cordwood. All subtlety was gone; the only skill they had was dying. Two explanations of this madness are possible: One, that the Lord of hosts is insatiable and does not hear his people. Two, that he hears and accepts the gift, but that his people are compulsive givers.

April 28

JAMES MONROE

James Monroe was born April 28, 1758 in Virginia and was an officer in the Revolutionary War. He later served in the Senate, as ambassador to France and England, as governor of Virginia, secretary of state under Jefferson, and as President from 1816 to 1824. His presidency, which saw the Floridas acquired from Spain and the Missouri Compromise enacted, was known as the "era of good feeling" because of the degree of domestic stability that prevailed. Monroe also issued the famous doctrine that warned foreign powers from encroachment in the Western Hemisphere.

PETITION: Bring tranquillity to your people, God, such as there existed in the days of your son James. Bring us together by means of your word; that way we can share a common hope even as we grapple with our differences.

RECESSIONAL: *Deut 10, 11* "Arise, go on your journey at the head of the people, that they may go in and possess the land, which I swore to their fathers to give them."

April 29

DUKE ELLINGTON

Edward Kennedy Ellington was born in Washington, D.C. on April 29, 1899. Even as a teen-ager he was an intelligent and talented young man whose elegant manners earned him the nickname "Duke." Offered a choice between art and music as a career, he chose music. He taught himself to be a jazz pianist and composer—in the opinion of historian Ralph Gleason "the greatest composer this American society has produced." He produced a wide variety of works ranging from popular numbers such as "Don't Get Around Much Anymore" to elaborate concert pieces and sacred music, all of which brought a new level of sophistication to what Ellington liked to call "negro music." He died, full of years and honors, in 1974.

OFFERTORY: All right then, don't take these gifts! They don't say what we mean, anyway; our deepest wishes can't be put in words. We'll find some elemental language constructed wholly out of tears and laughter, and sighs, counterpointed by the beating of our hearts. Then if we're not giving you what you want, at least you'll know you're hearing what we really are.

COMMUNION: *Eph 5, 18-19* Be filled with the Spirit, addressing one another in psalms and hymns and spiritual songs, singing and making melody to the Lord with all your heart.

April 30

JOHN CROWE RANSOM

John Crowe Ransom was born April 30, 1888 in Pulaski, Tenn. and graduated from Vanderbilt—the same college where he subsequently taught English from 1914 to 1937. Ransom was a poet of limited output and enormous influence. His exquisitely wrought verse offered ironic and dispassionate commentaries on human relations. His poems frequently evoked images of the aristocratic south, a setting Ransom championed in his genteel back-to-the-land philosophy. Equally influential as a critic, he taught for the last 37 years of his life at Kenyon College in Ohio and edited the *Kenyon Review*. He died in 1974.

PETITION: Inspire in us, Lord God, as you inspired in your servant John, dissatisfaction with the carelessly made thing. Strengthen our senses and our purpose that our creations may be purified by force until they stand by themselves, balanced precisely, cold and sharp as steel.

RECESSIONAL: Resume harvesters. The treasure is full bronze/Which you will garner for the Lady, and the moon/Could tinge it no yellower than does this noon;/But grey will quench it shortly—the field, men, stones./Pluck fast dreamers; prove as you amble slowly/Not less than men, not wholly.*

*Excerpt from "Antique Harvesters" © 1927 by Alfred A. Knopf, Inc. and renewed 1955 by John Crowe Ransom. Reprinted from *Selected Poems*, Third Edition, Revised and Enlarged, by John Crowe Ransom, by permission of the publisher.

MAY

May 1

GEORGE DEWEY

Admiral George Dewey was a Vermonter who went to Annapolis, who fought in the Civil War under David Farragut, and later rose to command the Asiatic Fleet. On May 1, 1898 he led a battle line of cruisers and gunboats into Manila Bay to rout the Spanish fleet in an action that overnight made the United States a world power. Dewey was not a modest man. Mentioned as a presidential candidate in 1900 he told reporters that he had studied the matter and was "convinced that the office of President is not such a very difficult one to fill." Dewey was born in 1837; he died in 1917.

PETITION: Give strength to our arms, Lord God. See fit to strengthen us in the hour of need. For the sea has been fed by tears, and the orphan on the mountain cries for someone to care for him. Give strength to our arms —the arms of consolation—on that day when the conquest is over and the burden of victory starts.

COMMUNION: *Is 23, 11* He has stretched out his hand over the sea, he has shaken the kingdoms; the Lord has given command concerning Canaan to destroy its strongholds.

May 2

JOSEPH MCCARTHY

Joe McCarthy had been an unremarkable senator until that day in 1950 when he announced that many "known Communists" were employed in the State Department. Those were days when Americans had seen the red tide sweep across China and eastern Europe and were willing to believe the worst. McCarthy rode their fears to dizzying heights of power, attacking anyone who opposed him and proving that when an accusation is sufficiently venemous evidence is not required. In the end it was the poison of his own manner that undid him before a national television audience. Mc-

Carthy died this day in 1957, 17 months after his formal condemnation by the Senate.

PROCESSIONAL: *Is 8, 12-13* "Do not call conspiracy all that this people call conspiracy, and do not fear what they fear, nor be in dread. But the Lord of hosts, him you shall regard as holy; let him be your fear, and let him be your dread." *Sir 28, 1-2* He that takes vengeance will suffer vengeance from the Lord, and he will firmly establish his sins. Forgive your neighbor the wrong he has done, and then your sins will be pardoned when you pray.

RECESSIONAL: In parting, let us once more renounce fear, putting a lid on that dark box and all its nightime ogres. If it will not go away, at least we will ignore it. And let us give ourselves instead to the task of increasing the light, to aid our own progress and the progress of all peoples.

May 3

J. EDGAR HOOVER

J. Edgar Hoover was only 29 years old when he became director of the Federal Bureau of Investigation—then a weak and ineffective branch of the Justice Department. Hoover changed that. For the next 48 years he supervised its operations against underworld gangs, World War II espionage agents, postwar Communists, campus radicals, and anyone else Hoover saw as a threat to the national security. In the process Hoover made the FBI into a personal fiefdom, powerful beyond imagination, accountable only to himself. He was admired, feared, and politically untouchable. After his death on May 3, 1972 he became the first civil servant honored by having his casket displayed in the Rotunda of the Capitol building.

PROCESSIONAL: *Is 21, 8* "Upon a watchtower I stand, O Lord, continually by day, and at my post I am stationed whole nights." *Ps 55, 9-11* Destroy their plans, O Lord, confuse their tongues; for I see violence and strife in the city . . . mischief and trouble are within it, ruin is in its midst; oppression and fraud do not depart from its market place.

PETITION: Protection, God, is what we seek. Save us from the armed man, from the one who might be armed, from the one who looks as if someday he may want to take up arms, from the one who never smiles, from the one who smiles too much, from the one who stays awake while we're asleep. From all these, Father, save us. Protection is what we seek.

May 4

WILLIAM MCGUFFEY

William McGuffey was the man who put together the McGuffey Readers in the mid-1800s, books that sold well over 100 million copies and which were the principal tools for reading instruction in the south and midwest. Although primitive by today's standards, the readers were a vast improvement over the textbooks of their day; they introduced students to real literature, and they had a strong moral tone—which stemmed from the fact that McGuffey was an ordained Presbyterian minister. McGuffey was born in 1800, was largely self-taught as a youth, and graduated from Washington College in Ohio. He was one of the founders of the public school system of Ohio, was president of Ohio University in Athens, O., and later taught philosophy at the University of Virginia. He died on May 4, 1873.

OFFERTORY: As usual the wishes that we offer you, Father, are confused: They are needs without shape, hopes without arrangement. You are the one who brought order out of chaos. Take this yearning, then, and give a name to it at least. Give us words so we will know what we are longing for, words and we'll be fed with knowledge when we eat.

RECESSIONAL: *Bar 1, 14* You shall read this book which we are sending you, to make your confession in the house of the Lord on the days of the feasts and at appointed seasons.

May 5

BRET HARTE

Bret Harte was not a great writer, but his gusty and colorful tales brought the California frontier vividly to life for readers in the 1860s, and for readers still today. Not even Mark Twain could match the authentic detail and earthy humor of *The Luck of Roaring Camp* or *Tennessee's Partner*. Harte came east to be lionized in 1870, but once removed from his sources he lost his inspiration. His writing sagged. Distressed, he took a diplomatic post and spent most of his remaining years in Europe, dying in London on May 5, 1902.

COMMUNION: Come with me all you who seek. Come beyond the rutted streets, past swinging doors, the cries and laughter, the music and the ladies fading. Promise awaits you in the hills. A stream issues from the rock, lavering the mountain, and in its wash there may be found the glint of possibility. Come.

May 6

HENRY DAVID THOREAU

Henry David Thoreau was born in Concord, Mass. and lived there most of his life, sometimes with his friend and teacher Emerson and for two years alone in the woods, which inspired his famous book *Walden*. Thoreau was a philosopher, a poet, and a naturalist who urged his readers to adopt the simple, self-reliant life and who was utterly opposed to the growing trends of urbanization and industrialization. Although a retiring man, his conscience could be galvanized by social issues; his essay on civil disobedience grew out of a day he spent in jail for refusing to pay taxes to support the Mexican War. Thoreau died on this day in 1862 of tuberculosis.

PROCESSIONAL: Living was so dear, I did not wish to live what was not life; nor did I wish to practice resignation.* *Ps 23, 2-3* He makes me lie down in green pastures. He leads me beside still waters; he restores my soul. He leads me in paths of righteousness for his name's sake.

PETITION: Enlighten us, we pray, as you did enlighten your servant Henry, who measured trees by embracing them, so that we too might embrace life wherever we find it, and struggle against forces which deny it.

RECESSIONAL: I went to the woods because I wished to live deliberately, to front only the essential facts of life, and see if I could learn what it had to teach, and not, when I came to die, to discover that I had not lived.*

May 7

GARY COOPER

Gary Cooper was born May 7, 1901 as the son of a Montana supreme court justice. He went to college in Iowa and worked on his father's ranch before moving to California in 1925 to work as a salesman. His ability to ride horses got him into the movies, and he graduated from bit parts to stardom with such films as *Mr. Deeds Goes to Town*, *For Whom the Bell Tolls*, *Pride of the Yankees*, *Sargeant York* and *High Noon*. In his roles Cooper portrayed men who were warmhearted, idealistic, perhaps even naive, but also strong and unyielding in the face of duty. Cooper died in 1961 in Hollywood.

*From *Walden* by Henry David Thoreau.

PETITION: Grant, O Lord, that our lives too, as was that of your son Gary, be paradigms of affirmation. Even in the darkest days, when everyone lines up against us, help us speak that simple word which says that we exist, that we believe. Yup.

COMMUNION: *Ps 119, 132-134* Turn to me and be gracious to me, as is thy wont toward those who love thy name. Keep steady my steps according to thy promise, and let no iniquity get dominion over me. Redeem me from man's oppression, that I may keep thy precepts.

May 8

HARRY S TRUMAN

Harry Truman, who was born today in 1884, was the very image of middle-class, small-town America. He was a farm boy and a family man. He liked to play poker and swap stories with his pals. He was a man of fierce loyalties—a quality that helped him become a judge, U.S. Senator, and then vice president of the United States. When Franklin D. Roosevelt died in 1945, the small-town boy became President. He tackled the complexities of the postwar world with the only talents he had: blunt candor and a cocky willingness to fight. The results, while not always artistic, were effective. And by the time he died in 1972 his public at last perceived that the small-town boy had developed more than a measure of greatness.

PROCESSIONAL: *Is 49, 2* He made my mouth like a sharp sword, in the shadow of his hand he hid me; he made me a polished arrow, in his quiver he hid me away. *Ps 41, 11-12* By this I know that thou art pleased with me, in that my enemy has not triumphed over me. But thou hast upheld me because of my integrity, and set me in thy presence for ever.

RECESSIONAL: Give us, God, the guts of Harry, your crony. No one will dare to push us around. Then we can stop all the fiddle-faddle we have to put up with—all the fancy language they make up to hide the truth. We know what's going on. From now on, let's call it as we see it.

May 9

WALTER REUTHER

When Walter Reuther was a foreman at the Ford Motor Co. he was fired for organizing workers. That wasn't unusual for 1932 when the labor movement was marked by unconcealed hostility and sporadic violence. In his rise to be head of the United Auto Workers and organizer of the CIO, Reuther survived several beatings and one assassination attempt. As a labor leader he combined toughness at the bargaining table with a visionary sense of humanity, being an active supporter of the black civil rights movement and a critic of other labor leaders who enjoyed high salaries and ostentatious living. Reuther died in an airplane crash on May 9, 1970.

PETITION: Don't put just our hands to work, Lord God. We have had enough of that—we want that understood. Surely you didn't make the world just because you had six days to kill. Well, we're creators too! Give us a chance to make our names as well as make our living. Then we will be able to look upon our labor and see that it is good.

COMMUNION: *Eccles 5, 18* Behold, what I have seen to be good and to be fitting is to eat and drink and find enjoyment in all the toil with which one toils under the sun.

May 10

ETHAN ALLEN

On the morning of May 10, 1775 a band of volunteer soldiers called the Green Mountain Boys surprised the British garrison at Fort Ticonderoga, N.Y. and captured it almost without a shot. The fort was useless, but the cannon it contained were precious as gold. The raid was the work of Ethan Allen, a husky, self-proclaimed colonel who wanted most of all to make Vermont a separate nation. Allen was a kind of frontier philosopher, much taken with the 18th-century Enlightenment but willing to use force when reason failed. He lived to be captured by the British, to see his Vermont dream fade, and to lose all his property as well. He died at the age of 51.

PROCESSIONAL: *Josh 6, 20* The people raised a great shout, and the wall fell down flat, so that the people went up into the city, every man straight before him, and they took the city. *Ps 106, 10, 12* So he saved them from the hand of the foe, and delivered them from the power of the enemy. Then they believed his words; they sang his praise.

RECESSIONAL: Nourished by the strength of our communion we are able to protect ourselves from those who would infringe upon our freedom. Help us to be welcoming, Lord God, but save us from the guest who starts to feel our home belongs to him.

May 11

OTTMAR MERGANTHALER

Who was the most significant inventor of 19th-century America? Eli Whitney? Cyrus McCormick? Probably Ottmar Merganthaler. A mechanic and engineer who emigrated from Germany, Merganthaler in the 1880s constructed a machine that actually set printers' type automatically, casting each line in hot metal and eliminating the tedious process of setting each letter by hand. This "linotype" machine revolutionized printing throughout the world, raising the literacy rate everywhere. Merganthaler, who was born May 11, 1854, died in Baltimore in 1899, much honored and greatly enriched by his creation.

PETITION: Lord God, you who honored Moses with words cut into stone, preserve your servant Ottmar who did the same with lead, and quickly. It's no small thing to be in publishing, whether from a loft or on a mountain peak; and if we have not improved upon your message, bless at least our progress in technique.

May 12

J.E.B. STUART

"Jeb" Stuart was the personification of the gentleman officer of the Confederacy: dashing in appearance, personally brave and pious, considerate to his own troops and to his enemies. For three years he led the southern cavalry in an unbroken series of victories, on at least two occasions riding around the entire Union army. As the war continued, however, Union horsemen began to match his in skill and in strength. On May 12, 1864 his command was defeated at the battle of Yellow Tavern in Virginia, and Stuart was killed. He was 31 years old.

PROCESSIONAL: *Deut 20, 1* "When you go forth to war against your enemies, and see horses and chariots and an army larger than your own, you shall not be afraid of them; for the Lord your God is with you." *Response* Hurrah! Hurrah! For Southern rights, Hurrah! Hurrah! for the Bonnie Blue Flag that bears a single star.*

OFFERTORY: In the beginning it was easy to give; we were strong and our riches were overflowing. But there came a day when we went to the storehouse and it was empty: The wheat and the wine had all been spent; the

*"Bonnie Blue Flag," a Confederate patriotic song, lyrics by Harry McCarthy.

morning and the sunlight had all been spent; our youth and our strength had all been spent. All we had left was the skill of giving. So in the end we gave that.

May 13

CYRUS MCCORMICK

Cyrus McCormick was the inventor of the McCormick reaper and other harvesting machinery that turned the American Great Plains into the world's most bountiful food-producing region. McCormick was a Virginian, the son of a mechanic who had tried himself for many years to perfect a mechanical reaper. In 1831 McCormick *fils* succeeded, although he did not take out a patent until three years later. By the mid-1840s McCormick reapers were used everywhere and were being produced in great quantities at McCormick's Chicago plant. The inventor died in Chicago on May 13, 1884.

PETITION: In your wisdom, Father, you scattered seeds throughout the earth, showering abundance on your nation. Grant that we who gather up what you have sown will share it among ourselves with the same munificence, and equal wisdom.

COMMUNION: *Ps 65, 11-13* Thou crownest the year with thy bounty; the tracks of thy chariot drip with fatness. The pastures of the wilderness drip, the hills gird themselves with joy, the meadows clothe themselves with flocks, the valleys deck themselves with grain, they shout and sing together for joy.

May 14

DAVID BELASCO

David Belasco was the best-known stage producer in America around the turn of the century, as well as a writer and designer for the stage. He was especially known for his realistic stage effects and lighting. It's estimated that he produced more than 300 plays in his lifetime. Belasco's own works were generally superficial and have not endured. However two of them were turned into operas by Puccini: *Madame Butterfly* and *Girl of the Golden West*. Belasco was born in San Francisco in 1853. He died in New York City on May 14, 1931.

PROCESSIONAL: *Acts 26, 16* Rise and stand upon your feet; for I have appeared to you for this purpose, to appoint you to serve and bear witness to the things in which you have seen me and to those in which I will appear to you. *Sir 42, 18-19* For the Most High knows all that may be known, and he looks into the signs of the age. He declares what has been and what is to be, and he reveals the tracks of hidden things.

OFFERTORY: The truth is clearer in the dawn than at midday. From that obscure first light we have pieced together stories of the garden, and the mountain, how the sea withdrew, and the voice that spoke in flames. Don't ask if they are facts. Ask instead: Do they live? Do they matter? This is why we act them out again, and we are born once more.

May 15

EDWARD HOPPER

Edward Hopper was the artist of the city. Not of the teeming, skyscraper city but of the empty city street, of angular shapes of buildings caught in the slanting sunlight and almost devoid of people. Because he preferred architectural forms to human forms, Hopper's paintings seem to radiate a special kind of loneliness. Yet to the discerning eye there is strength in them too, and security, and peace. Hopper was born in 1882 and lived nearly all his life in New York City, where he died on May 15, 1967.

PETITION: If you can't come to walk our streets, Lord God, send your word instead, or, failing that, send light. We've become inured to minimal revelation. Where some would speak of emptiness, we speak of expectation.

RECESSIONAL: *Eccles 11, 7-8* Light is sweet, and it is pleasant for the eyes to behold the sun. For if a man lives many years, let him rejoice in them all; but let him remember that the days of darkness will be many.

May 16

PHILIP ARMOUR

Philip Armour, the meat-packing magnate, was not a simple butcher at heart. What he was was a slick operator. Anticipating a drop in hog prices at the end of the Civil War, he parlayed meat futures into a cool $2 million for his small Milwaukee company. He invested that in the grain market and in a much larger meat-packing operation, this time in Chicago. He made Chicago hog butcher of the world, and within a few years Armour products were sold literally around the globe. Meanwhile, Armour got richer on the stock market. Armour was born on May 16, 1832; he died in 1901, worth about $50 million.

OFFERTORY: We are all attendants at the slaughter. What long ago was a hallowed act, we have made into a business. What was once accomplished on the altar, happens now on the assembly line. Receive this offering, Lord God, and condenscend to change it for our good, that it may cleanse our bodies and our minds, and free us from the blood of animals and men.

COMMUNION: *Sir 50, 15* He reached out his hand to the cup and poured a libation of the blood of the grape; he poured it out at the foot of the altar, a pleasing odor to the Most High, the King of all.

May 17

JOHN JAY

John Jay had the distinction of being his country's first Chief Justice, its first secretary of state (under the Articles of Confederation), and its first minister to Spain. He was also president of the Continental Congress, a member of the peace delegation that ended the Revolutionary War, and chief justice and governor of New York State. Despite his titles and his brilliance, Jay's career was somehow disappointing; always on the brink of greatness, he never achieved it. His finest hour came not in office but in writing *The Federalist* papers with Hamilton, urging the formation of a strong executive government. Jay died on this day in 1829 at the age of 83.

PETITION: God, you have bestowed upon your nation leaders; and on your people, by divine right, wisdom. Give each side in this arrangement sense to realize when it is most fit for them to act, and when it is most fit to follow.

May 18

JACQUES MARQUETTE

Did Father Marquette really want to convert the indians? Well, yes. But he was also sensitive to the expansionist aims of France in the New

World. With his friend Joliet in 1673 he explored the upper reaches of the Mississippi River, from Green Bay to within 700 miles of the Gulf. Worn out by dysentery, Marquette attempted another missionary journey to Illinois two years later but died on May 18th in 1675. In his memory were named a diocese, a college, a city, and a railroad.

PROCESSIONAL: *Is 43, 19-20* I will make a way in the wilderness and rivers in the desert. The wild beasts will honor me, the jackals and the ostriches; for I give water in the wilderness, rivers in the desert, to give drink to my chosen people. *Ps 46, 4* There is a river whose streams make glad the city of God, the holy habitation of the Most High.

RECESSIONAL: You are dismissed. Go not in sunlight, or to a destination that is known. Overhead, trees will shut off the sky, your course will bend and twist upon itself. Still, this is the way that must be followed. You are dismissed.

May 19

CHARLES IVES

Charles Ives was born the son of a bandmaster in Danbury, Conn., and as a boy he walloped a drum in his father's band on summer afternoons in the park. The hymns they played, the marches, the folk melodies, all found expression in his own music years later when Ives became one of the most creative, and most unnoticed, composers in 20th-century America. To compensate for obscurity Ives sold insurance and made a comfortable living. It was only in his last years, and after his death on May 19, 1954, that people began to listen to his extravagant, romantic music, and to appreciate it.

OFFERTORY: Purity, they say, is found in fire. In fire the dross is burned away till one element alone remains. Our business, though, is the opposite reaction when elements are joined, are mingled. Bring our gifts together, Lord; harmonize them, mix them up, so that your melting pot produces not dead purity, but life.

COMMUNION: *Sir 32, 5-6* A ruby seal in a setting of gold is a concert of music at a banquet of wine. A seal of emerald in a rich setting of gold is the melody of music with good wine.

May 20

CHARLES A. LINDBERGH

At 7:52 in the morning of May 20, 1927 a silver monoplane lifted heavily from the rain-slickened runway at Roosevelt Field, N.Y. The pilot was Charles A. Lindbergh, an unknown mail-service flier from Minnesota. When he landed 33½ hours later in Paris he was the most famous man in the world. Lindbergh was the archetypal American hero: handsome, intelligent, modest, and basically conservative. He was an earnest young man, a quality that made him both endearing and vulnerable. His campaign against U.S. involvement in Europe prior to World War II dented his popularity and drove him further into a shell of privacy from which he emerged only briefly before his death in 1974.

PROCESSIONAL: *Sir 24, 5* Alone I have made the circuit of the vault of heaven and have walked in the depths of the abyss. *Ps 63, 5-7* My mouth praises thee with joyful lips, when I think of thee upon my bed and meditate on thee in the watches of the night; for thou hast been my help, and in the shadow of thy wings I sing for joy.

COMMUNION: Out of the cloud that hides him will the Lord descend. His wings will cast light upon the upturned faces of his people.

May 21

JANE ADDAMS

Jane Addams was a pioneer in the American social-reform movement. The daughter of a prominent Illinois family, she established in 1889 a private welfare center called Hull House in a Chicago slum and worked there for 30 years, drawing artists and educators in to help her. Through her articles, books, and public speeches she also became an influential supporter of organized labor, women's sufferage, and the peace movement. In 1931 she was jointly awarded the Nobel Prize for Peace. She died on May 21, 1935.

OFFERTORY: These gifts of ours are simply tokens—pennies on the drum to salve our consciences. The real giving's done, Lord God, by people like your daughter Jane, donations made in blood, and time, and tears. You and we have opposite approaches to the needy: accidentally you're absent, but in fact you're truly here the theologians say. While we .`. . we make a show of giving; in fact we stay away.

RECESSIONAL: *Deut 15, 7-8, 10* You shall not harden your heart or shut your hand against your poor brother, but you shall open your hand to him, and lend him sufficient for his need, whatever it may be. You shall give to him freely, and your heart shall not be grudging when you give to him; because for this the Lord your God will bless you in all your work and in all that you undertake.

May 22

LANGSTON HUGHES

Langston Hughes was born in Missouri in 1902. He went to Columbia for a year but dropped out to work at odd jobs, sailing to Africa on a freighter and knocking around Europe. He was a busboy in Washington when Vachel Lindsay saw some of his poetry and arranged to have it published. Rapidly Hughes became the best-known black poet in the nation, winning several literary prizes and producing essays, plays, and newspaper columns as well. Hughes was a relentless promoter of other black writers and an apologist for their achievements. He died on May 22, 1967.

PETITION: Gather up/In the arms of your pity/The sick, the depraved,/The desperate, the tired,/All the scum/Of our weary city/Gather up/In the arms of your pity./Gather up/In the arms of your love—/Those who expect/No love from above.*

COMMUNION: *Is 27, 12* In that day from the river Euphrates to the Brook of Egypt the Lord will thresh out the grain, and you will be gathered one by one, O people of Israel.

May 23

KIT CARSON

Kit Carson was the prototype of the western hero—soft-spoken, illiterate, sandy-haired, and universally admired. After some years as a trapper in the northwest, he joined John Frémont as a guide on three expeditions to California. Once, when Los Angeles was beseiged by indians, he crawled through their lines to bring help. Carson spent his last years as an indian

---

*"Litany" © 1947 by Langston Hughes. Reprinted from *Selected Poems*, by Langston Hughes, by permission of Alfred A. Knopf, Inc.

agent in the Rockies, dreaming perhaps of the Arapaho girl he married and then lost as a young man in Idaho. He died May 23, 1868.

COMMUNION: *Ps 121, 1-2, 7-8* I lift up my eyes to the hills. From whence does my help come? My help comes from the Lord, who made heaven and earth. The Lord will keep you from all evil; he will keep your life. The Lord will keep your going out and your coming in from this time forth and for evermore.

RECESSIONAL: Something out there is calling me. From beyond the river, a voice calls. I have eaten the feast in readiness, and I turn my face to the shadows. Something out there is calling me. Across the wide river, it calls.

May 24

JOHN AND WASHINGTON ROEBLING

There were many people in that day who thought it was impossible to build a suspension bridge across New York's East River. A suspension bridge that size had never been built before. It was an enormous project, and, when it began, a tragic one. Men tumbled from the catwalks or died of caisson disease, or "bends," while digging to the bedrock. John Roebling, the bridge's designer and chief engineer, had his foot crushed, caught an infection, and died. His son Washington Roebling assumed command but was crippled by the bends and had to supervise work from the window of his home on Brooklyn Heights. But on May 24, 1883 the work was finished and Brooklyn Bridge was dedicated—the engineering marvel of its age.

OFFERTORY: Like a strand thrown across a chasm is our offering. Like a hand that reaches out in darkness, waiting for a touch. To be sure we make this gesture totally without condition; yet we expect the traffic, when it does begin, will advance not just from one beginning place, but two.

RECESSIONAL: *Ps 66, 5-6* Come and see what God has done: He turned the sea into dry land; men passed through the river on foot. There did we rejoice in him.

May 25

RALPH WALDO EMERSON

If Walt Whitman was the soul of Americanism, Ralph Waldo Emerson was its brain. In essays, poems, and public lectures, Emerson urged his countrymen to cut themselves adrift from conventional doctrines, to rely on their native wisdom, and to trust in their mystical togetherness. His message may sound naive to modern ears, but a century ago it suited an expansionist nation which had not yet realized its aptitude for evil. Emerson was born on May 25, 1803 in Boston; he died at his home in Concord in 1882.

PROCESSIONAL: *Job 13, 3, 6* I would speak to the Almighty, and I desire to argue my case with God. Hear now my reasoning, and listen to the pleadings of my lips. *Ps 37, 30-31* The mouth of the righteous utters wisdom, and his tongue speaks justice. The law of his God is in his heart; his steps do not slip.

PETITION: There are two laws discrete,/Not reconciled—/Law for man, and law for thing;/The last builds town and fleet,/But it runs wild,/And doth the man unking./ . . . Let man serve law for man;/Live for friendship, live for love,/For truth's harmony's behoof;/The state may follow as it can.*

May 26

AL JOLSON

Al Jolson was born May 26, 1886, the son of a Rabbi in Washington, D.C. He began singing as a boy in cafés and in vaudeville and minstrel shows. In San Francisco one night in 1909 he put on blackface, got down on his knee and sang a song called "Mammy." Overnight he was a star— a young man of boundless energy who loved to perform in front of audiences. After more than a decade on the Broadway stage he went to Hollywood in 1927 to make the first talking picture, *The Jazz Singer.* Even after the sentimental songs he sang lost their appeal, Jolson survived on style alone. He died in 1950.

PETITION: We've had enough of mournful music, God. Give us something lighter for a change. Let your toes tap on the floor. Enjoy yourself! Would you have been happier after all if your son Al turned out to be a cantor? Come down off your high horse! We'd walk a million miles for one of your smiles.

COMMUNION: *Ps 40, 1, 3* I waited patiently for the Lord; he inclined to me

---

*From "Ode" by Ralph Waldo Emerson.

and heard my cry. He put a new song in my mouth, a song of praise to our God.

May 27

CORNELIUS VANDERBILT

Cornelius Vanderbilt liked to be called "the Commodore," even though his nautical experience was limited to sailing a ferry between Staten Island and Manhattan. But Vanderbilt, who quit school at 11 and who could barely read, was shrewd enough to parlay that one ferry into a fleet of steamships plying the Hudson River, the eastern seaboard, and finally the oceans of the world. Always an opportunist, Vanderbilt went into railroads after the Civil War, bought the New York Central, built Grand Central Station, and along the way began one of the great family fortunes in American history. The Commodore was born this day in 1794; he died in 1877.

PROCESSIONAL: *Wis 14, 6* Even in the beginning, when arrogant giants were perishing, the hope of the world took refuge on a raft, and guided by thy hand left to the world the seed of a new generation. *Ps 135, 6* Whatever the Lord pleases he does, in heaven and on earth, in the seas and in all deeps.

RECESSIONAL: Refreshed and nourished, this pilgrim nation can renew its course once more, inspired by your son Cornelius. You be with us too, Lord God, lest our attention be taken fully with the method of our transport and not our destination.

May 28

NOAH WEBSTER

Noah Webster was born into an aristocratic Connecticut family that eagerly supported the American revolution. Noah himself was more interested in words than in politics. In 1783 he published a grammer based on the belief that good language is determined by usage, not by authority. His monumental dictionary in 1828 followed the same principle. Both met with astonishing success in the new republic anxious to break away from English influences and habits. Webster's work has been the foundation of all subsequent dictionaries published in the United States. He died on May 28, 1843.

OFFERTORY: We have been listening to your word for ages, God. In truth we are overfed with it, even jaded. Be silent and listen to us for a change. There is hidden in our babble a discernable note of exaultation that is none of us alone but all of us together. Listen God, and hear it. This song is our gift for you today.

COMMUNION: *Deut 5, 28* "I have heard the words of this people, which they have spoken to you; they have rightly said all that they have spoken."

May 29

PATRICK HENRY

By any standard Patrick Henry was a radical, hot-headed and passionate. He opposed the U.S. Constitution so strongly that he refused Washington's offer to become either secretary of state or Chief Justice. It was his earlier opposition to British rule that won him fame. His speech pleading for "liberty or death" in 1775 helped to carry Virginia into the Revolutionary War, and Henry served three terms as that state's governor. Henry was born on this day in 1736. Death came in 1799, extinguishing the last of his fires.

PROCESSIONAL: *Jer 8, 11-12* "They have healed the wound of my people lightly, saying, 'Peace, peace,' when there is no peace . . . Therefore they shall fall among the fallen; when I punish them, they shall be overthrown, says the Lord." *Ps 106, 4-5* Remember me, O Lord, when thou showest favor to thy people; help me when thou deliverest them; that I may see the prosperity of thy chosen ones, that I may rejoice in the gladness of thy nation, that I may glory with thy heritage.

OFFERTORY: We offer up these gifts: equivocation, cowardice, affluence. They are base metals; our poor alchemy cannot turn them into freedom. Take them, Lord; transform them in your fire. Our prayer is this: give us liberty again. Give us liberty.

May 30

THE UNKNOWN SOLDIER

His name is not recorded, yet there are facts about him that we know. He was carried in his mother's womb and he was born. He was loved and cared for; he learned how to run, he knew how to laugh. He went to school. He did everything we all did: scraped his knees, wept sometimes over nothing (his own frailty), and answered to his name. Surely he had hopes for his life. One final fact we know: he died. Tears ended. Hopes ended. Nothing left for him now. And for us not even the memory of him; but the fact.

COMMUNION: *2 Mac 7, 37* I, like my brothers, give up body and life for the laws of our fathers, appealing to God to show mercy soon to our nation.

RECESSIONAL: I saw battle-corpses, myriads of them,/And the white skeletons of young men, I saw them,/I saw the debris and the debris of all the slain soldiers of the war,/But I saw they were not as was thought,/They themselves were fully at rest, they suffer'd not,/The living remained and suffer'd, the mother suffer'd,/And the wife and the child and the musing comrade suffer'd,/And the armies that remained suffer'd.*

May 31

WALT WHITMAN

Walt Whitman was a poet whose works were both strongly American and strangely un-American. His prosaic, mystical verse celebrated the individual, but it had overtones of anti-materialism and sensuousness that ran counter to popular taste. Although he is seldom read today outside of classrooms, Whitman is perhaps the pivotal figure in American letters. His was the definitive turning-away from the European tradition, the first completely native voice in poetry. Whitman was born on Long Island on May 31, 1819. He spent his life tramping around the country, working as a journalist, as a civil servant, and during the Civil War as a nurse in Union hospitals. He died in 1892.

PROCESSIONAL: One's-self I sing, a simple separate person . . ./Of Life immense in passion, pulse, and power,/Cheerful, for freest action form'd under the laws divine,/The Modern Man I sing.** *Song 2, 10-12* My beloved speaks and says to me: "Arise my love, my fair one, and come away; for lo, the winter is past, the rain is over and gone. The flowers appear in the earth, the time of singing has come, and the voice of the turtledove is heard in the land."

*From *Leaves of Grass* by Walt Whitman.

**From "One's-Self I Sing" from *Leaves of Grass* by Walt Whitman.

PETITION: We who are alone, who will always, ultimately be alone, ask you to help us discover in our very loneliness our uniqueness, and in our solitude a song.

JUNE

June 1

BRIGHAM YOUNG

Brigham Young was born June 1, 1801 in Vermont and was raised in up-state New York. His family was poor and Young had little education, but he was strong-willed and had a talent for leadership. Converting to Joseph Smith's Mormon Church at the age of 31, Young became one of its first twelve apostles and was a missionary to England. When Smith died in 1844, Young took his place. The Mormons were suffering persecution in Illinois, so Young led them to Missouri and then on an epic trip across the plains to Utah where they established their home. It was a totally planned community with Young as its autocratic ruler. He served two terms as Utah's territorial governor until he was ousted by President Buchanan in a dispute over the Mormon practice of polygamy. Young died in 1877, survived by 17 wives and 47 children.

PROCESSIONAL: *Num 10, 31-32* "Do not leave us . . . for you know how we are to encamp in the wilderness, and you will serve as eyes for us. And if you go with us, whatever good the Lord will do to us, the same we will do to you." *Ps 50, 4-5* He calls to the heavens above and to the earth, that he may judge his people: "Gather to me my faithful ones, who made a covenant with me by sacrifice!"

RECESSIONAL: We'll find the place which God for us prepared/Far away, in the west,/Where none shall come to hurt or make afraid,/There the Saints will be blessed!/We'll make the air with music ring,/Shout praises to our God and King!/Above the rest each tongue will tell/All is well! All is well!*

June 2

GEORGE S. KAUFMAN

George S. Kaufman started out to be a lawyer, but after having some

*From "Come, Come, Ye Saints," a Mormon hymn by William Clayton, 1848.

100

funny quips printed in newspapers he decided he might as well be a full-time humorist. For the next 50 years while he worked as a columnist, theater critic, playwright, screenwriter, and director, he aimed his satirical thrusts at America's latest social extravagances, and usually scored. Kaufman did most of his writing as a collaborator with people such as Marc Connelly, Edna Ferber, Ira Gershwin, and Moss Hart. Among his best-known works are *Of Thee I Sing*, *The Man Who Came to Dinner*, and *You Can't Take It With You*. Kaufman died on June 2, 1961.

PETITION: Well Sir, we've been getting along pretty good for quite some time now, and we're certainly much obliged. Remember, all we ask is just to go along and be happy in our own sort of way. Of course we want to keep our health but as far as anything else is concerned we'll leave it up to You. Thank You.*

COMMUNION: In his hands laughter is instruction and foolishness is wisdom. He takes our weakness and turns it into strength.

June 3

JEFFERSON DAVIS

Jefferson Davis didn't want to be president of the Confederacy and wasn't suited for it. He took politics too much to heart, letting personal likes and dislikes color his reasoning. Davis was trained to be a soldier and graduated from West Point. After the Mexican War he was elected to the Senate from Mississippi and served for a time as Pierce's secretary of war. In all those positions he was capable, but running the Confederacy was beyond his means—probably beyond anyone's. After the war he was treated with the sort of puzzled awe one reserves for the survivor of a terrible accident. Davis was born on this day in 1808. He died, still unreconciled to the Union, in 1889.

PROCESSIONAL: *Zech 11, 7* I became the shepherd of the flock doomed to be slain . . . And I took two staffs; one I named Grace, the other I named Union. And I tended the sheep. *Ps 89, 38-39* But now thou hast cast [him] off and rejected [him], thou art full of wrath against thy anointed. Thou hast renounced the covenant with thy servant; thou hast defiled his crown in the dust.

OFFERTORY: Delicately God you turned your back on those offerings, too polite to say "no" outright to our faces and yet too fair-minded to accept

*Grandpa's prayer from Act I of *You Can't Take It With You* by George Kaufman and Moss Hart. Reprinted by permission of the copyright owners, Anne Kaufman Schneider and Catherine Carlisle Hart.

them, representing as they did our baser qualities. Ah, we were too much in love with them to see their flaws. Not until time turned them rotten before your altar did we realize the truth. Then we were left in anguish with the waste. Once presented, there was no way to take them back.

June 4

JAMES LAWRENCE

James Lawrence joined the navy as a midshipman in 1798 and saw action as a young man in the war against the Barbary pirates in Tripoli. During the War of 1812 he commanded the frigate *Chesapeake* stationed at Boston. On June 4, 1813 he accepted the challenge to do battle with the British frigate *Shannon*. In a brief but bloody fight that saw both sides take severe losses the *Chesapeake* was beaten and Lawrence fatally wounded. His admonition of "don't give up the ship" was in vain, but his valor raised the spirits of Americans, and his dying words inspired Oliver Hazard Perry's ensuing victory over the British on Lake Erie.

PETITION: Don't give us up, God, when we are beaten down by opposition, or by doubt, or simply by the pressures of enduring day-to-day. We can live with something less than triumph, and even with defeat. But we need to know that the pain and the trying were not pointless. When we have nothing else, give us that assurance.

June 5

ROBERT F. KENNEDY

On June 5, 1968 Bob Kennedy was shot and mortally wounded in a Los Angeles hotel. The next day the New York *Daily News* described the dead Senator as "the perfect Irish-American, a gut fighter with brains and a heart that could bleed for a cause." Kennedy was a man people loved and hated with equal passion. He was disliked and sometimes feared for the vehemance of his manner, and yet he seemed to be a man of almost limitless compassion. Whatever his motives, the depth of his commitment was unquestioned, and thus he looked to be the person best suited to bring Americans together in the tumultuous late 1960s. Bob Kennedy died and that hope was not realized.

COMMUNION: *2 Sam 1, 23, 25* "Saul and Jonathan, beloved and lovely! In life and in death they were not divided; they were swifter than eagles, they were stronger than lions. How are the mighty fallen in the midst of the battle!"

RECESSIONAL: Come, my friends,/'Tis not too late to seek a newer world./Push off, and sitting well in order smite/The sounding furrows; for my purpose holds/To sail beyond the sunset, and the baths/Of all the western stars, until I die.*

June 6

DWIGHT D. EISENHOWER

On June 6, 1944 a onetime farm boy from Kansas initiated the largest military operation in the history of mankind. The day was D Day. The man, of course, was Eisenhower. Dwight Eisenhower wasn't the most able field commander of the war, but he was a superlative staff officer who excelled at making diverse elements work together smoothly. He emerged from the war as a leader of almost mythic proportions, and it was no wonder that Americans, shaken by the cold-war jitters, called on him to be their President in 1952 and again in 1956. He turned out to be fairly good at the job—not imaginative perhaps, but perceptive and strong when he had to be. He retired in 1961 with his popularity still intact, and he died in 1969.

PROCESSIONAL: *Wis 8, 14* I shall govern peoples, and nations will be subject to me; dread monarchs will be afraid of me when they hear of me; among the people I shall show myself capable, and courageous in war. *Ps 101, 6* I will look with favor on the faithful in the land, that they may dwell with me; he who walks in the way that is blameless shall minister to me.

PETITION: Almighty Lord be with us when our fortune hangs in balance, when the future of our lives will be decided by one day's events or by the passing of a single morning. It is too late then to take precautions. The moon and the tides will tell us whether land will rise to meet our step or whether we will stumble into nothingness. Be with us then.

June 7

EDWIN BOOTH

Edwin Booth was one of the finest actors ever produced in America and

*From "Ulysses" by Alfred, Lord Tennyson.

one of the greatest Shakespearian actors of all time. With his father and three brothers he was a member of a distinguished acting family. Booth was especially known for his *Hamlet*, but almost equally for *King Lear* and *Othello*. He was a scholar of the theater, a sensitive and somewhat aloof man who for a time was emotionally disabled by his brother's assassination of Abraham Lincoln. Yet he came back to perform another 20 years before his death on June 7, 1893. His home in New York City is still used as a private club for actors.

OFFERTORY: The moment of sacrifice approaches. A hush descends upon the watchers as the symbols of the slaughter are brought forth. Bread and wine will wear a royal mask again. The great Lord will be a victim . . . Watchers, don't be fooled by what is happening or believe that your part in this is all vicarious. When the final words are done he will get up to play the ritual another time. The one who seems to die lives forever. It is you, who seem to live, who will die a little on this day. To you this time will never be restored.

COMMUNION: *Ps 56, 12-13* My vows to thee I must perform, O God . . . For thou hast delivered my soul from death, yea, my feet from falling, that I may walk before God in the light of life.

June 8

THOMAS PAINE

It seemed that Tom Paine was a rebel almost by nature. He was tactless, contentious, loud, sometimes drunk, and by all accounts unusually ugly. Yet his writing had a wonderful fervor that seemed to stir men, and his arguments were framed in the compelling fashion of the Enlightenment. Paine was born in 1737 in England. When his pamphleteering made him unpopular there, he came to America. He arrived in Philadelphia in 1774, just in time to sustain his new homeland in the dark days of its revolution. Once that was accomplished he went to France where he took part in that rebellion, narrowly escaping the guillotine himself. Paine was born for conflict; he was not built for placid times. He died poor and forgotten in New York City on June 8, 1809.

PROCESSIONAL: These are the times that try men's souls. The summer soldier and the sunshine patriot will in this crisis shrink from the service of his country; but he that stands it now deserves the love and thanks of man and woman.* *Ps 94, 16-17* Who rises up for me against the wicked? Who

*From "The Crisis" No. 1, 1776, by Tom Paine.

stands up for me against evildoers? If the Lord had not been my help, my soul would soon have dwelt in the land of silence.

RECESSIONAL: Freedom has been rooted out in every nation of the globe. The earth stands barren. Here in this place let freedom be cultivated and nurtured by reason, light, and law, so that in time this people can bring nourishment—the sweet, heady fruit of liberty—to all the world.

June 9

CARRY NATION

Carry Nation was the most forceful and most colorful temperance advocate of the 19th century. Operating mostly around Kansas, she would march into barrooms, sternfaced and armed with a hatchet, to hurl insults at patrons and chop up their furniture. She also appeared on stages and at carnivals to lecture on such evils as drinking, smoking, eating foreign food, wearing corsets, or looking at nude paintings. Her rigid fundamentalism may have been a way of compensating for an unhappy childhood and for two marriages that were destroyed by alcoholism and desertion. Carry Nation died on June 9, 1911.

PETITION: Can't you, God, just post a notice somewhere telling us that we're sinners instead of hurling these avenging angels at our heads? We don't claim to be a blameless nation, but why must we be mortified in public for our sins? Tell you what: If you will overlook our smaller faults we will try to stop the big ones. We should be able to settle matters of this kind quietly, behind closed doors, like gentlemen.

COMMUNION: *Rev 14, 19-20* So the angel swung his sickle on the earth and gathered the vintage of the earth, and threw it into the great wine press of the wrath of God; and the wine press was trodden outside the city, and blood flowed from the wine press.

June 10

MARCUS GARVEY

Marcus Garvey was a black leader ahead of his time. He was an exponent of separatism and black pride when most of his brothers were trying to fit into white society. Garvey had little education, but he had a perceptive mind and was a skillful organizer. In 1914 he founded an association to promote black capitalism and repatriation to Africa. By 1920 the organization had branches in most large American cities. Fearful whites and middle-class blacks attacked him. In 1925 he was convicted of mail fraud and deported to Jamaica where he had been born. Ten years later he moved to London where he died, poor and forgotten, on June 10, 1940.

OFFERTORY: My offering is painful for the multitude. They turn their eyes away because it is too raw for them, because it represents my real feelings, while they are satisfied with token things which are safe and unexpressive. They cry "No, no! You must not violate our sacred place! It is a sacrilege!" And they fall upon the present; they tear it apart and hurl it into the darkness. But in that moment before the shadows fell, did you, Lord, accept that offering and cherish it? Did you?

June 11

VINCE LOMBARDI

"Winning isn't everything," said Vince Lombardi, "but losing is nothing." More than anything else this gravel-voiced, gap-toothed, New York Italian-American loved to win. In nine years as head coach of the Green Bay Pakers his teams won six division titles and five National Football League championships. Lombardi was born June 11, 1913. He reached his peak as a coach in that era after World War II when America thought it would always win, when defeat was unthinkable for the national ego. Lombardi was the god of victory. Man and god, he died suddenly of cancer in 1970.

PROCESSIONAL: *Is 28, 2* Behold, the Lord has one who is mighty and strong; like a storm of hail, a destroying tempest, like a storm of mighty, overflowing waters, he will cast down to the earth with violence. *Ps 140, 7* O Lord, my Lord, my strong deliverer, thou hast covered my head in the day of battle.

PETITION: Lord God you have so arranged the fates of peoples that we all will come to know the taste of weakness and of failing at the end. Triumph slips away from us like a fistful of sand, but we have a great capacity for loss. Give us some enduring prize. We will forsake our expectations if we know that you will hold our mornings and our noontimes in your memory even when we're overcome with darkness.

June 12

SAUL ALINSKY

Saul Alinsky was born and educated in Chicago and spent many years there as a labor organizer. In the 1960s he pioneered new methods of social action by applying labor-organizing tactics to community problems. It was an era when government bureaucracies had grown increasingly out of touch with the concrete needs of citizens. Alinsky's strategies bridged the gap without resorting to violence, and they found adherents among the Irish in Chicago, blacks in Rochester, chicanos, indians, and other ethnic and racial minorities. Alinsky died on June 12, 1972.

COMMUNION: *Ps 72, 13-14* He has pity on the weak and the needy, and saves the lives of the needy. From oppression and violence he redeems their life; and precious is their blood in his sight.

RECESSIONAL: His people are made stronger by his presence in their midst. He gathers them together and fashions them into a people.

June 13

WINFIELD SCOTT

Winfield Scott was the hero of two American wars. He first came to public notice during the battle of Lundy's Lane in the War of 1812 and became the nation's foremost military leader at Veracruz and Mexico City during the Mexican War. Dubbed "Old Fuss and Feathers" because of his insistence on military protocol, Scott was nevertheless popular with his soldiers. Less so with voters: Nominated for the presidency in 1852, he was soundly trounced by Franklin Pierce. Scott was born June 13, 1786. He retired in 1861, too old to lead Union armies in the Civil War but not too old to see the winning strategy he devised carried out by Grant.

PETITION: It goes to his credit, God, that your servant Winfield responded to our call so often, and to our discredit that we felt compelled to call him. Give him rest from his long labors. And with him gone give us a larger measure of prudence so that we won't have to call on others to finish what we start.

June 14

BENEDICT ARNOLD

Benedict Arnold was one of the ablest generals of the American revolution. He served with distinction during the invasion of Canada and was a hero of the American victory at Saratoga. Reprimanded for some minor infraction, Arnold brooded; he felt unappreciated. In 1777 he conspired with the British commander in New York to hand over the American fort at West Point in return for £20,000, and when the conspiracy was discovered Arnold fled. He served for a short time thereafter as an officer in the British army, but lived most of his remaining life in failure and ostracism, dying in London on June 14, 1801.

PROCESSIONAL: *Jer 12, 7* "I have forsaken my house, I have abandoned my heritage; I have given the beloved of my soul into the hands of her enemies." *Ps 38, 21-22* Do not forsake me, O Lord! O my God, be not far from me! Make haste to help me, O Lord, my salvation!

OFFERTORY: The garden where we once were young is closed to us. The action of a moment was decisive: doors slammed, curtains fell, and the secret place was gone. Behold us, Lord, in an alien land. Accept these sacrificial offerings and bless them. That way you will come to us who cannot come to you. In your presence our memory will live again, and our expectation.

June 15

JAMES K. POLK

Harry Truman always believed James K. Polk to be one of America's greatest presidents—perhaps because Polk combined combativeness and political acumen in much the same way Truman did. Polk came out of Tennessee, a protégé of Andrew Jackson, to serve 14 years in the House and become its Speaker. He was only 49 when elected President in 1844. His accomplishments were largely territorial: he settled the northwest boundary dispute with England and acquired California and parts of the southwest through war with Mexico. But Polk couldn't cope with Yankee critics back home unhappy with his vascillating policies on slavery. Exhausted by his single term, Polk retired in 1849 and died three months later on June 15.

PETITION: Watch over our domain, Lord God, while we are off crusading. We have heard the call to empire as people do from time to time. Glorious possibilities are ours for the taking. But you must protect our homelands while we're gone. Maintain them in your care lest they revert to wilderness; then we would have gained a small reward and lost a treasure.

RECESSIONAL: *2 Sam 23, 3-4* When one rules justly over men, ruling in the fear of God, he dawns on them like the morning light, like the sun shining forth upon a cloudless morning, like rain that makes grass to sprout from the earth.

June 16

VERNON L. PARRINGTON

Vernon L. Parrington was born in Aurora, Ill. in 1871, went to Emporia College in Kansas and to Harvard. He spent the remainder of his life teaching American literature, mostly at the University of Washington. While greatly admired by his students, Parrington wasn't widely known until 1927 when he published *Main Currents in American Thought*, a literary and historical study that won him the Pulitzer Prize and established his reputation. He proposed that democratic idealism was the greatest single shaping force in American letters. Parrington died suddenly in England on June 16, 1929.

COMMUNION: *Ps 78, 2-3* I will open my mouth in a parable; I will utter dark sayings from of old, things that we have heard and known, that our fathers have told us.

RECESSIONAL: O I see flashing that this America is only you and me,/Its power, weapons, testimony, are you and me,/Its crimes, lies, thefts, defections, are you and me,/Its Congress is you and me, the officers, capitols, armies, ships, are you and me,/Its endless gestations of new states are you and me,/The war (that war so bloody and grim, the war I will henceforth forget), was you and me,/Natural and artificial are you and me,/Freedom, language, poems, employments are you and me,/Past, present, and future, are you and me.*

June 17

JOSEPH WARREN

Joseph Warren was the most respected and influential citizen in colonial Boston. A doctor by profession, he was an ardent patriot and a leader of the resistance against English rule. Warren was president of the third provincial congress of Massachusetts (tantamount to being governor) and was appointed major general of the army. He seemed headed for leadership in the American revolution. On June 17, 1775 British troops attacked the American fort on Bunker Hill, and since his commission hadn't come through Warren volunteered to serve as an ordinary rifleman. It was there that a British musket ball found him and Warren was shot dead.

PROCESSIONAL: The Lord has set me upon the height and he has cast me

---

*"By Blue Ontario's Shore" (#17) from *Leaves of Grass* by Walt Whitman.

down, and yet I do not fear. For he will make my name live among his people. *Ps 27, 13-14* I believe that I shall see the goodness of the Lord in the land of the living! Wait for the Lord; be strong, and let your heart take courage; yea, wait for the Lord!

OFFERTORY: Lord accept these presents as you accepted the gift of Joseph your servant. Frequently we strain to make you an offering of noble deeds when the one you seek is the one most natural to give. Instill in your people the habit of generosity; then you may pick and choose among our gifts.

June 18

ROBERT M. LaFOLLETTE

Robert M. LaFollette was born in Wisconsin in 1855. Entering politics, he served three terms in the House of Representatives and then opened a 10-year campaign against his own Republican leadership in Wisconsin, charging corruption and political bossism. Elected governor in 1910, he instituted a wideranging program of reform that included such innovations as direct primary elections and a state civil service. In the U.S. Senate he carried reform into national politics. Although a Republican, he supported Roosevelt's Bull Moose Party and Woodrow Wilson's Democrats. In 1924 the Progressive Party nominated him for President and LaFollette polled nearly five million votes. He died on June 18, 1925.

COMMUNION: *Sir 24, 11-12* In the beloved city likewise he gave me a resting place, and in Jerusalem was my dominion. So I took root in an honored people, in the portion of the Lord, who is their inheritance.

RECESSIONAL: Nourished by the unity we find around your table Lord, grant that we may find new life in your nation—not by claiming all wisdom and power for ourselves but by joining ourselves to those who are powerless so that we might share in the kingdom you have established among them.

June 19

JULIUS AND ETHEL ROSENBERG

Julius and Ethel Rosenberg were born and grew up not far from each other in New York City—he shy, studious, an electrical engineer, and she plump, outgoing, interested in music and dance. They met in college, married, and had two children. After World War II her brother David Greenglass accused them of recruiting him to steal atomic-bomb secrets which he said they funnelled to Soviet agents. They were tried and convicted in 1951 during a wave of anti-communist xenophobia. Despite the circumstantial nature of the evidence and over the protests of liberal and leftist groups, the two walked out of their cells in Sing Sing Prison on June 19, 1953, one day after their fourteenth wedding anniversary, and were taken one-by-one to the electric chair. They were the first and only U.S. civilians ever executed for spying.

PROCESSIONAL: *Hos 13, 14* Shall I ransom them from the power of Sheol? Shall I redeem them from Death? O Death, where are your plagues? O Sheol, where is your destruction? Compassion is hid from my eyes. *Ps 33, 20-22* Our soul waits for the Lord; he is our help and shield. Yea, our heart is glad in him, because we trust in his holy name. Let thy steadfast love, O Lord, be upon us, even as we hope in thee.

PETITION: Do not turn away, Lord God, from those who are casually trampled when dragons collide. Whether innocent or guilty—it does not matter. They are caught in the middleground and left there bleeding while the battle moves elsewhere. We have seen their eyes glazed with terror. We have seen their children crying by the roadside. We have seen them reaching out, pleading for rescue we could not give. They are guilty of being victims of forces which we in our innocence started and can't contain. Do not turn away from them in their perdicament, or us in ours.

June 20

"KING" PHILIP

Philip was the son of Massasoit, the indian chief who befriended the Mayflower pilgrims. Philip apparently wished to maintain the peace his father established, but colonial expansion and the enclosure of indian land led to friction between indians and settlers. On June 20, 1675, following the execution of three indians by a colonial court, general warfare broke out over eastern Massachusetts, Connecticut, and Rhode Island. It was called "King Philip's War" although Philip exercised no overall command and may indeed have tried to restrain the tribes. This largest indian war ever to strike New England raged indecisively for more than a year until the indians were routed in a battle near Kingston, R.I. Philip was killed and his wife and child were sold into slavery.

OFFERTORY: Insatiable God, we offered you an honorable gift but you demanded more. Everything we had was stripped from us. Our gardens and towns were plundered and we were sold into captivity. Will you redeem this time of suffering, Lord God? When our humiliation is over, will you make a new home for us?

RECESSIONAL: *Gen 4, 9-10* Then the Lord said to Cain, "Where is Abel your brother?" He said, "I do not know; am I my brother's keeper?" And the Lord said, "What have you done? The voice of your brother's blood is crying to me from the ground."

June 21

REINHOLD NIEBUHR

Reinhold Niebuhr was born June 21, 1892 in Wright City, Mo., the son of a Lutheran pastor. Entering the ministry himself, he spent 13 years as a social-activist pastor in Detroit before moving to New York and Union Theological Seminary where he gave the next 40 years to teaching, writing, and lecturing. Theologically Niebuhr was moderately orthodox in the tradition of Augustine. However he firmly believed religious men must carry their convictions into social and political spheres, and he influenced several generations of Protestant clergymen along those lines. Niebuhr was influential in Democratic party politics and was a founder of the Liberal party of New York. He died in 1971.

PETITION: Be our protector, God, our mighty fortress. But be our leader, too, so we will not cower behind the shelter of your walls. They do more than hold off the enemy; they hold us in. With your blessing we can sally forth to grapple with the foe, relishing our struggle and our freedom.

COMMUNION: *Ps 28, 8-9* The Lord is the strength of his people, he is the saving refuge of his anointed. O save thy people, and bless thy heritage; be thou their shepherd, and carry them for ever.

June 22

PAUL MORPHY

For a brief moment in history Paul Morphy's play illuminated the game of chess with an intensity rarely seen before or since. In the winter of 1858-59 he went as an unknown to Europe and defeated the world's greatest masters with a brilliant, aggressive style of play. It was an improbable role for Morphy, who was a young New Orleans lawyer, born June 22, 1837, the son of a judge and the product of a Jesuit college. He hoped to repeat his performance on another European trip but the American Civil War intervened, and when he did go after the war his mental health was deteriorating. He lapsed into madness, dying in 1884.

OFFERTORY: Behold we push forward a gift, Lord God—a tempting morsel for your taking. Please, don't regard it with a wary eye that way. Admittedly we'll demand a fair exchange; there will be things we want from you. But in the end our powers cannot compare with yours: Our forces are weak, our tactics slipshod. So take this gift. You can afford to leave an opening for us and still retain your glory.

COMMUNION: *Ps 24, 7-8* Lift up your heads, O gates! and be lifted up, O ancient doors! that the King of glory may come in. Who is the King of glory? The Lord, strong and mighty, the Lord, mighty in battle!

June 23

WILLIAM PENN

On June 23, 1683 William Penn, the religious leader and founder of Pennsylvania, signed a treaty at the indian village of Shackamaxon on the Delaware River pledging friendship between the white and indian peoples. It was a typical gesture for Penn. His Quaker sensibilities genuinely abhorred violence, and he looked upon indians as friends and equals. Penn lived in America for less than four years, only for enough time to lay out a street plan for Philadelphia and establish his benign jurisdiction over the colony. Most of his life was given to religious and political controversy in England where he was simultaneously admired for his character and distrusted for his liberal ideas. Penn (who was also born this day in 1644) died in London in 1718.

PROCESSIONAL: *1 Sam 2, 35* I will raise up for myself a faithful priest, who shall do according to what is in my heart and in my mind; and I will build him a sure house, and he shall go in and out before my anointed for ever. *Ps 37, 37* Mark the blameless man, and behold the upright, for there is posterity for the man of peace.

RECESSIONAL: The Lord has been faithful to his covenant. He has treated his people not as children but as brothers and sisters. He has placed his unbroken faith in them.

June 24

E.I. DuPont de Nemours

Eleuthère Irénée DuPont de Nemours was born in Paris June 24, 1771, the son of a French economist and statesman. Young DuPont studied chemistry under Lavoisier and worked for a time in the royal powder factory before the revolution drove his family to America. In 1802 he opened a gunpowder mill near Wilmington, Del., developed a superior brand of blasting powder, and made a fortune during the War of 1812. The company he founded was built by his descendants into the world's largest chemical company.

Petition: We glory in our transforming power. We can change coal into clothing, acetylene into rubber, and make explosives out of sulphur. Keep close watch on our wizardry, Lord God (our hands are almost quicker than your eye), but also teach us how to unmake what we make. Because it seems our sons and daughters are being killed off by explosives, while our plastic bottles live forever.

Communion: *2 Cor 3, 17-18* Now the Lord is the Spirit, and where the Spirit of the Lord is, there is freedom. And we all, with unveiled face, beholding the glory of the Lord, are being changed into his likeness from one degree of glory to another.

June 25

George A. Custer

George Armstrong Custer lived his life in the shadow area between bravado and ignorance. Things went his way so regularly that he stopped weighing his chances. Custer was a brilliant cavalry officer in the Civil War. Flamboyant with long blond hair, he was a major general at the age of 26. After the war he led the 7th Cavalry Regiment in the indian campaigns. On June 25, 1876 he came against a Sioux encampment on the Little Big Horn River in Montana, not knowing it held more indians than the 7th Cavalry had bullets. Boldly and stupidly he divided his command and ordered a charge. The detachment under his leadership was wiped out to the man. It was the largest defeat ever recorded by indians against white soldiers.

Processional: *Jer 48, 14-15* "How do you say, 'We are heroes and mighty men of war'? The destroyer of Moab and his cities has come up, and the choicest of his young men have gone down to slaughter." *Ps*

89, 41-42 All that pass by despoil him; he has become the scorn of his neighbors. Thou hast exalted the right hand of his foes; thou hast made all his enemies rejoice.

OFFERTORY: The cup of offering was full and still they poured, until the wine flooded across the altar and the whole place of sacrifice was stained as with blood. Idiots! And not them only. How often have we proffered a gift that was not needed, or wanted, or even usable? The Lord sits drumming his fingers, wishing that he had a holy nation but seeing that they do not know the difference between giving and throwing away.

June 26

BABE DIDRICKSON ZAHARIAS

Babe Didrickson was the finest female athlete ever produced in America, and perhaps anywhere. She was a sprinter, a javelin thrower, a high jumper (a winner of two gold medals at the 1932 Olympics), a boxer, a swimmer, a golfer, a tennis player, skater, fencer, bowler—she could play anything, and usually win. After her marriage to George Zaharias she became a top professional golfer, winning the U.S. Women's Open Golf Championship three times and the British Ladies Golf Championship once. She was born on June 6, 1913 in Port Arthur, Tex. She died in 1956.

COMMUNION: *Wis 7, 26-27* She is a reflection of eternal light, a spotless mirror for the working of God, and an image of his goodness. Though she is but one, she can do all things.

RECESSIONAL: Instructions for a holy card: Make her all bones and angles, with a loud laugh, skin the color of oak, muscles like cords, and eyes like August afternoons. And then put all her parts in motion. No saint ever should be pictured standing still.

June 27

HELEN KELLER

When Helen Keller was 19 months old a severe illness left her unable to see, or speak, or hear. She remained in her dark, incomprehensible world until she was six when Anne Sullivan, a 20-year-old teacher from Boston, broke through her several walls. Helen learned how to spell out words with her fingers, to read Braille, to lip-read with her fingers, and finally to talk. She graduated from Radcliffe with honors, wrote 10 books, lectured widely, and was one of the most admired women of her day. Helen Keller was born on June 27, 1880. She died at her Connecticut home in 1968.

PROCESSIONAL: *Is 29, 18-19* In that day the deaf shall hear the words of a book, and out of their gloom and darkness the eyes of the blind shall see. The meek shall obtain fresh joy in the Lord. *Ps 30, 1-2* I will extoll thee, O Lord, for thou hast drawn me up, and hast not let my foes rejoice over me. O Lord my God, I cried to thee for help, and thou hast healed me.

OFFERTORY: Out of this great darkness our hands reach for the Lord, seeking to discern his countenance. Our gift is emptiness waiting to be filled, silence waiting for his word. Put your sign upon us Lord, heal us with your touch. Open up to us your garden so that we in our joy can give names to all the things of your creation.

June 28

ALEXIS CARREL

Alexis Carrel was born in France on June 28, 1873. He was trained as a surgeon, but finding little interest in France for medical research he came to the United States in 1904. In Chicago and then in New York Carrel developed the first techniques for suturing blood vessels and transplanting living organs. He was awarded the Nobel Prize for medicine in 1912. Carrel had distinctly elitist ideas of society and was a shaping force behind his friend Charles Lindburgh's isolationism. During World War II Carrel returned to France, served in the Vichy government, and became a target of scorn at the war's end. He died in 1946.

PETITION: Don't bother, God, to save us if all you want is functionaries for your kingdom. That's not what we mean by redemption. Yes, we appreciate your efforts, but don't expect our gratitude if you snatch us from the jaws of liberty. If that's what your kingdom is all about, then count us out.

COMMUNION: *Eph 1, 7-8* In him we have redemption through his blood, the forgiveness of our trespasses, according to the riches of his grace which he lavished upon us.

June 29

HENRY CLAY

Henry Clay played a decisive role in the creation of American economic, foreign, and domestic policies for 40 years prior to his death on June 29,

1852. As Speaker of the House, Clay led the "War Hawk" congressmen who demanded war with England in 1812. After the war his high tariff protected native industry and financed westward expansion. Clay was an ardent believer in national unity and (although a Virginian) a conciliator on the divisive issue of slavery. He was the principal formulator of the Missouri Compromise and the Compromise of 1850 which for a time averted a civil war. Clay failed twice to be elected President, but his service in the House and Senate assure him a place as one of his country's greatest statesmen.

PROCESSIONAL: *Eph 2, 14* He is our peace, who has made us both one, and has broken down the dividing wall of hostility. *Ps 120, 6-7* Too long have I had my dwelling among those who hate peace. I am for peace; but when I speak, they are for war!

OFFERTORY: This is an offering of water to pour upon the flames, water on the passions that inflame our people. We raise it up knowing that you, Lord, may still prefer the holocaust; it may be in your plan to let the fires rage until justice is restored. Take this offering anyway. If it can't be used to quench the flames then give it back to us as rain upon our leafless desolation when the holocaust is over.

June 30

LEE DE FOREST

Lee De Forest, the man most responsible for the development of commercial radio and talking pictures, was born in Council Bluffs, Ia. and went to Yale. In 1906 he invented an electron tube for generating and amplifying radio signals, and this opened the door to the rapid expansion of the radio communications industry. De Forest lost fortunes as rapidly as he made them, failing as a manufacturer while succeeding as an inventor. Among his 300 patents are significant contributions to the development of television, motion pictures, radar, the phonograph, and the telephone. He died on June 30, 1961.

RECESSIONAL: We listened to the Lord in our assemblies. From outside this place his voice came to us—beyond our touching or our seeing. We did not grasp his presence. Yet we knew him by the caress of his transcendence, and we know him now by the void that is left when his voice is stopped.

JULY

July 1

HARRIET BEECHER STOWE

Harriet Beecher Stowe was the product of a pious and aristocratic Connecticut family. Her father was a Calvinist minister and anti-slavery crusader. At the age of 41, in angry response to the passage of the Fugitive Slave Act, she wrote a novel called *Uncle Tom's Cabin*, purporting to show the evils of slavery—a book which more than any other created a moral climate for the American Civil War. Translated into 23 languages, it made its author an international celebrity. She wrote several other mildly popular but now-forgotten novels before her death at the age of 85 in Hartford on July 1, 1896.

PROCESSIONAL: *Ex 6, 6-7* I will deliver you from their bondage, and I will redeem you with an outstretched arm and with great acts of judgment, and I will take you for my people. *Response* I looked over Jordan and what did I see?/Coming for to carry me home./A band of angels coming after me,/Coming for to carry me home.

RECESSIONAL: Firestorms were loosed upon the fields, and those who looked back on those places died. With our sister Harriet to guide us, let us find shelter in a new country, and pray that the fire next time will spare us still.

July 2

AMELIA EARHART

Amelia Earhart was a former army nurse and social worker who became one of America's pioneer aviators. In 1932, only five years after Lindburgh, she flew alone across the Atlantic, and three years later became the first person ever to solo from Hawaii to the U.S. mainland. She was an intelligent and capable woman, the author of two books, served as an airline executive, and was married to a wealthy publisher. In 1937 Amelia Earhart attempted an around-the-world flight with one companion, but on

118

July 2, somewhere north of New Guinea, trouble developed and radio contact was lost. The plane and its passengers were never found.

PETITION: Be with us Lord as we step into the unknown. Monitor our progress. With your finger trace our ascent and our descent and all the forces that push and pull on us. And watch at last that final falling when all our power's spent, so that if we don't fall into the arms of our countrymen, then into yours Lord God.

COMMUNION: *Ps 9, 13-14* Be gracious to me, O Lord! O thou who liftest me up from the gates of death, that I may recount all thy praises, that in the gates of the daughter of Zion I may rejoice in thy deliverance.

July 3

GEORGE M. COHAN

George M. Cohan had more than his share of blarney. He always claimed July 4th as his birthday when actually he was born on the 3rd, in 1878 in Providence. Cohan was a genial, sentimental Irishman who was anxious to prove (as were many Irish of his day) that he was just as patriotic as anyone else—perhaps more so. Born in a vaudeville family, he graduated to the Broadway stage where he wrote more than 40 plays, acting, singing, and dancing in most of them. The plays are long forgotten, but the songs he wrote for them still live, among them: "Give My Regards to Broadway," "I'm a Yankee Doodle Dandy," "Over There," and "Grand Old Flag."

PROCESSIONAL: *Deut 4, 6-7* "Surely this nation is a wise and understanding people." For what great nation is there that has a god so near to it as the Lord our God is to us, whenever we call upon him? *Ps 30, 11-12* Thou hast turned for me my mourning into dancing; thou hast loosed my sackcloth and girded me with gladness, that my soul may praise thee and not be silent.

OFFERTORY: Receive this gift of loyalty, delivered with a fanfare. And pardon the flashy presentation. The rich, you see, can afford anonymous donations; the poor, with just one chance, perforce must make a show. Be comforted in knowing that underneath the glitter there's real flesh and real blood measured out, waiting for that moment when the spectacle is done and sacrifice begins.

July 4

NATHANIEL HAWTHORNE

Nathaniel Hawthorne was born July 4, 1804 in Salem, Mass. He was only four years old when his father died and his mother became a recluse, and so at an early age he developed a solitary, brooding outlook associated with stories such as *The Scarlet Letter* and *The House of Seven Gables*. Hawthorne stressed the dark, irrational side of human nature as an antidote to the witless optimism of Emerson and the transcendentalists, with whom he profoundly disagreed. Hawthorne saw mankind as flawed, and capable of salvation only by acknowledging its flaw. In private life he was a affable man, a personal friend of President Franklin Pierce (who appointed him to a counsular position in England) and of Herman Melville. He died in 1864.

PROCESSIONAL: In the midst of the darkest forest the road divides. Which way shall we go? Always we are forced to choose before we can know the consequences of our choice. *Ps 82, 4-5* "Rescue the weak and the needy; deliver them from the hand of the wicked." They have neither knowledge nor understanding, they walk about in darkness.

PETITION: Father grant to us who obscure our faces from each other the strength to tear away the veils of fear and ignorance. It is time to end the charade. Wounds exposed to sunlight and fresh air find healing; those left hidden will bring about destruction.

July 5

P.T. BARNUM

"There's a sucker born every minute," said P.T. Barnum, and in time he took money from most of them. In return he showed them "General Tom Thumb" the celebrated dwarf, Jenny Lind the singer, and Joyce Heath, a black nanny said to be 160 years old who, when she died in 1836, proved to be only 70. It was a long way from Bethel, Conn. where Barnum was born on July 5, 1810 to his final eminence as proprietor of the "Greatest Show on Earth." Barnum enjoyed every minute of it. So did the suckers.

OFFERTORY: Yessiree God, step right up for the most fabulous offering ever put together! For the very first time anywhere, behold with your own eyes these perfectly untainted gifts raised up in the midst of a blameless assembly. What's that you ask? Do we really believe this pitch? Well, look at it this way: As long as you seem to buy it (and you always do), we're going to keep saying it.

RECESSIONAL: *1 Kings 1, 40* And all the people went up after him, playing on pipes, and rejoicing with great joy, so that the earth was split by their noise.

July 6

LOUIS ARMSTRONG

Louis Armstrong was born on the 4th of July, 1900, in New Orleans. He learned to play the trumpet in reform school, and soon he was playing with the best bands of the day: "King" Oliver, Kid Ory, and Fletcher Henderson. For equipment he had a soaring trumpet and a gravely voice, punctuated by an ever-present white handkerchief he used to mop his head. Armstrong was a founder of the music known as jazz, and by the time of his death on July 6, 1971 he was an international celebrity and ambassador of good will—a man who was able to grin at the King of England and announce: "Here's one for you, Rex."

PETITION: When we were low or feeling sad, you, God, gave us Louis with his gap-tooth grin and his horn to make us happy. Promise us that someday, when the saints at last assemble, we will hear his notes again and know that Louis and all the rest of us have been included in your number.

COMMUNION: *Ps 98, 4-6* Make a joyful noise to the Lord, all the earth; break forth into joyous song and sing praises! Sing praises to the Lord with the lyre, with the lyre and the sound of melody! With trumpets and the sound of the horn make a joyful noise before the King, the Lord.

July 7

SANFORD DOLE

On this day in 1898 President McKinley signed a bill that formally annexed the territory of Hawaii to the United States. That act was a personal triumph for Sanford B. Dole, the Massachusetts-educated lawyer who (although his surname today is more often remembered in connection with canned fruit) was once president of the Republic of Hawaii. Dole was the son of American missionaries. Born and raised on the islands, he served as chief justice during the native monarchy and as a member of the

121

legislature. When the territorial government was established in 1900, Dole became Hawaii's first governor.

RECESSIONAL: Strengthened by our common purpose, we go forth to summon people to our banner, baptizing them in our tradition, which, because it is so dominant, must therefore be the best. God protect these innocents, newborn to the faith. But most of all protect us, your apostles, guardians of the ancient code, who exalt our banners on the mountain but whose hidden hearts have doubts, have awful doubts.

July 8

JOHN D. ROCKEFELLER

In 1859 some businessmen in Cleveland sent one of their accountants into the Pennsylvania oil fields to see if there was any future there. The clerk came back with a negative report, then secretly scraped together $2000 of his own and went into the oil business. His name was John D. Rockefeller, and 11 years later his firm was incorporated as the Standard Oil Company of Ohio with a capitalization of $1 million. Compared to the moguls of his day, Rockefeller was dignified and pious. He liked to keep his bible by his bedside, right on top of his strongbox. Even after giving $530 million of his fortune to charity, when he died he was, perhaps, the richest man the world had ever seen. Today is the day he was born in 1839.

PROCESSIONAL: *Job 29, 2, 5-6* "Oh, that I were as in the months of old . . . when the Almighty was yet with me, when my children were about me; when my steps were washed with milk, and the rock poured out for me streams of oil!" *Ps 115, 14-15* May the Lord give you increase, you and your children! May you be blessed by the Lord, who made heaven and earth!

OFFERTORY: I have given money to the needy, Lord, and kept a little for myself. Hear the cry of a just man! I have read your sacred precepts. I have listened to the pleadings of your people and heaped offerings upon your altar. I have filled the coffers of your people from my storehouse. And kept just a little for myself.

July 9

EARL WARREN

When Earl Warren was appointed Chief Justice of the Supreme Court in

1953, there was no reason to expect he would be anything more than handsome. Warren had served three terms as a popular but unremarkable governor of California; once he ran for vice president and lost. However Warren proved to be the most influential Chief Justice since John Marshall. Taking a generally progressive stance, the "Warren court" produced decisions that reorganized state governments across the land, that enlarged the rights of accused criminals, and most important—in the epochal *Brown vs. Board of Education* ruling of 1954—that outlawed racial segregation in public schools. Warren retired from the court in 1969; he died on July 9, 1974.

PETITION: Deliver us, Lord God, from our once harmless habits that have endured to demean us. What is permitted to a child is not condoned among adults. The casual injustice, the well-meaning prejudice, the residual evil of our gestures—we did not see these things because they were not intended, but simply allowed. Open our eyes, we pray; help us to grow in mind, in body, and in conscience.

COMMUNION: *Jer 20, 13* Sing to the Lord; praise the Lord! For he has delivered the life of the needy from the hand of evildoers.

July 10

FINLEY PETER DUNNE

Finley Peter Dunne was the most popular political humorist in America before Will Rogers. Born of Irish immigrant parents in Chicago, Dunne was a newspaperman in 1893 when he created "Mr. Dooley," a fictitious homespun philosopher who commented on the day's events in an Irish dialect. Mr. Dooley's gentle but accurate barbs were directed against sham and pretense in public life. Dunne, who was born on July 10, 1867, was always discouraged by the fact that more people knew Dooley's name than his own. He stopped writing Mr. Dooley columns in 1915, and he died in 1936.

RECESSIONAL: Not even you, God, can escape the sting of ridicule. You've been known to make some blunders in your day. Take the church (your well-beloved daughter) for example, still claiming her virginity despite the knowing winks. Or think how several of your saints floated in the air, competing with the birds for perches. And then, of course, you did create the platypus. And the Irish. These works are cause enough for blushing, and we who were given laughter as a mark of our humanity do not intend to spare you from the full expression of our nature.

JOHN QUINCY ADAMS

John Quincy Adams was born July 11, 1767. His father was the second President of the United States, and John Quincy became a diplomat, Member of Congress, secretary of state, and President in his own right. He was, in the words of John F. Kennedy, "a Puritan statesman . . . harsh and intractable, like the rocky New England countryside which colored his attitude toward the world at large." His presidency was undistinguished, since Adams was engaged in an unceasing struggle with the emerging Jacksonian party. However, as a Member of Congress for 18 years after he left the White House, Adams became a leader in the first battles against slavery, displaying a singleminded persistence which in the end antagonized nearly everyone but won the respect of all.

OFFERTORY: Surely, Lord, you have no use for bread and wine. What gift of ours can stand the test of time? It must be a sense of principle so strong that neither force, nor fashion, nor outside pressures can divert it. Rolled toward the future, it will grow on its own momentum long after the one who shaped its core is forgotten, or written off in histories as a fool.

COMMUNION: *Ps 37, 18-19* The Lord knows the days of the blameless, and their heritage will abide for ever; they are not put to shame in evil times, in the days of famine they have abundance.

July 12

ALEXANDER HAMILTON

Alexander Hamilton was totally unsuited for life in a democracy. He was a poor political manager, opinionated and unwilling to compromise. And yet this man, who was born in 1757 in the West Indies, did more to shape the American democracy than anyone except Jefferson. His insistance on a strong executive and a loose construction of the Constitution endures to this day, and as America's first secretary of the treasury he laid down fiscal policies that assured the early survival of the United States. He was always a contentious person, and the ill will between him and Aaron Burr culminated in a duel in 1794 during which Hamilton was mortally wounded. He died on July 12th.

PROCESSIONAL: *2 Chron 14, 11* "O Lord, there is none like thee to help, between the mighty and the weak. Help us, O Lord our God, for we rely on thee, and in thy name we have come against this multitude." *Ps 105,*

43-44 So he led forth his people with joy, his chosen ones with singing. And he gave them the lands of the nations; and they took possession of the fruit of the people's toil.

RECESSIONAL: What you have brought about by grace, Lord God, now stabilize by law. We can't subsist on charism forever. The progress of your people needs a firm hand in control, and that will be impossible if the Spirit speaks at random. Restrain your guidance, God; hold back your light, lest we be blinded and lose what we already have.

July 13

JOHN C. FRÉMONT

As an explorer, politician, and general, John C. Frémont was one of the most popular men of his day. His expeditions in the 1840s mapped the first routes over the Sierra Nevada to the West Coast, winning him the title of "The Pathfinder." He was the Republican party's first presidential nominee, losing to Buchanan in 1856. And with the outbreak of the Civil War, Frémont for a time commanded the Union armies along the Mississippi. Unsuccessful in war as in politics, Frémont eventually lost his fortune acquired in the California gold fields. He died in relative obscurity in New York on July 13, 1890.

PETITION: You need not separate the seas for us, Lord God, or build a pretty footpath for our trip. No, despite the arid mountains, the desert, and the plain, we'd much prefer to strike out on our own. But leave your mark at random on the landscape, so even if we're wandering and lost we'll be encouraged to continue, strengthened by your presence and your promise.

COMMUNION: *Is 51, 3* The Lord will comfort Zion: he will comfort all her waste places, and will make her wilderness like Eden, her desert like the garden of the Lord; joy and gladness will be found in her.

July 14

WOODY GUTHRIE

Woody Guthrie was the greatest American ballad-maker of the 20th century. Born July 14, 1912 in Oklahoma, he left home in his early teens to go walking through the southwest, playing his harmonica and guitar for meals and living with simple folk. Guthrie's songs reflected his concern for the oppressed—migrant workers, hobos, and union men. Traveling to New York in the 1930s he gradually found an audience for such ballads as "So Long (It's Been Good to Know Ya)," "Hard Traveling," and "This Land Is Your Land." By the time of his death in 1967 he had become greatly admired for his humanity as much as for his music.

PROCESSIONAL: *Is 62, 10* Go through the gates, prepare the way for the people; build up, build up the highway, clear it of stones, lift up an ensign over the peoples. *Ps 85, 8-9* Let me hear what God the Lord will speak, for he will speak peace to his people, to his saints, to those who turn to him in their hearts. Surely his salvation is at hand for those who fear him, that glory may dwell in our land.

RECESSIONAL: Nobody living/Can ever stop me/As I go walking/my freedom highway,/Nobody living/Can make me turn back,/This land was made for you and me.*

July 15

JOHN J. PERSHING

In the army barracks of his day, John J. Pershing was known as "Black Jack." It wasn't a reference to his card-playing abilities but to the fact that he once commanded black cavalrymen in the war against the Apaches—a command of which he was inordinately proud. He also saw action in Cuba, the Philippines, and in Mexico. But it was as commander of the American Expeditionary Force in World War I that Pershing won lasting fame. He was a stiff, rather humorless man. But stubbornness was a virtue in 1917, and Pershing returned to America heaped with honors, being the first General of the Armies since George Washington held that rank. He died on July 15, 1948.

COMMUNION: *Ps 138, 7* Though I walk in the midst of trouble, thou dost preserve my life; thou dost stretch out thy hand against the wrath of my enemies, and thy right hand delivers me.

RECESSIONAL: Save us, O Lord, from the wrath of our enemies as your servant John saved us of old. But save us too from the arts of warfare which he mastered, lest the next war to end war becomes a war to end humanity.

July 16

MARY BAKER EDDY

Mary Baker Eddy was born July 16, 1821 and grew up near Concord, N.H. She was a precocious child, but sickly, and her ailment persisted into adult life. In 1862 she was apparently cured with the help of a faith healer. The experience changed her life. In the next decade she developed her own theory of faith healing, culminating in 1875 with the publication of *Science and Health*. Her book argued that the mind alone is real, that the body and bodily pain are phantoms controlled by the mind. Linking this idea with New Testament theology, she established in 1879 the Church of Christ Scientist and remained as its effective and autocratic leader until her death in 1910.

PROCESSIONAL: *Wis 8, 7* She teaches self-control and prudence, justice and courage; nothing in life is more profitable for men than these. And if any one longs for wide experience, she knows the things of old, and infers the things to come. *Prov 4, 20, 22* My son, be attentive to my words; incline your ear to my sayings. For they are life to him who finds them, and healing to all his flesh.

PETITION: Reach down to touch our bodies and our spirits, God, as you have done for your servants from the beginning of time. And grant us a sense of our own power that we may turn to those who are ailing in our midst, and touch them too, and bring them healing.

July 17

TY COBB

Ty Cobb had that quality which is absolutely indispensible to the making of great nations and great athletes: a fierce competitiveness that refuses to admit the possibility of defeat. Cobb was friendly enough off the field, but when the game began every opponent was a hated enemy to be attacked and, if need be, humiliated. Using sheer aggressiveness he elevated his ordinary physical assets to a level of skill perhaps unmatched in the history of baseball. In 22 seasons he won 12 batting championships. He played in more games, had more hits, and had the highest lifetime batting average of any player before or since. Cobb was born in Georgia in 1886; he died there on July 17, 1961.

OFFERTORY: The immolation of the saints, so highly praised, excites our curiosity. See, where others make a token gift they hurl themselves upon the holocaust, proving love through lavish spending. Oh applaud their total giving surely, but from a distance. For who knows if what was boldly cast upon the altar was really cherished, or if that passion offered for the public good served to satisfy some inner need, hidden from us all?

COMMUNION: *Ps 77, 18* The crash of thy thunder was in the whirlwind; thy lightnings lighted up the world; the earth trembled and shook.

July 18

HORATIO ALGER

Horatio Alger grew up in Revere, Mass., the son of a Unitarian minister, and went on to study at Harvard and become a minister himself. Secretly he always wanted to be a writer. In 1867 he produced a dreadfully written juvenile story about a newsboy who became rich. Published in an era of great industrial growth, the book was an instant success—so successful in fact that Alger virtually reproduced it in more than 100 other dime novels before the end of the century. All of them exaulted the virtues of honesty and hard work and the goodness of money. Alger himself became the victim of an unhappy love affair, had a nervous breakdown, and died on July 18, 1899.

PETITION: Lord God of hosts, shower your benevolence on us who are working our way to the top. Grant us patience to play the game until you call us to the head of the table, and humility enough to enjoy the taste of life wherever we sit.

RECESSIONAL: May these mysteries serve to remind us, Lord, as your servant Horatio has done so redundantly, that transformation is possible for the one who perseveres. We give you thanks for thus being raised from rags to riches.

July 19

SAMUEL COLT

Sam Colt was born July 19, 1814 in Hartford, Conn. As a young man he got an idea for a new kind of pistol that would utilize revolving chambers and a single barrel. He devised a model and secured patents but sold very few guns (which he mass produced, using interchangeable parts). With the advent of the Mexican War, however, the army finally placed a large order and Colt's fortunes soared. His revolver has been called the 19th century's major development in weaponry, and the Colt .44, called the "peacemaker," turned out to be the principal weapon of the American west.

PROCESSIONAL: *Jer 50, 25* The Lord has opened his armory, and brought out the weapons of his wrath, for the Lord God of hosts has a work to do in the land of the Chaldeans. *Ps 44, 3* For not by their own sword did they win the land, nor did their own arm give them victory; but thy right hand, and thy arm.

COMMUNION: Give us peace, almighty Father: not the peace of eternal sleep but the peace of present awareness. Send your prince of peace among us to shelter us with his arms.

July 20

ALEXANDER HOLLEY

With Andrew Carnegie, Alexander Holley was a prime mover in the beginnings of the American steel industry. Carnegie was the manager, Holley was the engineer. A technical writer for the *New York Times*, Holley in 1863 secured the American patent for the Bessemer process of steelmaking. Within four years the first rails were being produced at Holley's Troy, N.Y. plant. In the following years he designed and built steel mills in many parts of the country, making several improvements on the Bessemer process. Holley was born in Connecticut on July 20, 1832. He died in Brooklyn, N.Y. in 1882.

OFFERTORY: We have made soft things for you, Lord God, hard things for us; bread and wine for you, and for us steel blades. Our tools display our different purposes no doubt, though face-to-face it's hard to say whether yours or ours is better suited to keep the peace, or whose cuts deeper.

July 21

ERNEST HEMINGWAY

For Ernest Hemingway experience was the unformed plasma of writing. His life was a kind of dress rehearsal for his art—the first expansive and boistrous, the second taut and disciplined. All his adventures, whether in the Michigan woods, as an ambulance driver in World War I, or while fishing off Cuba, were worked into his stories. And yet they were elevated, too, with a painful craftmanship that made Hemingway perhaps the most influential prose stylist in the 20th century. Hemingway was born July 21, 1899 in Oak Park, Ill. In 1961, ill and with his powers failing, he took his own life.

PROCESSIONAL: *Eccles 1, 3-5, 8* What does man gain by all the toil at which he toils under the sun? A generation goes, and a generation comes, but the earth remains for ever. The sun rises and the sun goes down . . . All things are full of weariness. *Ps 17, 6* I call upon thee, for thou wilt answer me, O God; incline thy ear to me, hear my words.

RECESSIONAL: Perfection is an icy summit, cold and unyielding. Those who seek it must beware, stripping away comforts as they climb. There was a leopard that passed that way once, brilliant and raging. Out of his element he perished, striving for the House of God.

July 22

JOHN DILLINGER

During a 12-month span beginning in July 1933, America was gripped in delicious terror. John Dillinger was on the loose, robbing banks, breaking out of jail, and thumbing his nose at lawmen who tried to capture him. In the parlance of the day, Dillinger was a small-time racketeer, without mob connections. His solitary bravado somehow appealed to a depression-ridden country. And there were some mixed feelings when, on July 22, 1934, federal agents trapped Dillinger outside the Biograph Theater in Chicago and shot him dead.

PETITION: Although denied to your son John, deign to reward us, Father, with the rich fullness of years given with regularity to the gouging landlord and the corrupt politician. Like them, may we live to enjoy the fruits of our labors, to rest in the comfort of our homes, and to play with our grandchildren.

RECESSIONAL: *Deut 30, 19-20* I call heaven and earth to witness against you this day, that I have set before you life and death, blessing and curse; therefore choose life, that you and your descendants may live, loving the Lord your God, obeying his voice, and cleaving to him.

July 23

JAMES GIBBONS

James Gibbons was born July 23, 1834, the oldest son of Irish immigrant parents in Baltimore, Md. He was ordained a priest at 27, was made a bishop at the age of 34, became archbishop of Baltimore at the age of 43, and a cardinal at 51. Gibbons was an intelligent, even-tempered man and a good administrator. As leader of America's oldest diocese, he presided over the Catholic church during a period of turmoil and controversy marked by massive immigrations from Europe and anti-democratic attitudes in Rome. He prevailed to such a degree that Theodore Roosevelt could describe him in 1917 as "the most respected, and venerated, and useful citizen our our country." Gibbons died in 1921.

PROCESSIONAL: *Sir 45, 7-8* He made an everlasting covenant with him, and gave him the priesthood of the people. He blessed him with splendid vestments, and put a glorious robe upon him. He clothed him with superb perfection, and strengthened him with the symbols of authority. *Ps 78, 5* He established a testimony in Jacob, and appointed a law in Israel, which he commanded our fathers to teach to their children.

RECESSIONAL: Woe to him who would breed dissention among the leaders of Israel by introducing a spirit of nationalism into the camps of the Lord. Brothers we are, whatever may be our nationality, and brothers we shall remain.*

July 24

MARTIN VAN BUREN

Martin Van Buren was one of the ablest and most wiley politicians of the young American republic. He got his training in New York politics, Machiavellian even in those days, climbing through the posts of state senator, state attorney general, U.S. Senator, and governor. In Washington Van Buren became an ally and confidant of Andrew Jackson. He was Jackson's secretary of state in 1827, vice president in 1832, and succeeded Jackson to the presidency in 1836. However once in the White House Van Buren was hobbled by an economic panic and by the rising tide of slavery. He was defeated in 1840, more by election hoopla than by William Henry Harrison. He died in Kinderhook, N.Y. on July 24, 1862.

*From a sermon by Cardinal Gibbons, Aug. 20, 1891.

PETITION: Give us perseverance, God, and talent, like you gave to your son Martin, that we may render service to your people. Give us good fortune too, which he did not have, so that when the point of ministry is reached the people will be willing to receive what it is we have to give.

COMMUNION: *Is 42, 18-19* Hear, you deaf; and look, you blind, that you may see! Who is blind but my servant, or deaf as my messenger whom I send? Who is blind as my dedicated one, or blind as the servant of the Lord?

July 25

THOMAS EAKINS

Thomas Eakins, one of America's greatest and (in his day) least appreciated painters, was born in Philadelphia on July 25, 1844. As an art student Eakins was inspired by the Spanish realists Velasquez and Goya. His own style was meticulously precise, and to his students at the Pennsylvania Academy of Fine Arts Eakins stressed geometrical perspective and anatomical studies. Eakins was dismissed from the academy for having nudes pose in a coed class, and he remained a dour outcast of Philadelphia society for the rest of his life. But his finely wrought portraits and his paintings of doctors and athletes at work guaranteed him a place in the front rank of American artists. He died in 1916.

PROCESSIONAL: *Jn 8, 45-46* Because I tell the truth, you do not believe me. Which of you convicts me of sin? If I tell the truth, why do you not believe me? *Ps 119, 29-30* Put false ways far from me; and graciously teach me thy law! I have chosen the way of faithfulness, I have set thy ordinances before me.

OFFERTORY: We will not come to you, Lord God, attired in special clothes and singing songs that celebrate our virtues. We are tempted to, but we will not. In some encounters all pretense must fall. Look at us: The certainty of our early days is gone, and the beauty of our youth. Our only hope is that when all the loveliness is stripped away honesty might still redeem us. At the very least it might sharpen our perception of your coming. For it surely is the case that any people seeking to see you must first of all see themselves.

July 26

GEORGE CATLIN

George Catlin was born July 26, 1796 in Wilkes Barre, Pa., and although

132

trained as a lawyer he decided abruptly as a young man to be a painter. Catlin had always been fascinated by indians. In 1832 he set out to sketch and describe in his notebooks the way of life of the still-unconquered tribes of the American west. He lived with the indians and won their trust before attempting to paint them. While not great art, his pictures offer an anthropological record of a way of life that was vanishing even as it was fixed in oil. Catlin died in 1872.

PETITION: You created all peoples, Lord God, settling them in different places of the earth. And they, reaching out for the things they saw around them, formed their manner of living. Teach us respect for both creations —yours and theirs. Once joined, they can't be separated. Should the customs of the people die, the people too will die.

RECESSIONAL: The flower-fed buffaloes of the spring/In the days of long ago,/Ranged where locomotives sing/And prairie flowers lie low:—/The tossing, blooming, perfumed grass/Is swept away by the wheat,/Wheels and wheels and wheels spin by/In the grass that still is sweet./But the flower-fed buffaloes of the spring/Left us long ago./They gore no more,/They bellow no more,/They trundle around the hills no more:—/With the Blackfeet, lying low,/With the Pawnees, lying low,/lying low.*

July 27

GERTRUDE STEIN

Gertrude Stein was a large woman with a loud voice and striking features. She wore plain clothes, talked and laughed a great deal, and was never without an opinion. She was born in Pennsylvania, studied medicine and literature, and then went to Paris in the 1920s with a considerable fortune in her pocket to establish a salon for artists and writers. On her own she wrote prose and an odd kind of rhythmic poetry that won her a minor reputation. As a patroness, however, she was a major figure, especially for the support she gave to artists such as Picasso, Hemingway, Cézanne, Matisse, Sherwood Anderson, Faulkner, Paul Robeson, and many others. She died on July 27, 1946.

PROCESSIONAL: *Wis 8, 8* She understands turns of speech and the solutions of riddles; she has foreknowledge of signs and wonders and of the outcome of seasons and times. *Prov 31, 16-17* She considers a field and buys it; with the fruit of her hands she plants a vineyard. She girds her loins with strength and makes her arms strong.

---

*"The Flower-Fed Buffaloes of the Spring" by Vachel Lindsay. Reprinted by permission of Nicholas C. Lindsay.

133

OFFERTORY: I am Rose my eyes are blue/I am Rose and who are you/I am Rose and when I sing/I am Rose like anything*

July 28

ANDREW J. DOWNING

Andrew Jackson Downing was the foremost practitioner of romantic country architecture in the 19th century. Downing grew up in Newburgh, N.Y. and spent several years as a landscape gardener. He popularized wilder, more baroque gardens in place of the formal, federal styles previously in vogue. With Calvert Vaux as a partner, Downing designed and built neo-gothic country houses that featured assymetrical spaces, towers, gingerbread roofs, and open porches—a style that influenced American home building for a half century. Downing died at the age of 37 in a ship accident on July 28, 1852.

COMMUNION: *Song 4, 13-15* Your shoots are an orchard of pomegranates with all choicest fruits, henna with nard, nard and saffron, calamus and cinnamon, with all trees of frankincense, myrrh and aloes, with all chief spices—a garden fountain, a well of living water.

RECESSIONAL: Astonish us. Make your creation tremble with surprises. Fill our days with unforseen angles, sudden bursts of sunlight, moving shadows. There is nothing that so resembles death as regularity.

July 29

BOOTH TARKINGTON

Booth Tarkington lived most of his life in Indianapolis, being born there July 29, 1869 and dying there in 1946. Tarkington was a pure storyteller, and the stories that he told were washed with the genteel humor and sentiment of life in America's midland. His most popular books were built around boyhood adventures, like *Penrod* and *Seventeen*. He also produced adult novels such as *The Magnificent Ambersons* which won one of his two Pulitzer Prizes. Tarkington also wrote numerous plays, frequently adaptations of his novels.

PETITION: Oh yes we want shady streets and tall white houses with porches on them where we can drink lemonade on summer evenings. Give us, Lord, this perfect place—but on the one condition that should thunder rumble in the distance we do not sit unheeding in the soft and secret darkness, sipping at our glass as if the lightning could not strike.

July 30

HENRY FORD

Let us now praise Henry Ford, born this day in 1863. Ford was a man of contradictions. He was a lover of nature whose cars did more to ruin the environment than did any other 20th-century device. He claimed to be a pacifist yet reaped huge profits in two world wars. He was an avowed champion of the working man who hired a private army to fight labor unions. He was an idealist, a Jew-baiter, a technological genius, a bigot. He devised the production line to mass-produce cars for working men, and in the process turned working men into machines. Praise him.

PROCESSIONAL: *Jer 46, 8-9* "He said, I will rise, I will cover the earth, I will destroy cities and their inhabitants. Advance, O horses, and rage, O chariots!" *Ps 144, 14-15* May there be no cry of distress in our streets! Happy the people to whom such blessings fall!

OFFERTORY: Have compassion on your people, God, who no longer offer you the products of their hands. Our wine and our wafers are manufactured for us now. With mechanical gestures we lift them up, trusting that you will understand. It seems that in our genius we provided bounty for the feast but lost the feeling for it.

July 31

ROBERT A. TAFT

Robert A. Taft was the voice and perhaps even the conscience of the Republican party during the long era of the Roosevelt and Truman administrations when Republican fortunes were on the wane. As a man he was intellectual and somewhat colorless; as a politician he was conservative, and proud of it. Taft called the New Deal "socialism." He was opposed to the United Nations, to NATO, and to internationalism generally. As a senior member of the Senate he sponsored legislation that curbed the power of labor unions. Taft was the son of William Howard Taft, and he wanted badly to be President like his father, but he failed to win struggles for the nomination in 1948 and 1952. He died on July 31, 1953.

COMMUNION: *Ps 19, 8* The precepts of the Lord are right, rejoicing the heart; the commandment of the Lord is pure, enlightening the eyes.

RECESSIONAL: Lead us into your light, Lord God, into the brightness so great that we are annihilated in your gaze. What is the value of human flesh when compared to truth?

AUGUST

August 1

HERMAN MELVILLE

Largely ignored during his lifetime, Herman Melville was finally acknowledged after his death as a towering figure in American literature. He was the first to explore fully the dark, compulsive forces that underlaid the American dream, the violence inherent in the American adventure, and the death of American innocence. Melville was born in New York City on Aug. 1, 1819. He had a grade-school education and spent six years at sea as a youth. The first stories of his travels were well received, but the public was unprepared for the bleak symbolism of *Moby-Dick*. The book was a failure and Melville was reduced to near poverty. He lived his last years in obscurity at a government job, dying in 1891.

PROCESSIONAL: I muse upon my country's ills—/the tempest bursting from the waste of Time/on the world's fairest hope linked with man's foulest crime.* *Jer 2, 7* I brought you into a plentiful land to enjoy its fruits and its good things. But when you came in you defiled my land and made my heritage an abomination.

COMMUNION: After you have taken retribution, after the payment has been exacted, after the waters have covered the earth and drowned the voices of the idolaters, grant that we may be buoyed by the very sign of death, and nourished by its knowledge.

August 2

HORACE MANN

Horace Mann did more than any other person to shape the character of American public-school education. When Massachusetts created the first state board of education in 1837 the school system there, as in most states, was in sad disrepair. Few teachers had any real training, and each village school had its own standards. Mann, a state legislator who himself rose up

---

*From "Misgivings" by Herman Melville.

from poverty and dismal schools, became secretary of the first state board and effected a revolution that was widely copied in other states. Teacher training schools were established; corporal punishment and sectarian textbooks were eliminated. Mann later succeeded to John Quincy Adams' seat in Congress for two terms, ran for governor and lost, and ended his career as president of Antioch College in Ohio. He died on Aug. 2, 1859.

OFFERTORY: Like a stale crust thrown upon the table we make an offering of our ignorance. It's not a pretty gift, and not one we are proud of. But it's our part to give and your part to give our giving meaning. Looked at in the proper way, ignorance can be lifted up to wisdom. So in return for our offering we gain a new perspective on what we give away.

RECESSIONAL: *Ps 25, 4-5* Make me to know thy ways, O Lord; teach me thy paths. Lead me in thy truth, and teach me, for thou art the God of my salvation; for thee I wait all the day long.

August 3

AUGUSTUS SAINT-GAUDENS

Considered by many people to be America's greatest sculptor, Augustus Saint-Gaudens learned his art as a cameo cutter in New York City and at schools in New York and Paris. Influenced chiefly by French classicism, his works include the hooded figure known as "Amor Caritas" in Washington, D.C., "The Puritan" in Springfield, Mass., the statues of Lincoln and Gen. Logan in Chicago, and the equestrian statue of Gen. Sherman at the Plaza entrance to Central Park in New York City. Saint-Gaudens was born in Ireland in 1848. He died on Aug. 3, 1907.

PETITION: Grant us, God, the power of articulation. Give us words to speak of beauty and of sorrow as you did for your son Augustus for whom a chisel was his tongue and a mallet his breath. Give us power to feel what we see, and power to speak what we feel.

COMMUNION: *1 Kings 7, 14* He was full of wisdom, understanding, and skill, for making any work in bronze. He came to King Solomon, and did all his work.

August 4

PETER ZENGER

By himself Peter Zenger did nothing memorable. Emigrating from Germany, Zenger worked as a printer in Maryland and New York, surfacing as editor of the *New York Weekly Journal* during a political squabble in 1734. His editorials were so unpopular with the colonial governor that issues of the paper were confiscated and Zenger himself was arrested for libel. In a celebrated trial in 1735 Zenger's attorney advanced the novel idea that the jury should not determine whether the editorials hurt the governor but whether or not they were true. On August 4th the jury handed down its decision: Not guilty. Zenger was let go, and the principle of a free press was established on American shores.

COMMUNION: *Jn 8, 31-32* "If you continue in my word, you are truly my disciples, and you will know the truth, and the truth will make you free."

RECESSIONAL: Encourage your people, Lord, to be unafraid of the truth when it is spoken in their midst. May those gathered around your table find honesty an occasion to grow in love and mutual forgiveness.

August 5

MARILYN MONROE

Marilyn Monroe was born Norma Jean Mortenson in Los Angeles in 1926 and was raised by 12 different sets of foster parents. An early marriage ended in divorce. She did some modeling, played bit parts in movies, and in 1948 found herself out of work. At the age of 24 she was a failure. The career that rose out of those ashes was a spectacular triumph, but not the life. She made 23 movies from 1950 onward and became the movie industry's premier sex goddess. She was wed in turn to a sports hero and a famous playwright. And yet it seemed she never stopped being Norma Jean Mortenson, and never outgrew failure. On Aug. 5, 1962 she took a massive overdose of sleeping pills and died alone in her home.

OFFERTORY: We have little enough to give. And because we have a modest amount we make a spectacle of giving, magnifying our delivery until it eclipses those who have more than we do to offer. It fools no one, God— surely not you. But, ah, we cannot help it! The strange thing is: Your glance cuts through the outward show and perceives the small, pure gift we had at the beginning. You accept that gift and you cherish it. And in your sight we are redeemed.

August 6

ENRICO FERMI

Enrico Fermi had already won the Nobel Prize for physics when he came to the United States in 1938, fleeing the Fascist government of his native Italy. In 1939 he was one of the scientists who alerted President Roosevelt to the potential destructive power of atomic energy—an act that resulted in the creation of the Manhattan Project to develop the atomic bomb. In December of 1942 Fermi directed a team of scientists in Chicago who achieved the first controlled nuclear chain reaction. Fermi later helped to design the bomb itself. On this day in 1945 an atomic bomb was dropped on Hiroshima in Japan. Nearly 100,000 persons died.

PROCESSIONAL: *Jer 16, 21* "Therefore, behold, I will make them know, this once I will make them know my power and my might, and they shall know that my name is the Lord." *Ps 18, 7-9* Then the earth reeled and rocked; the foundations also of the mountains trembled and quaked, because he was angry. Smoke went up from his nostrils, and devouring fire from his mouth; glowing coals flamed forth from him. He bowed the heavens, and came down; thick darkness was under his feet.

RECESSIONAL: We have touched an awesome power. Together we beheld mystery, and we bore it into our dwellings to illuminate our future. We are Neanderthal after the lightning storm, gazing at the burning taper he salvaged from the forest—in his rapture not yet comprehending that the fire which warms him can burn him too, and can destroy him.

August 7

RALPH BUNCHE

Ralph Bunche, who was born the son of a Detroit barber on Aug. 7, 1904, went to school at UCLA and at Harvard, from which he took a Ph.D. in government in 1934. In the following years he filled a number of jobs— teaching at college, working with the U.S. State Department, and helping Swedish anthropologist Gunnar Myrdal. In 1946 Bunche began a long association with the United Nations, first in the Trusteeship Council and then as a political aide to the Secretary General. In that capacity he handled crucial negotiations in Palestine, the Congo, Suez, and Cyprus. For his successful effort in halting the first Arab-Israeli war he was awarded the Nobel Peace Prize in 1950. He died in 1971.

PETITION: Inspire us, Lord God, with the memory of your servant Ralph who did not give into resentment for the indignities he suffered but instead served the cause of peace. May we be guided by his wisdom, strengthened by his perseverence, and humbled by the tears he would not shed.

COMMUNION: *Is 2, 4* He shall judge between the nations, and shall decide for many peoples; and they shall beat their swords into plowshares, and their spears into pruning hooks; nation shall not lift up sword against nation, neither shall they learn war any more.

August 8

ERNEST O. LAWRENCE

Ernest O. Lawrence, the man who built the first cyclotron (or "atom smasher" as the public called it), was born Aug. 8, 1901 in Canton, S.D. After studies at Chicago and Yale, he went to the University of California as professor of physics and director of its radiation laboratory. In 1933 Lawrence constructed the first large-scale cyclotron which accelerated atomic particles by alternating magnetic fields. The device enabled scientists to bombard large atoms with fast-moving particles, leading to the discovery of many radioactive isotopes. Lawrence won the Nobel Prize for physics in 1939. During World War II he helped to develop plutonium for the first atomic bombs. He died in 1958.

PROCESSIONAL: *Wis 7, 17* It is he who gave me unerring knowledge of what exists, to know the structure of the world and the activity of the elements. *Ps 29, 5, 7-8* The voice of the Lord breaks the cedars, the Lord breaks the cedars of Lebanon . . . The voice of the Lord flashes forth flames of fire. The voice of the Lord shakes the wilderness.

OFFERTORY: Lord of the Universe, you who set stars and planets spinning in the void, behold these little worlds we bring before you as gifts. They are much less than anything you created. Yet there's mystery in them that the common eye cannot perceive. Peel away their layers and one discovers stars and planets spinning in the void and you, Lord of the Universe.

August 9

WILLIAM MORTON

William Morton, a pioneer in the use of general anesthesia, was born Aug. 9, 1819 in Massachusetts and practiced dentistry in Boston. The gas called "ether" had been known for some time, but it was not widely used until Morton started to administer it to his patients and to surgical cases in Boston hospitals. Other doctors criticized him because he lacked medical credentials, and he was sued by persons who claimed prior discovery of the anesthetic. Impoverished by the long legal battles that followed, Morton died in New York in 1868.

PETITION: Don't protect us too much, God. Stand aside and let us walk alone. We'd be bored to death in a cotton-candy world. We want to feel pain and tiredness, laughter and loneliness, love (of course) but also loss. Come to our help if you see we're on the verge of breaking, but for the rest leave us alone. Before we can be your people, we must first of all be people.

RECESSIONAL: *Sir 38, 6-8* He gave skill to men that he might be glorified in his marvelous works. By them he heals and takes away pain . . . His works will never be finished; and from him health is upon the face of the earth.

August 10

HERBERT HOOVER

Herbert Hoover was born Aug. 10, 1874 in Iowa and was raised by an uncle in Oregon, his parents having died. After working his way through college, Hoover became a mining engineer and eventually president of his own international mining firm. By now wealthy, Hoover directed massive American relief operations in Europe during and after World War I and became secretary of commerce under Presidents Harding and Coolidge. In 1928 he was elected President. Hoover believed in rugged individualism. One year into his term the stock market collapsed and Hoover had no faith to fit the crisis. Turned out of office, he lived for another 32 years as a Republican elder statesman, personally respected but shorn of influence.

OFFERTORY: With these gifts of bread and wine you, Lord God, will feed your holy nation and nourish it. Take some of it also and set it aside for leaner times like Joseph did in Egypt. Reserve some against that day when our lives will be barren and our hands empty before your altar. Then you can borrow from your storehouse and your people will not be left to starve.

COMMUNION: *Gen 41, 56-57* When the famine had spread over all the land, Joseph opened all the storehouses, and sold to the Egyptians, for the famine was severe in the land of Egypt. Moreover, all the earth came to Egypt to Joseph to buy grain, because the famine was severe over all the earth.

August 11

ANDREW CARNEGIE

Andrew Carnegie was born in Scotland in 1835 and came to western Pennsylvania with his family when he was 13. Undeterred by his lack of schooling, he rose to become a division manager of the Pennsylvania Railroad. Carnegie recognized early that steel was the commodity of the future. The bridge-building company he formed in 1865 became a major steel producer and was worth a cool $225 million when sold to J.P. Morgan in 1901. While not enlightened in his dealings with labor, Carnegie proved to be generous in retirement, building libraries in many cities and establishing endowments for education and peace. He died Aug. 11, 1919.

PROCESSIONAL: *Sir 33, 22-23* Excel in all that you do; bring no stain upon your honor. At the time when you end the days of your life, in the hour of death, distribute your inheritance. *Ps 2, 8-9* "Ask of me, and I will make the nations your heritage, and the ends of the earth your possession. You shall break them with a rod of iron, and dash them in pieces like a potter's vessel."

PETITION: Grant to us, Lord God, not only the grace of generosity but also the willingness to admit that the treasure each person claims as his own has in fact been amassed through the labor of many people. All of these things—wealth, talent, reputation, and time itself—come to us from others, and must be returned.

August 12

CECIL B. DEMILLE

Cecil B. deMille, the maker of movie spectaculars, was born Aug. 12, 1881 in Massachusetts. His father was a playwright and deMille himself wrote several plays before joining Jesse Lasky and Samuel Goldwin to create a cinema company. DeMille productions contributed to the development of serious filmaking and helped to introduce the phenomenon of movie "stars." His most popular films were costume dramas with "casts of thousands." Among them: *The King of Kings*, *The Sign of the Cross*, *The Ten Commandments*, and *The Greatest Show on Earth*. He produced more than 70 films by the time of his death in 1959.

COMMUNION: *Dan 2, 6* If you show the dream and its interpretation, you shall receive from me gifts and rewards and great honor.

RECESSIONAL: Behold the mighty host parading toward the future, dressed in goatskins, vinyl, wigs, and false furs. (The sun goes down on cue. Hosannah!) The Lord in his heaven is watching, helpless with laughter. He won't even get a credit for special effects. But wait! Now he ponders gravely. He nods his head. He sighs. His glance perceives the truth hidden even from us: Only the sunset is fake. The march is real.

August 13

ANNIE OAKLEY

The girl who became known as Annie Oakley was born Phoebe Anne Oakley Mozee in Ohio on Aug. 13, 1860. She appears to have been a phenomenal shot even as a child. She paid off the mortgage on her parents' farm by hunting. In 1885 she joined Buffalo Bill's Wild West Show, giving marksmanship exhibitions. At 30 paces she could hit a playing card edge-on. She hit dimes thrown into the air, and she regularly shot cigarettes from the lips of her husband Frank Butler. She was so proficient at shooting holes through playing cards tossed into the air that punched complimentary tickets ever after became known as "Annie Oakleys." She died in 1926.

PETITION: Descend upon your trigger-happy nation, God, and bring us peace. You sent your daughter Annie to inspire us, but we didn't take the hint: We still prefer shooting Presidents to cards. We do it skillfully. Now we require stronger medicine. Come into our midst with compassion so genuine we'll be too surprised to pull the trigger. In time we'll learn to live in harmony with your disarming love.

August 14

WILLIAM RANDOLPH HEARST

William Randolph Hearst was not content. He was not content simply to be a millionaire newspaper publisher who started wars with his left hand and summoned politicians with his right. He wanted to shape American politics, to control public opinion. He wanted to be the greatest patron of the arts since the Medicis. He wanted . . . actually, no one knows what he wanted. Perhaps not even him. Money, power, and reputation he had already. He created an empire, and it bored him. When he died Aug. 14, 1951 one had the feeling that he still was not content.

PROCESSIONAL: *Is 40, 6-7* All flesh is grass, and all its beauty is like the flower of the field. The grass withers, the flower fades, when the breath of the Lord blows upon it; surely the people is grass. *Ps 50, 3* Our God comes, he does not keep silence, before him is a devouring fire, round about him a mighty tempest.

RECESSIONAL: You brought us to the mountain and revealed the kingdoms of the earth spread like a carpet at our feet. Your glory shone about us. Your power lay within our grasp. But it was lonely on the mountain, and cold. We looked in vain for one embrace or some sign of warmth. So at length we turned our back on all of it. We're coming down the mountain, Lord. Coming down the mountain.

August 15

GEORGE WASHINGTON GOETHALS

On Aug. 15, 1914 President Theodore Roosevelt formally declared the Panama Canal open to world shipping. It was a triumphant moment for George Washington Goethals, the 56-year-old army engineer who had supervised the last seven years of the construction. Goethals had to resolve political differences relating to the location and size of the canal. Then he had to deal with the more physical dangers of flooding, landslides, and tropical diseases. The finished canal proved to be a great boon to commerce and enabled the American navy to move its ships more easily from coast to coast. Goethals was born in Brooklyn, N.Y. in 1858 and graduated from West Point. He retired from the army in 1919 as a major general, and he died in 1928.

PETITION: Lord God of Hosts, you who held back the walls of the sea to make a pathway for your people, give honor to your servant George who pushed back mountains to make a waterway for ships. As for us, we need engineering of an inner sort: Our past and our future have lost connection; our geography is in disarray. We appeal to anyone who will join our shores together, or our oceans.

COMMUNION: *Ps 78, 15-16* He cleft rocks in the wilderness, and gave them drink abundantly as from the deep. He made streams come out of the rock, and caused waters to flow down like rivers.

August 16

WILLIAM F. HALSEY

William F. Halsey was the aggressive and impetuous commander of U.S. carrier forces in the Pacific during World War II. He was dubbed "Bull" Halsey by the press because of his blunt manners, but he was "Bill" to friends. Halsey liked the strategy of attack even when his back was against the wall as it was at Guadalcanal. Later at Leyte Gulf he was victorious in the largest naval battle ever fought, but he almost lost it too through recklessness. Halsey was born in 1882 in New Jersey. He died as a retired five-star admiral on Aug. 16, 1959.

PROCESSIONAL: *Job 41, 31-33* He makes the deep boil like a pot; he makes the sea like a pot of ointment. Behind him he leaves a shining wake . . . Upon the earth there is not his like, a creature without fear. *Ps 78, 53* He led them in safety, so that they were not afraid; but the sea overwhelmed their enemies.

OFFERTORY: Accept our impulsiveness, Lord God. Take our clumsy eagerness and refine it if you can, or harness it. For some people it's an endearing quality, for some it's not, but it seems to be ingrained in our character. If you want a cosmopolitan people, look elsewhere. But if you're willing to accept commitment that's acted out with puppy-dog enthusiasm, then be our God.

August 17

DAVY CROCKETT

Davy Crockett was sure-enough born on a mountaintop in Tennessee on Aug. 17, 1786. He grew up on the frontier without much learning, but he sure could handle a rifle and an axe. They say he killed a lot of bears and it's probably true, and it's a fact that he scouted for Andy Jackson in the Creek War. But mainly Davy liked to joke and tell stories. The folks in Tennessee liked him so much they sent him to Congress for two terms, in 1826 and 1832. Miffed after losing a try for reelection, he packed up his gear and went to try his luck in Texas. And wound up in the Alamo.

COMMUNION: *Ps 107, 35-36* He turns a desert into pools of water, a parched land into springs of water. And there he lets the hungry dwell, and they establish a city to live in.

RECESSIONAL: The mountains and the forests are behind me. I have turned my back on the places of my youth that closed me in on all sides. The way before me now is clouded with mystery. Help me, Lord God. The mountains and the forests are inside me. The places of my youth will never leave me.

August 18

MERIWETHER LEWIS

Meriwether Lewis was a son of the Virginia aristocracy, born Aug. 18, 1774. He was Thomas Jefferson's private secretary in 1801 when the Louisiana Territory was purchased, and Jefferson asked Lewis to explore it. Assisted by William Clark (like Lewis, a soldier), he set out in 1804 with 40 men up the Missouri River to the high plains and the Rocky Mountains. It took them two years to cross the mountains, to canoe down the Columbia River to the Pacific, and then to make the return journey to St. Louis. The entire party returned safely. The expedition yielded a great deal of knowledge about the vast land of the northwest. Lewis subsequently served for two years as governor of the territory. On a trip to Washington in 1809 he met with an accident and was killed.

PROCESSIONAL: *Is 32, 16-17* Then justice will dwell in the wilderness, and righteousness abide in the fruitful field. And the effect of righteousness will be peace . . . quietness and trust for ever. *Ps 89, 24-25* My faithfulness and my steadfast love shall be with him, and in my name shall his horn be exalted. I will set his hand on the sea and his right hand on the rivers.

OFFERTORY: Accept these familiar offerings, Lord God—the same things you have seen before. Our gifts must seem monotonous in your sight. But in return you give us things strange and new. Unexpected vistas unfold to our astonishment, lands full of danger, full of possibility. We're grateful for this exchange, but we wonder if you find it boring to get bread again while we are given whole new worlds laid open for exploring.

August 19

BERNARD BARUCH

Bernard Baruch was a valued advisor to American presidents in every administration from Wilson's to Kennedy's. To the public Baruch was a grandfatherly figure who sat on park benches and dispensed homespun advice. Baruch, however was no simpleton. His speciality was international finance, and he was sharp enough at it to be a millionaire by the age of 40. He never held a cabinet-level position, but his influence in government was powerful nonetheless. Baruch was born on Aug. 19, 1870 in South Carolina. He died in 1965.

PETITION: Put words into our mouths at the crucial moment God, as you gave words to your son Bernard. When we are called to give accounts, put words into our mouths. We, for our part, will devote our time to looking at things and will not worry about explanations. If we see things truly as they are, your words will come to us.

August 20

PAUL TILLICH

Paul Tillich was born Aug. 20, 1886 in Brandenberg, Germany, took his degree in theology in 1911 and served as a military chaplain in World War I. After the war his teaching on religious and social issues did not endear him to the Nazis; he came to the United States in 1933 to begin the major phase of his career. Tillich took his theological nourishment from many sources: depth psychology, existential philosophy, and political activism. His books were a blend of mysticism and down-to-earth practicality. His many published works, including *Courage to Be* and his three-volume *Systematic Theology* rank him among the 20th century's greatest religious thinkers. Tillich died in Chicago in 1965.

PROCESSIONAL: *Ex 3, 13-14* Then Moses said to God "If I come to the people of Israel and say to them, 'The God of your fathers has sent me to you,' and they ask me, 'What is his name?' what shall I say to them?" God said to Moses, "I AM WHO AM." And he said, "Say this to the people of Israel, 'I AM has sent me to you.' " *Ps 71, 15* My mouth will tell of thy righteous acts, of thy deeds of salvation all the day, for their number is past my knowledge.

RECESSIONAL: *Rev 21, 1-3* Then I saw a new heaven and a new earth; for the first heaven and the first earth had passed away, and the sea was no more. And I saw the holy city, new Jerusalem, coming down out of heaven from God . . . and I heard a voice from the throne saying, "Behold, the dwelling of God is with men. He will dwell with them, and they shall be his people, and God himself will be with them."

August 21

NAT TURNER

On Aug. 21, 1831 Nat Turner and about 75 fellow slaves in Virginia began the bloodiest slave revolt recorded in the ante-bellum south. Turner was a man of superior intelligence with apparently a mystical bent. He had some knowledge of reading and writing. Oppressed by a cruel owner, he had "visions" of a racial war. During two days in 1831 he and his followers killed 55 white persons before their capture on the road to Jerusalem, Va. They were tried and convicted. Turner and 14 of his followers were hanged in Jerusalem less than two months after the revolt began.

PROCESSIONAL: *Neh 9, 36* Behold, we are slaves this day; in the land that thou gavest to our fathers to enjoy its fruit and its good gifts, behold, we are slaves. *Ps 105, 18-19* His feet were hurt with fetters, his neck was put in a collar of iron; until what he had said came to pass the word of the Lord tested him.

PETITION: Now you, God, must make your choice. We have followed you to this point in good faith; now you must follow us or deny the words you spoke to us in private. Because we cannot go on the way we were and still be called your people. We are resolved to risk our very lives to attain our possibilities. This much is clear to us: If you are to be our master, then no one else can be; if you are not, then we will be our own.

August 22

SAMUEL P. LANGLEY

Samuel P. Langley was one of the most remarkable scientists America ever produced. With only a high-school education he trained himself to be a civil engineer and went on to teach mathematics at Harvard and at the U.S. Naval Academy. In 1867 he took a position as astronomer at Western University in Pennsylvania and over the next 20 years became a world authority on the sun and solar radiation. In 1887 Langley began a long association with the Smithsonian Institution in Washington, continuing his solar research. He also experimented with heavier-than-air flight. He built successful models of planes and might have accomplished the first powered flight had his money not run out. Langley was born on this day in 1834. He died in 1906.

OFFERTORY: Lord come to us in light and air: Use light to scatter through our darkness and air to invigorate our days. Our gift to you is our capacity, our readiness for your fire and breath. Lord come to us with warmth and breezes: Warmth to melt our frozen hearts and breezes that will lift them up. In return we offer you expectancy. Our calm waits upon your storm.

COMMUNION: *Amos 5, 8* He who made the Pleiades and Orion, and turns deep darkness into the morning, and darkens the day into night . . . the Lord is his name.

August 23

EDGAR LEE MASTERS

Edgar Lee Masters was born Aug. 23, 1869 in Kansas and grew up in Illinois. He practiced law for several years in Chicago. Even before that time he had been writing stories and poems without attaining much notice, but his *Spoon River Anthology* in 1915 was an instant success and ended his law practice forever. It was a book of poetic monologues spoken from beyond the grave by citizens of a small midwestern town, revealing the truth of their inner lives. It was a bleak and ironic portrait of small-town America. Although Masters produced more poetry, novels, biographies, and an autobiography, nothing he ever wrote approached *Spoon River*. He died in 1950.

RECESSIONAL: I went to the dances at Chandlerville,/And I played snap-out at Winchester./One time we changed partners,/Driving home in the moonlight of middle June,/And then I found Davis./We were married and lived together for seventy years,/Enjoying, working, raising the twelve children,/Eight of whom we lost/Ere I reached the age of sixty./I spun, I wove, I kept the house, I nursed the sick,/I made the garden, and for holiday/Rambled over the fields where sang the larks,/And by Spoon River gathering many a shell,/And many a flower and medicinal weed—/Shouting to the wooded hills, singing to the green valleys./At ninety-six I had lived enough, that is all,/And passed to sweet repose./What is this I hear of sorrow and weariness,/Anger, discontent and drooping hopes?/Degenerate sons and daughters,/Life is too strong for you—/It takes life to love life.*

*"Lucinda Matlock" from *Spoon River Anthology* by Edgar Lee Masters. Reprinted by permission of Ellen C. Masters.

August 24

CHARLES F. MCKIM

Charles F. McKim was America's leading architect in the last quarter of the 19th century and the foremost exponent of the neoclassical revival in architecture. McKim designed many magnificent public buildings, including the Boston Public Library, the Morningside Heights campus of Columbia University, and New York's Pennsylvania Station. He also supervised the restoration of the White House in 1903 and drew up the first plans for the Lincoln Memorial. McKim was born Aug. 24, 1847 in Chester County, Pa. He was educated at Harvard and in Paris. He died in 1909.

PROCESSIONAL: *2 Chron 6, 2* "I have built thee an exalted house, a place for thee to dwell in for ever." *Ps 61, 2-4* Lead thou me to the rock that is higher than I; for thou art my refuge, a strong tower against the enemy. Let me dwell in thy tent for ever! Oh to be safe under the shelter of thy wings!

OFFERTORY: We shall construct a new mansion for mankind founded on the principle of liberty. All people will have an equal place inside it. The raw materials we start with are the same as our fathers used—but watch! Something new will happen to them. In their transformation we will be made one.

August 25

ALLAN PINKERTON

Allan Pinkerton was born Aug. 25, 1819, the son of a police sergeant in Glascow, Scotland. Emigrating to the United States, he became a barrel maker and a deputy sheriff in Illinois, working on the side to help slaves escape from the south. In 1850 he opened his own private detective agency, specializing in railroad thefts. With the coming of the Civil War Pinkerton moved into military intelligence work with a notable lack of success (he invariably overestimated the size of Lee's army), but peacetime brought a welcome return to domestic crime. In his last years he put Pinkerton detectives to work battling labor unions at the request of business moguls. Pinkerton died in 1884.

RECESSIONAL: Having come here out of respect, Lord God, allow us to depart with the same respect from you. We don't require your surveillance in the coming days. Nor would we appreciate you poking into our half-formed intentions or listening to the tumult of our subconsciousness. It was you, after all, who first wrapped yourself in secrecy and spoke in thunder from behind the clouds. Grant us the right to be mysterious as well.

August 26

WILLIAM JAMES

William James was born in New York City in 1842. He was the son of a wealthy Swedenborgian philosopher and the older brother of novelist Henry James. William was trained as a medical doctor, but as time passed his focus of interest changed to psychology, to religion, and eventually to philosophy. As a professor at Harvard he wrote *Principles of Psychology* (1890) and *The Varieties of Religious Experience* (1902), both considered classics in their fields. James took up and popularized the philosophy of pragmatism first expounded by C.S. Pierce. As an idea-system pragmatism appealed to Americans; it held that truth, far from being an abstract reality, was synonymous with success. James retired after 35 years at Harvard in 1907. He died on this day in 1910.

PETITION: Don't show your face to us directly, God. Keep your presence hidden. Our senses can't embrace theophany, and your glory would confuse our faith, not clarify it. Instead reveal yourself as you always have in the lives of people whom we know and can touch. Through their experience we perceive if not your face at least the outlines of your being.

COMMUNION: *Rom 2, 12-13* All who have sinned without the law will also perish without the law, and all who have sinned under the law will be judged by the law. For it is not the hearers of the law who are righteous before God, but the doers of the law who will be justified.

August 27

LYNDON B. JOHNSON

In the closing year of his administration Lyndon B. Johnson was likened to a tragic king of literature who was ruined in spite of his greatness. Johnson was a man of enormous abilities. He had physical presence, great persuasive powers, a capacity for work, and political sagacity. Yet Johnson found himself trapped in a war that was increasingly unpopular at home but which to him was a test of his commitment—an important consideration for a man like Johnson. There was also an ego problem. Johnson's was large, and he was sensitive as only a Texan can be sensitive who comes under attack by eastern liberals. The drama played out to its denouement. The king was defeated, but in defeat was still a king. Lyndon Johnson was born this day in 1908. He died in 1973.

PROCESSIONAL: *Jer 8, 20-21* "The harvest is past, the summer is ended, and we are not saved." For the wound of the daughter of my people is my heart wounded, I mourn, and dismay has taken hold on me. *Is 1, 18* "Come now, let us reason together, says the Lord: though your sins are like scarlet, they shall be as white as snow; though they are red like crimson, they shall become like wool."

RECESSIONAL: We have come out of that valley where all things were green and strong, the valley of our abundance, of our strength. We have climbed up from that valley (where women and children were sprawled in a ditch) and came to this place, cool and desolate, stripped of abundance. Here the air is cleaner. This is the mountain of withdrawal. Here we make our habitation in a cave, a cave with light at its other end.

August 28

FREDERICK LAW OLMSTED

Frederick Law Olmsted was the finest landscape architect America ever produced. He created public parks and gardens in many of America's principal cities, including Fairmont Park in Philadelphia, Mont Royal Park in Montreal, the campus of Stanford University in Palo Alto, Calif., the grounds of the U.S. Capitol building in Washington, Prospect Park in Brooklyn, and Central Park in New York City. Olmsted was a genial and rather absentminded man. Besides being a designer he was a skilled writer and administrator. He was secretary of the U.S. Sanitary Commission (the precursor of the American Red Cross) during the Civil War. Olmsted was born in Connecticut in 1822. He died on Aug. 28, 1903.

OFFERTORY: Renew yourself in our dead soil, Lord God. Bring life to our dried limbs, our withered roots. Our offerings, like seeds, won't begin to grow until you transform them in your spirit, until you ignite them with a touch as delicate as spring and gentle as the rain.

COMMUNION: *Sir 24, 19-20* "Come to me, you who desire me, and eat your feed of my produce. For the remembrance of me is sweeter than honey, and my inheritance sweeter than the honeycomb."

August 29

CHARLIE PARKER

Charlie Parker was born in Kansas City on Aug. 29, 1920 and was playing the alto saxophone in bands by the time he was 17. They called him "Yardbird," or simply "Bird." His playing was intricate, soaring, and endlessly creative. Moving to New York, he joined with Dizzy Gillespie, Thelonias Monk and others to create a new jazz sound called "bop." Parker was the most influential jazz musician of his day, but his day was short. Ravaged by drugs and alcohol, he died in 1955 at the age of 34.

PROCESSIONAL: Sadness and fear find me in the morning and follow me through the day. Only in the darkness do I find freedom. *Ps 150, 3-5* Praise him with trumpet sound, praise him with lute and harp! Praise him with strings and pipe! Praise him with sounding cymbals.

PETITION: Give us, Lord God, the means to say what is deepest in ourselves, to speak what has no name. Whether in a word, or a song, or a shout, or in tears, help us to speak what we need to speak, hear what we need to hear.

August 30

HUEY LONG

Huey Long was born Aug. 30, 1893, the son of a poor farmer in Winnfield, La. Huey wasn't meant to stay on the farm, or to stay poor. He worked his way through law school by the age of 22, was elected to the state railroad commission at 25, and was governor at 35. During the next seven years as governor and U.S. Senator he became a dictator unique in American history, mixing folksy manners with an instinct for violence, destroying his enemies by any means—but also building roads, hospitals, and schools for the poor. He was beginning to challenge Franklin D. Roosevelt for national leadership in 1935 when the son of a political enemy shot him dead on the steps of the Louisiana capitol.

OFFERTORY: We had an offering prepared for you, Lord God. We entrusted it to one who promised to carry it to your altar and present it in our name. But when he got there he claimed it as his own. We have learned two things from this transaction: First, ministry and honesty are not synonymous. Second, don't make an offering without getting a receipt.

COMMUNION: *1 Sam 22, 2* And every one who was in distress, and every one who was in debt, and every one who was discontented, gathered to him; and he became captain over them.

August 31

ABRAHAM CAHAN

Abraham Cahan had to flee his native Lithuania in 1881 for political reasons, and like many other eastern European Jews of that period he ended up in New York. With a friend he founded a Yiddish-language newspaper of a socialist bent, and in 1887 he moved to the *Jewish Daily Forward*. After a five-year hiatus on English-language papers he returned to the *Forward* as editor and made it the most successful and influential foreign-language newspaper in America. For millions of half-educated Jews, the *Forward* was a textbook on the arts, politics, and economics. Cahan also wrote many stories of immigrant life that were popular with non-Jewish readers. He died on Aug. 31, 1951 in New York City.

PETITION: *Deut 9, 26, 29* "O Lord God, destroy not thy people and thy heritage, whom thou hast redeemed through thy greatness, whom thou hast brought out of Egypt with a mighty hand. For they are thy people and thy heritage, whom thou didst bring out by thy great power and thy outstretched arm."

RECESSIONAL: As we go out in search of some new land we find comfort in the fact that the Lord still speaks in the language of our fathers. But what will happen when the method of his revelation changes? How will we hear him? And how can we know that the one we are hearing is him, as we go out in search of some new land?

SEPTEMBER

September 1

AARON BURR

Aaron Burr is known best as the man who fatally shot Alexander Hamilton in a duel in 1804. He also stood trial for his alleged attempt to create an independent nation in the southwest territories; he was found innocent of that charge in a tumultuous hearing that ended this day in 1807. Burr was a headstrong, ambitious man. He was a good hater. He served one term in the Senate from New York, and then was nearly elected President in 1800, until archrival Hamilton threw his support to Thomas Jefferson. After the treason trial Burr gradually dropped out of sight, dying in 1836.

PROCESSIONAL: The violent men will rise up, and the meek will find shelter. Save me from the violent man; save me, too, from the meek. *Ps 51, 11-12* Cast me not away from thy presence, and take not thy holy Spirit from me. Restore me to the joy of thy salvation, and uphold me with a willing spirit.

RECESSIONAL: Do not let us, O Lord, who have found fellowship at your supper, be tools for each other's ambitions. But do not let us lack ambition either. These two things we shall carry away from this place: compassion on one hand, passion on the other.

September 2

HENRY GEORGE

Henry George, one of the earliest and most eccentric American economists, was born Sept. 2, 1839 in Philadelphia and worked while a young man as a merchant seaman, lighthouse keeper, typesetter, and editor. In 1871 he published a manifesto declaring that land was the root of all wealth and that rent for the use of land was an obstacle to progress. As his ideas gained popularity George gravitated toward politics, running twice (unsuccessfully) for mayor of New York. Largely discredited today, George's economic theories have a utopian ring, harkening back to an era when land, not industry, was America's most important product.

OFFERTORY: Forgive us, Father—you who hid precious gems for our finding, who gave us soil and seeds, and rain and sunlight. Forgive us that the things you gave us are things we keep from each other. May these gifts today be a new beginning. Teach us again to share. Teach us that everything is ours to use, but nothing is ours to keep.

COMMUNION: *Ps 37, 28-29* The righteous shall be preserved for ever, but the children of the wicked shall be cut off. The righteous shall possess the land, and dwell upon it for ever.

September 3

LOUIS SULLIVAN

Louis Sullivan was the father of the modern skyscraper building and one of the most influential designers in American history. Born in Boston on Sept. 3, 1856, he spent most of his career in Chicago where several of his buildings still stand. Sullivan eschewed useless decoration, believing that a structure's use and its building materials should determine its style. He also felt that buildings should blend in with their environments—a belief carried on by his most famous disciple, Frank Lloyd Wright. Sullivan died in 1924.

PETITION: Inhabit them, Lord God, these sacred spaces we construct that hold the darkness and the light. Descend upon our firmament; find dwelling in our tabernacles. The first creation was too grand for us, so we're reduced to pleading for your presence within these makeshift worlds we build inside of yours.

RECESSIONAL: *1 Kings 8, 12-13* "The Lord has set the sun in the heavens, but has said that he would dwell in thick darkness. I have built thee an exalted house, a place for thee to dwell in forever."

September 4

DANIEL BURNHAM

Daniel Burnham is considered the founder of the modern practice of city planning. Born in New York on Sept. 4, 1846, Burnham grew up in Chicago and was trained as an architect. He was involved in some of the first high-rise office buildings: the Montauk Building in Chicago and the Flatiron Building in New York. His real accomplishment was the design for the World's Columbian Exposition in Chicago in 1892 which stimulated interest in the grouping of buildings and parkland. Later he produced urban designs in Washington, D.C., Cleveland, San Francisco, and Manila. Burnham died in 1912.

OFFERTORY: Receive, Lord God, these first fruits from our gardens, planted when the world was new. The offerings are lovely, but alas the gardens have gone to ruin. They were plundered for their goods and left in wild disorder to spoil and decay. Come, bring your design into our chaos. Change these gifts back into seeds and plant them in us so that we may grow anew, lest these first fruits will also be our last.

COMMUNION: *Gen 1, 9-10* And God said, "Let the waters under the heavens be gathered together in one place, and let the dry land appear." And it was so. God called the dry land Earth, and the waters that were gathered together he called Seas. And God saw that it was good.

September 5

JESSE JAMES

Popular legend made Jesse James seem like Robin Hood, a romantic bandit who contested the power of railroad barons. The truth is simpler than that: he was just a thief and a killer. Born Sept. 5, 1847 in Missouri, in a family with Confederate sympathies, he learned his violent art with Quantrell's Raiders during the Civil War. When that fighting was over he started his own gang, looting trains and banks in Kansas. At last they posted a $10,000 reward for him and spread the news around until one of Jesse's own men shot him in the back.

PROCESSIONAL: The people held their breath when they heard of Jesse's death,/They wondered how he ever came to fall;/Robert Ford, it was a fact, shot Jesse in the back/While Jesse hung a picture on the wall.* *Zech 5, 3* "This is the curse that goes out over the face of the whole land; for every one who steals shall be cut off henceforth according to it, and every one who swears falsely shall be cut off henceforth according to it."

RECESSIONAL: For those injuries they caused, they asked forgiveness; for the injuries they suffered, they demanded retribution. The judge answered

*Traditional folk ballad.

them, saying: "What course shall I take when you bring injury to your-selves?"

September 6

MARGARET SANGER

Margaret Sanger was born Margaret Higgins in New York in 1883 and was trained as a nurse. Working largely in ghetto areas, she was appalled by the degrading conditions she found and by the number of deaths from self-induced abortions. Flouting prevailing laws which classified con-traceptive data as obscene, she became a controversial advocate of birth control, serving a term in jail as a consequence. For 50 years she wrote books, lectured publicly, and founded organizations (including the Planned Parenthood Federation) in support of her cause. She died on Sept. 6, 1966.

PROCESSIONAL: *Job 17, 6-7* "He has made me a byword of the peoples, and I am one before whom men spit. My eye has grown dim from grief, and all my members are like a shadow." *Ps 35, 11-14* Malicious witnesses rise up; they ask me of things that I know not. They requite me evil for good; my soul is forlorn. But I, when they were sick—I wore sackcloth, I afflicted myself with fasting. I prayed with head bowed on my bosom, as though I grieved for my friend or my brother.

COMMUNION: *Ps 74, 21* Let not the downtrodden be put to shame; let the poor and needy praise thy name.

September 7

JOHN GREENLEAF WHITTIER

John Greenleaf Whittier spent his early years as a firebrand editor of anti-slavery newspapers in Boston, Washington, and Philadelphia. When the Civil War was over he returned to the rustic themes of his childhood and was much honored in his day for poems such as *Snowbound, Barbara Fritchie, Barefoot Boy*, and others. He lived his last years as a celebrated poet of rural New England, dying at the age of 85 on Sept. 7, 1872.

RECESSIONAL: We are weak, but Thou art strong;/Short our lives, but Thine is long;/We are blind, but Thou hast eyes;/We are fools, but Thou art wise!/Thou our morrow's pathway knowing/Through the strange world round us growing,/hear us, tell us where we are going.*

September 8

Peter Stuyvesant

Peter Stuyvesant came to New Amsterdam in 1647, an irascible and despotic Dutchman with a pegleg and a talent for leadership. As representative of the Dutch East India Co. he ruled his colony with an iron hand, quelling local demands for self-government just as he quelled Indian uprisings. When an English fleet hove into sight in 1664 Stuyvesant could not rouse his fellow citizens to resist, and so on Sept. 8th he surrendered and went off in great ill-humor to live as a farmer. The English promptly renamed his town New York.

PROCESSIONAL: *Dan 3, 28* "Thou hast executed true judgments in all that thou hast brought upon us and upon Jerusalem, the holy city of our fathers." *Ps 22, 4-5* In thee our fathers trusted; they trusted, and thou didst deliver them. To thee they cried, and were saved; in thee they trusted, and were not disappointed.

PETITION: In times of stress grant to us, O Lord, men like your servant Peter to rule over us with righteousness and strength. But please Lord, we beg you, find something else for them to do when the times of stress are over.

September 9

Edward H. Harriman

Edward H. Harriman was a player with railroads unparalled in American history. Beginning as a Wall Street clerk at the age of 15, he played the market until he was able to buy control of the Lake Ontario Southern Railroad, then the Union Pacific, then the Southern Pacific and Central Pacific. By 1905 he controlled over 60,000 miles of track, and he used his power ruthlessly to dominate competitors and subordinates. After coming under attack by the Interstate Commerce Commission, and in public disfavor for his business methods, he died suddenly on Sept. 9, 1909.

*From *Song of Slaves in the Desert* by John Greenleaf Whittier.

September 10

OLIVER HAZARD PERRY

Born into a Rhode Island family that produced a long line of naval officers, Oliver Hazard Perry was only 28 years old when he was given command of a hastily created force of ships on Lake Erie during the War of 1812. Using for the most part men who had never fought in ships before, he utterly routed the opposing fleet on Sept. 10, 1813, thereby wrecking British plans for an invasion of the northern states. Perry died on his 34th birthday in 1819.

COMMUNION: *Ps 18, 39-40* Thou didst gird me with strength for the battle; thou didst make my assailants sink under me. Thou didst make my enemies turn their backs to me, and those who hated me I destroyed.

RECESSIONAL: We came here, God, expecting bread, but you nourished us with flesh and blood. We came expecting friendship, and you presented us with love. We came fully expecting defeat but hoping to find in it some meaning. Sheer wonderment! We have got victory instead!

September 11

O. HENRY

O. Henry was the pen name of William S. Porter, born Sept. 11, 1862 in North Carolina. Convicted of embezzling money from a Texas bank, Porter began writing stories to pass the time in jail. In New York after his release he perfected a formula: the compact, slick tale with a surprise twist at the end. O. Henry wrote of the little people in the big cities, the forgotten, the downtrodden. He was the poet laureate of the emerging urban society. He died of tuberculosis in New York in 1910.

PETITION: Teach us the song of your city, God. Help us to hear the cadence of the cars, to sense the color, the lights, the crowds, the crooks, the cops, the noise, the daily dance of your sinewy, smartass people. When you fashioned men from clay, Lord God, you got your hands dirty. We rejoice in the work of your hands.

COMMUNION: *Ps 87, 1-3* On the holy mount stands the city he founded; the Lord loves the gates of Zion more than all the dwelling places of Jacob. Glorious things are spoken of you, O city of God.

September 12

H. L. MENCKEN

A caustic observer of American excesses, literary and social, H. L. Mencken railed against the academic elite in his day nearly as much as he scored middle-class Babbittry. He was proud of being a simple journalist. As a critic, Mencken was the virtual arbiter of taste in the 1920s, writing for such magazines as *Smart Set*, *The Nation* and *American Mercury*. He is known particularly for his book on *The American Language*. He was born Sept. 12, 1880; he died in 1956.

OFFERTORY: If it's true, God, that you can do all things, won't you make our vices into virtues? All our small-town, pigheaded, chauvinistic, bigotries—there must be some good in them somewhere. Won't you take those faults, along with these gifts we make now, and give them back to us in a new way?

RECESSIONAL: When everything was finished they found their weaknesses were strengths, their strengths were weaknesses. Neither stronger nor weaker were they, but were moved by the mystery of themselves.

September 13

WALTER REED

Walter Reed was born Sept. 13, 1851 in Virginia. He received training in public health medicine in New York City and then in 1875 joined the

162

army. There he served competently and unspectacularly for nearly 30 years. Then in 1889 he headed a team of doctors investigating the causes of yellow fever, a disease that was epidemic among U.S. servicemen in Cuba. Aided by human volunteers (several of whom lost their lives), Reed proved that one species of mosquito carried the deadly parasite. With this knowledge doctors mounted a dramatic counterattack on the disease. In 1900 Havana alone had 1400 cases of Yellow Fever; by 1902 there were no cases in all of Cuba. Reed died suddenly in Washington, D.C. in 1902 of appendicitis.

PETITION: You did protect us God from the lions and the wolves that prowled our caves, and then from lesser beasts—serpents, and rodents, and insects, and last of all from microbes, too small for our seeing. And when all of these are gone, when all external threats are eradicated, then the only predators that threaten us will be ourselves and our own dark impulses, beyond the reach of science. O protect us then.

September 14

ISADORA DUNCAN

Isadora Duncan was born in San Francisco in 1878 and became a professional dancer at the age of 17. During years of poverty and obscurity she struggled to bring naturalistic movement back into her art form which had become mired in classical formalism. Gradually her ideas took hold, and at various times she had dance schools in Moscow, Berlin, in France, and at Tarrytown, N.Y. Her life, however, was a series of personal tragedies. Her two children died of drowning. Her politics and behavior caused such a stir that she fled America only to die herself in an automobile accident on Sept. 14, 1927 in France.

PROCESSIONAL: *Eccles 3, 2, 3-4* There is a time to be born, and a time to die; a time to weep, and a time to laugh; a time to mourn, and a time to dance. *Ps 69, 7-8* It is for thy sake that I have borne reproach, that shame has covered my face. I have become a stranger to my brethren, an alien to my mother's sons.

RECESSIONAL: Lord, you have nourished my body with life. Let me feel its beauty, its quickness, its strength. We, your people, will be justified not by our existence, but by how we move.

September 15

JAMES FENIMORE COOPER

James Fenimore Cooper was born Sept. 15, 1789 in New Jersey and grew up in Cooperstown, N.Y., a village named after his father. From 1820 onward he produced a series of novels about the American frontier, called the Leatherstocking Tales, that catapulted him to international fame. Seen in their day as simple romances, they are recognized now as profound moral conflicts between native American virtues and the coming materialistic society. Cooper was the first to portray the tragic hero as the mediator between personal freedom and the remorseless requirements of civilization.

PROCESSIONAL: Within the darkness there was light. Among the shadows of the trees walked his people. The destroyer came among them dressed in sunlight and righteousness. *Ps 140, 4-5* Guard me, O Lord, from the hands of the wicked; preserve me from violent men, who have planned to trip up my feet. Arrogant men have hidden a trap for me, and with cords they have spread a net, by the wayside they have set snares for me.

PETITION: Comfort your people, God, who are held captive by their own horizons. What they freely chose is what confines them, and the moment of choice is long since past. Comfort them who glory in their deeds but whose deeds now bind them in at every turn.

September 16

ANNE BRADSTREET

Anne Bradstreet was America's first poet, arriving in Massachusetts with her husband only 10 years after the first pilgrims landed. She was an educated woman who at first was dismayed by the rugged life of the colonies. In time she adapted to it and raised a family of eight children. Her writing was simple and human and filled with gentle humor—in marked contrast to the prevailing Puritan sternness. She died on Sept. 16, 1672.

PETITION: Preserve us in adversity, Lord God, as you preserved your daughter Anne in the New World. May the hardness of life serve to toughen us rather than discourage us. And keep our sensitivities from being eroded in the daily grind, so that even in the most trying circumstances we may not fail to plant in the wilderness at least one flower.

COMMUNION: Thy love is such I can no way repay;/The heavens reward thee manifold I pray./Then while we live, in love let's so persever,/That when we live no more, we may live ever.*

*From "To My Dear and Loving Husband" by Anne Bradstreet.

September 17

RUTH BENEDICT

Ruth Benedict was one of the world's best-known anthropologists. Her book *Patterns of Culture*, translated into more than a dozen languages, probed the varieties of cultural forms and their relationship to the human personality. A later work *Race: Science and Politics* rebutted the claims of racists and argued for the essential unity of all human beings. Benedict was born in New York City in 1887 and did much of her writing at Columbia University where she held the rank of full professor. She died suddenly on this day in 1948 at the age of 61.

OFFERTORY: You, Almighty Father, made us one people from the first dawning of history. Now take our divergencies, our disagreements, and make us one again. Because division and unity are matters of perspective. In our eyes we are many; in your eyes we are one.

RECESSIONAL: *Wis 7, 1, 5-6* I also am mortal, like all men, a descendant of the first-formed child of earth . . . For no king has had a different beginning of existence; there is for all mankind one entrance into life, and a common departure.

September 18

ADOLPH S. OCHS

On Sept. 18, 1851 a new journal appeared on the streets of New York, called the *Times*. The *Times* flourished for a few years, then faltered. Obviously it would never amount to much as a newspaper. In 1896 the *Times* was bought by Adolph S. Ochs, a 38-year-old Chattanooga publisher who thought a respectable paper could compete with the yellow journalism then in vogue. Almost from the first he visualized the *Times* as a "paper of record"—a historical document that recorded the events of the day for posterity. Ochs, who was also a founder and longtime president of the Associated Press, died in 1935 at the age of 77. The *Times*, of course, lives.

COMMUNION: *Sir 39, 2, 4* He will preserve the discourse of notable men and penetrate the subtleties of parables . . . for he tests the good and the evil among men.

RECESSIONAL: Present at our table we have the Lord. Contained in our own deeds that are preserved and recounted we have his revelation.

September 19

JAMES A. GARFIELD

James A. Garfield came out of poverty in Ohio to get a good education, serve creditably in the Civil War (emerging as a major general), and to spend 17 years in the House of Representatives. When the 1880 Republican convention failed after 35 ballots to choose between John Sherman, Ulysses Grant, or James G. Blaine, it turned to old party loyalist Garfield as a compromise candidate. He was elected by a slim majority. Six months after his inauguration he was shot by an assassin in a Washington railroad station. He died on Sept. 19, 1881.

PETITION: Bestow from time to time upon your people, God, leaders of modest talents, without great vision or great flaws, cut from ordinary cloth. Give us average men like James, your servant. For we know if such men are elected then we, too, are elected. And by this token you will have fixed upon our rude fabric an eternal design.

RECESSIONAL: *2 Pet 1, 10-11* Therefore, brethren, be the more zealous to confirm your call and election, for if you do this you will never fall, so there will be richly provided for you an entrance into the eternal kingdom of our Lord and Savior Jesus Christ.

September 20

DONALD MCKAY

Of all the creations of American workmanship, none was more beautiful than the clipper ship—that graceful lord of the sea topped by a cloud of canvas that set sailing records unequalled to this day. No one in the world designed and built clipper ships as well as Donald McKay at his yard in Boston. His ship *Flying Cloud* sailed from San Francisco around Cape Horn to New York in just 89 days, and the *Lightning* once covered 436 nautical miles in 24 hours. Those were the final, halcyon days of sailing ships, soon to be overcome by iron and steam. McKay closed his shipyard in 1869, and he died on Sept. 20, 1880.

OFFERTORY: Borne by fragile vessels our offerings approach your throne, Lord God. They are ordinary gifts, workmanlike, the unromantic products of our days and weeks. In their place you return to us exotic offerings as from the east, perfumed, rich with mystery and promise. These you entrust to us, your fragile vessels, your people. You place them in our care for this, our perilous journey.

166

COMMUNION: *Ezek 27, 4-5, 7* Your builders made perfect your beauty. They made all your planks of fir trees from Senir; they took a cedar from Lebanon to make a mast for you . . . Fine embroidered linen from Egypt was your sail, serving as your ensign.

September 21

CHIEF JOSEPH

Chief Joseph of the Nez Percé was a noble and brilliant indian leader. He was committed to peace with the whites but when forced into battle proved to be a tenacious and innovative fighter. Driven from their tribal lands in 1877, Joseph's band of 750 persons set out on a march of 1500 miles, during which they twice crossed the continental divide and fought 18 pitched battles against a vastly superior foe, winning most of them. The tribe was finally surrounded just 30 miles short of Canadian sanctuary. Joseph surrendered with dignity. He spent the next 27 years on government reservations, dying on Sept. 21, 1904.

PROCESSIONAL: We are all sprung from a woman . . . We cannot be made over again . . . We are just as we were made by the Great Spirit, and you cannot change us.* *Ps 76, 3-4* There he broke the flashing arrows, the shield, the sword, and the weapons of war. Glorious are thou, more majestic than the everlasting mountains.

RECESSIONAL: Why should the children of one mother and father quarrel? Why should one try to cheat the other? I do not believe the Great Spirit gave one kind of men the right to tell another kind of men what to do.*

September 22

NATHAN HALE

There was nothing extraordinary about Nathan Hale. He grew up in Connecticut, went to Yale, became a schoolteacher. Like other young men he joined the army when war broke out. When George Washington wanted a spy to go behind British lines, Hale volunteered. When the British caught him, Hale said yes, he was guilty. On Sept. 22, 1776 his captors led him to the gallows, and Hale, only 21 years old, looked down at them and said, according to legend: "I only regret I have but one life to lose for my country." And he lost it.

*Quotations from Chief Joseph.

167

OFFERTORY: Behold your people, God. We do not have a life to give. We are broken and torn, divided, suspicious. If we were made one we would have one life to give you, one life to share with each other. Come, send your spirit among us and make us worthy of this moment.

COMMUNION: *Joel 2, 28* "I will pour out my spirit on all flesh; your sons and daughters shall prophesy, your old men shall dream dreams, and your young men shall see visions."

September 23

VICTORIA WOODHULL

Had Victoria Woodhull been born in Russia, she would have been Catherine the Great. Intelligent, beautiful, and eccentric—she was everything the typical 19th-century woman was not. She was an advocate of free love and was married three times; with her sister Tennessee she directed a successful stock-brokerage firm, edited a weekly magazine, preached women's rights. In 1872 she became the first woman ever nominated for the presidency, running on a ticket with Frederick Douglass. Victoria was born in Ohio, the daughter of itinerant medicine-show performers, on Sept. 23, 1838. She died in England as the wife of a wealthy British banker in 1927.

PETITION: Judge our case, Lord; we refuse to accept the verdict of conventional wisdom. We have danced long enough to clumsy music; your appraisal is the only one that matters. We may be weak, but we are not powerless. We may be servants, but we are not passive. In your gaze all flesh will be stripped away until the inner part alone remains. We will abide by your decision.

COMMUNION: *Prov 9, 1-2* Wisdom has built her house, she has set up her seven pillars. She has slaughtered her beasts, she has mixed her wine, she has also set her table.

September 24

JAY GOULD

In the age of business moguls, Jay Gould was in a class by himself—wheeling and dealing, manipulating the stock market by legal and illegal means, and fighting for control of corporations. With Jim Fisk he tried to corner the gold market in 1869 and failed, causing a crisis on Sept. 24th that ruined thousands of small investors. It was a typical Gould maneuver. Three years later he was forced out of the Erie Railroad after that company sold $5 million of fraudulent stocks. Gould spent his declining years simply—as director of the Union Pacific, the Missouri Pacific, Western Union Telegraph Co., and the New York City elevated-train system. He died in 1892.

RECESSIONAL: You revealed your law to us Almighty God. Is that all there is? Now it's our turn to use it as we will. Just as we take your trees and carve them into different shapes, so we will take your law. Legality is our beginning point. The end is limited by our inventiveness, and our lack of scruples.

September 25

WILLIAM FAULKNER

William Faulkner was born Sept. 25, 1897 and grew up in Oxford, Miss. Except for brief periods he spent the rest of his life there, writing a succession of profound and grotesque novels that pictured the decay of Southern society in mythic terms. The unscrupulous Snopes clan that populated fictional Yoknapatawpha County portended, in Faulkner's eyes, the emergence of the uncultured bourgeoisie. The density of Faulkner's novels hindered wide popular acceptance but won him critical renown, including the Nobel Prize in 1949 and the Pulitzer Prize in 1954. He died in 1962.

PROCESSIONAL: *Ex 11, 1, 5-6* "Yet one plague more I will bring upon Pharaoh and upon Egypt" . . . "And all the first-born of the land of Egypt shall die . . . And there shall be a great cry throughout all the land of Egypt, such as there has never been, nor ever shall be again." *2 Sam 18, 33* "O my son Absalom, my son, my son Absalom! Would I had died instead of you, O Absalom, my son, my son!"

OFFERTORY: What can we offer you, Father, when the land is arid and despoiled, when neither wheat nor grapes are suitable for gifts? We will offer you an empty plate, but with a gesture of such grace and beauty that you will smile upon your barren land, your barren people, and save us from destruction.

September 26

GEORGE GERSHWIN

George Gershwin lived only 38 years. He was born Sept. 26, 1898 in

Brooklyn, N.Y. of Jewish immigrant parents; he died in Hollywood, a world-famous composer of songs and concert music. Gershwin was a warm, extroverted person with unbounding curiosity. He devoted himself to searching for a new language that would celebrate his own sense of life in America, its rhythms and noble qualities. In his striving he led millions of persons to sing, dance, smile. Nice work if you can get it.

PETITION: Not again will we apologize for the way we live. God, help us to stop. Your son George saw the truth: Underneath our plastic veneer there is real tears, real tenderness. If we have been foolish, we have also known moments of greatness. The memory of all that will not leave us. No, no, they can't take that away.

RECESSIONAL: The radio and the telephone/And the movies that we know/May just be passing fancies/And in time may go./But, Oh my dear,/Our love is here to stay./Together we're/Going a long, long way./In time the Rockies will crumble,/Gibraltar will tumble./They're only made of clay,/But our love is here to stay.*

September 27

THOMAS NAST

Thomas Nast was America's first great political cartoonist, active during the latter part of the 19th century with *Harper's Weekly* and other periodicals. It was Nast who first pictured the Democratic mule, the Republican elephant, and the Tammany tiger, and it was Nast whose cartoons brought about the downfall of Boss Tweed and his ring of corrupt politicians. Nast was born on Sept. 27, 1840; he died, sick and nearly broke, in 1902.

PROCESSIONAL: Wicked men found safety behind rigid lines where nothing was out of place. But underneath the form which they ordained, corruption flourished; their order was a shield for corruption. *Response:* Behold the Lord has brought confusion to their ways, like a pond whose mirror makes the mountains dance. In his reflection we perceived the truth.

September 28

JOHN PAUL JONES

John Paul Jones, the first naval hero in American history, was born in Scotland in 1747 and came to Virginia at the age of 12. Since he had experience as a ship's officer in the slave trade, he was offered command of a warship in the American revolution, and he earned his reputation as a raider along the English and Scottish coasts. His most notable victory came over the British frigate *Serapis* on Sept. 28, 1779 after Jones, in his sinking flagship *Bon Homme Richard*, declared "I have not yet begun to fight."

OFFERTORY: In the shadow of defeat the gift is made. Everything gambled, the final offering is lifted up—a gesture to hold back the void. The gifts don't even belong to us. We have pawned our very faith, trusting that you will rescue us again. See fit to take this offering, we pray, that we may have at least a taste of triumph, and that our hopes may be saved from drowning this one more time.

COMMUNION: *2 Mac 10, 38* When they had accomplished these things, with hymns and thanksgivings they blessed the Lord who shows great kindness to Israel and gives them the victory.

September 29

WINSLOW HOMER

On Sept. 29, 1910 Winslow Homer died at his home on the Maine coast. He was a semi-recluse in his last years, never marrying, a man of few words. In his art, however, Homer was a glorious romantic, producing a masterful collection of oils and luminous watercolors of Americans in communion with nature—sometimes at peace in the forest, sometimes struggling against the mindless might of the sea. Of all the painters of his day, he was the most American in his vision and choice of subjects. Among his best-known works are *Snap the Whip, Eight Bells,* and *Gulf Stream.*

COMMUNION: *Jer 31, 35* Thus says the Lord, who gives the sun for light by day and the fixed order of the moon and the stars for light by night, who stirs up the sea so that its waves roar—the Lord of hosts is his name.

RECESSIONAL: We thank you Lord for these gifts: bread and wine, green grass, blue sky, lakes and hills, sunlight and starlight. Do not let us walk through our days blind to the wonders of your world. Open our hearts. Let us see.

September 30

WILLIAM WRIGLEY

William Wrigley was the emperor of chewing gum, turning that dubious habit into a worldwide addiction. He was the prototype of the American supersalesman who used snappy advertising and dealer kickbacks to corner the market. Wrigley was born Sept. 30, 1861 in Chicago. By the time of his death in 1932 his chewing gum business was grossing $75 million annually. Just for kicks he also owned the Chicago Cubs baseball team, Santa Catalina island in California, and built the Wrigley Building in Chicago, one of the world's largest.

OFFERTORY: You, O cosmic Juicy Fruit, if you come to us, we will not deposit later beneath movie seats, lunch counters, or in other hidden places. No, accept this promise: Nourish us this day and our union will become a public sticking place to confound mankind. And passers-by will grudgingly confess that you have truly been impressed on us, and we on you.

OCTOBER

October 1

RUFUS CHOATE

Rufus Choate was a brilliant courtroom lawyer who kept juries spellbound in early 19th-century America. Choate was born Oct. 1, 1799 in Massachusetts and died just before the Civil War. Although a loyal servant of the Whig party and a famous orator, he declined to serve in Congress and even on the Supreme Court because he couldn't face giving up his law practice. So persuasive was he in court that one jury freed a client of his because Choate convinced them that the man was sleepwalking at the time he committed the evil deed.

PETITION: Be our advocate, Lord God, when we are called to account for all our failings. Plead our cause before the throne of judgment. Stir the waters of compassion on our behalf. Call forth the gentle rain from heaven. Persuade your angels to testify as expert witnesses. Attire us in rainbows. Magnify our better parts. Do anything! Just get us off.

RECESSIONAL: *Ps 54, 21* His speech was smoother than butter, yet war was in his heart; his words were softer than oil, yet they were drawn swords.

October 2

CORDELL HULL

Cordell Hull was Franklin D. Roosevelt's wartime secretary of state. Hull was a stern, crusty old character from Overton County, Tenn. He was a hard-liner, a hawk in an age when hawks ruled the air. Yet his most notable achievement was laying the groundwork for the United Nations, an achievement for which he won the Nobel Prize in 1945. Hull was born Oct. 2, 1871. Before moving to the State Department he served 13 years in Congress and was the author of the first federal income-tax law. He resigned from the cabinet in 1944 and died in Bethesda, Md. in 1955.

PROCESSIONAL: *Jer 31, 16-17* "Keep your voice from weeping, and your eyes from tears; for your work shall be rewarded, says the Lord, and they shall come back from the land of the enemy. There is hope for your future, says the Lord, and your children shall come back to their own country." *Ps 85, 8-9* He will speak peace to his people . . . Surely his salvation is at hand for those who fear him, that glory may dwell in our land.

COMMUNION: The Lord has protected his people in their time of trial. His steadfastness has brought us to the day when the lights go on again all over the world.

October 3

THOMAS WOLFE

Thomas Wolfe was born Oct. 3, 1900 in Ashville, N.C., a city he fled from as a young man and then celebrated in a series of semi-autobiographical novels. Wolfe was an intuitive and undisciplined writer whose gargantuan stories brimmed with life and feeling. In an age when farms and small towns all over America were losing their young people to the cities, Wolfe wrestled with new-found feelings of freedom and alienation—a sense of triumph and loss that also reflected America's new role in the 20th-century world.

OFFERTORY: Not again will we offer you this bread, this wine Lord. Not again will we sit like this for your supper. We will meet again, but not us: all things change. Make this bread your flesh, and our flesh too, so that, consuming it, the real presence of each other may refresh our spirits on the road that leads each of us in separate ways.

RECESSIONAL: . . . Something has spoken in the night,/And told me I shall die, I know not where./Saying:/"To lose the earth you know, for greater knowing;/To lose the life you have, for greater life;/To leave the friends you loved, for greater loving;/To find a land more kind than home, more large than earth . . ."*

October 4

FREDERIC REMINGTON

Frederic Remington went west in 1880, aware that the influx of railroads would soon dilute the untamed way of life there and anxious to capture it

*First and second stanza of "Toward Which" (p. 166) from *A Stone, A Leaf, A Door* by Thomas Wolfe, Selected and Arranged in Verse by John S. Barne. Copyright 1945 by Maxwell Perkins as Executor (Charles Scribner's Sons). Originally in prose in *You Can't Go Home Again* by Thomas Wolfe. Copyright 1940 by Maxwell Perkins as Executor. By permission of Harper & Row, Publishers, Inc.

first on canvas. Over the next few years he produced paintings and bronze figures of cowboys, indians, and soldiers that were filled with motion and precise detail. These works and the illustrations Remington did during the Spanish-American War (which he covered for the Hearst papers) won public acclaim for him in America and Europe. Remington was born Oct. 4, 1861 in upstate New York; he died in 1909.

OFFERTORY: Behold this gift-horse frozen in its gallop, eye and nostral eternally dilated. Your servant Frederic fashioned it to his own glory and yours. We your people, Lord God, are not such rigid gifts; what we are today we may recant tomorrow. Take us then before this moment passes. Take us while you can.

COMMUNION: *Jer 48, 8* The destroyer shall come upon every city, and no city shall escape; the valley shall perish, and the plain shall be destroyed, as the Lord has spoken.

October 5

ROBERT H. GODDARD

Robert H. Goddard was born Oct. 5, 1882 and taught physics at Princeton and Clark universities. He is considered the father of the modern science of rocketry. Goddard was the first to devise two-stage rockets, the first to use liquid oxygen fuels, and the first to send aloft instrument packages containing thermometers, barometers, and cameras. Although he took out more than 200 patents, Goddard was generally ignored during his lifetime. In 1969, fourteen years after his death, the *New York Times* formally retracted a 1920 editorial ridiculing his claim that rockets could fly to the moon.

PETITION: God of the heavens, give your servant Robert the honor he deserves, and to all your nameless servants here on earth who, beaten down by indifference and neglect, dare still, from their unspoken places, to reach their arms out to the stars.

COMMUNION: *Ps 68, 32-33* Sing to the Lord, O kingdoms of the earth; sing praises to the Lord, to him who rides in the heavens, the ancient heavens; lo, he sends forth his voice, his mighty voice.

October 6

GEORGE WESTINGHOUSE

Born Oct. 6, 1846 in upstate New York, George Westinghouse was only

18 years old when he became third assistant engineer for the Navy Department during the Civil War. In 1869 he patented a new air brake for railroad trains, and soon thereafter he organized the Westinghouse Air Brake Co. Within his lifetime it became one of the largest electric and hydraulic manufacturing firms in the world. He also built dynamos for the Niagara Falls power plants and for the New York City and London subway systems.

PROCESSIONAL: Power lay in the earth and in its waters; power rode on the winds and in the flame; the power of the Lord was given to his people. *Ps 111, 6-7* He has shown his people the power of his works, in giving them the heritage of the nations. The works of his hands are faithful and just.

RECESSIONAL: We have gone out, Lord God, and tamed the rivers and the oceans; we have brought the wind under harness, and herded the clouds like sheep. Of all your creatures only we men careen unchecked through the earth, borne by jungle currents that surge and batter against the walls of our days. Strengthen our hands and our wills, O Lord, that this energy may be used to build up your kingdom.

October 7

EDGAR ALLAN POE

Although most readers today know him for his poetry, Edgar Allan Poe was one of America's foremost literary critics in the last century and a formidable short fiction writer. He is credited with having invented the detective story. His interest in the music of language and his obsession with mood and melancholy made him a favorite of French symbolists Baudelaire and Mallarmé. Poe's personal life was tragic: an orphan, his periods of work were overshadowed by long bouts of alcoholism and depression, finally leading to his death in Baltimore on Oct. 7, 1849.

PROCESSIONAL: *Job 10, 20-22* "Let me alone, that I may . . . go whence I shall not return, to the land of gloom and deep darkness, the land of gloom and chaos, where light is as darkness." *Wis 2, 5* For our allotted time is the passing of a shadow, and there is no return from our death, because it is sealed up and no one turns back.

RECESSIONAL: "Over the Mountains of the Moon,/Down the Valley of the Shadow,/Ride, boldly ride . . ./If you seek for Eldorado."*

*From "Eldorado" by Edgar Allan Poe.

October 8

ALVIN C. YORK

Alvin York grew up in the mountains of Pall Mall, Tenn. where he scratched out a living from the land, hunted with his rifle, and went to church regularly. When the Great War came along he asked twice for conscientious-objector status but was twice refused, and so ended up in the 82nd Division in France. On Oct. 8, 1918 Sgt. York led a squad of seven men who, when pinned down by machine-gun fire, charged the German positions, killed 25 of the enemy and captured 132 more. When the War To End All Wars shuddered to a halt a few weeks later, Alvin York was hailed as America's foremost war hero.

PETITION: Save your people, Lord God, who in their striving to secure the blessings of liberty on themselves and their children did make a killer out of your gentle son Alvin. There is no place left for innocence in your world. Comfort us on our road from Eden. We have all become serpents in order to survive. But, O Lord, even as we struggle in this wilderness, let us never cease remembering that once perfect place.

October 9

AIMEE SEMPLE MCPHERSON

Aimee Semple McPherson . . . Rarely is the name heard today. But in the decade between 1923 and 1933 it was hardly ever out of the newspapers. She was Sister Aimee, "the world's most pulchritudinous evangelist," founder of the International Church of the Foursquare Gospel in Los Angeles. Her religion was primarily spectacle, and so was her life. She was three times married, once supposedly kidnapped and miraculously returned, and was continually involved in lawsuits with her followers and her family. Her career in the end was the story of a magnetic and sad woman who used other people's loneliness as a balm for her own. She was born this day in 1890; she died in 1944 from an overdose of sleeping pills.

PETITION: Do not promise us happiness, Lord God. Do not promise us comfort, or warmth, or security. Loneliness is a natural condition for mankind. Give us your unchanging promise, as you did for Sister Aimee, the sad disciple, whose advertisements promised sunshine but whose days were dark with shadow. Help us to live with reality, so that we can thereby truly live.

October 10

JAMES B. DUKE

James Buchanan Duke changed the social habits of millions, maybe billions, of persons: he invented cigarettes. Or at least he made them practical. As manager of his father's tobacco business in North Carolina in the 1880s, Duke marketed the first machine-rolled cigarette, a product that quickly supplanted pipes and cigars and made Duke a millionaire. He went on to form the giant American Tobacco Company and to lavish, before his death on Oct. 10, 1925, great sums of money on little Trinity College in Durham, N.C., which subsequently changed its name to Duke University.

OFFERTORY: How often do our gifts displease you, Lord God? How often have we given you moldy bread, sour wine? Naively our fathers laid upon your altar the genius of their mediocrity, believing it worthy of your sight. Accept these gifts now, we pray. Do not turn your face from them. Do not wrinkle up your nose as from incense that spirals upward to your throne. It is the incense of our generation. Mentholated.

October 11

CASIMIR PULASKI

Count Casimir Pulaski leaped into the American revolution after first failing to overthrow his own monarch in Poland and suffering exile for his efforts. Offering his services to Washington, Pulaski fought at Brandywine and wintered at Valley Forge. In 1779 he commanded a corps of French and American cavalry in the south. Wounded in the siege of Savannah, he died on Oct. 11. Pulaski achieved no great success in the American war, yet he came to symbolize the kind of devotion poured out by heroes from the old world to win independence for the new.

COMMUNION: *Eph 2, 19-20* So then you are no longer strangers and sojourners, but you are fellow citizens with the saints and members of the household of God, built upon the foundation of the apostles and prophets.

RECESSIONAL: May the brotherhood we find at your table, Lord, help to break down our differences and teach us, as we leave this place, that our struggle is not for one people or one nation or one system but is the struggle for liberty, in all places, for all people.

October 12

CHRISTOPHER COLUMBUS

Early in the morning of Oct. 12, 1492 a fleet of three ships commanded by Genoese mariner Christopher Columbus made landfall on the small island of San Salvador in the Bahamas. These were not the first Europeans to reach the New World, but they were the first to do anything about it. For Columbus the discovery meant fame, wealth, magnificent titles, and administrative control over the new-found territories. He proved to be a skilled navigator but a poor manager. He made three more voyages, was arrested and removed as governor, was stripped of much of his wealth, and died believing the lands he discovered were parts of China.

PROCESSIONAL: *Zech 9, 10* He shall command peace to the nations; his dominion shall be from sea to sea, and from the River to the ends of the earth. *Ezek 26, 18* Now the isles tremble on the day of your fall; yea, the isles that are in the sea are dismayed at your passing.

PETITION: Grant to us, O Lord, the eyes of discovery with which your servant Christopher first saw fresh, new lands. Give us again the grace of astonishment. Thus prepared, each moment of our day will be filled with wonder, each person we meet will be a new world.

RECESSIONAL: You are sent forth into the unknown; you shall leap out into the darkness. Only faith shall suspend you, only faith cushion your fall.

October 13

ED SULLIVAN

Ed Sullivan was one of those people on the fringe of show business without an ounce of performing talent themselves. Someone called him a "rock-faced Irishman." He was so dreadfully ill at ease before television cameras that people felt sorry for him. Sullivan's real business was journalism. He wrote for many papers over the years, ending up as Broadway columnist for the New York *Daily News*. In 1948 he started a television variety show called "Toast of the Town." It was an instant success—a blending of ballet dancers, rock stars, and animal acts that played to 45 million people every week for 23 years. And Sullivan in his own way was the glue that held it together. His "rally big shew" was the arbiter of American popular taste in the 1950s and early 1960s. Sullivan died on Oct. 13, 1974.

OFFERTORY: Our performance never varies from week to week. The same faces, the same songs, the same offerings are displayed for the Lord's approval. The astonishing thing is not that we continue performing the ritual but that he continues to accept it. Don't turn away, Almighty God. Don't let boredom win you over. Mixed with our hackneyed routines there are some moments fresh and new that will delight even your ancient eyes.

October 14

E. E. CUMMINGS

He was born Edward Estlin Cummings, the son of a Harvard professor, on Oct. 14, 1894. He became a man. He went to war, wrote poetry, wrote plays, a novel, lived in Greenwich Village, and generally enjoyed life. At heart Cummings was a romantic, a Cambridge aristocrat who affected the manners and language of the proletariat. His poems about whores, clowns, and street peddlers were written with a cynical zest that was both funny and strangely moving. E.E. Cummings died in 1962.

COMMUNION: Reach out a perhaps hand to your people, God, we who stand tense and anxious waiting for your arrival upon the clouds, and surprise us with one scarlet flower that rises up, pushing between the paving stones of our souls.

RECESSIONAL: *1 Cor 3, 18-19* If any one among you thinks that he is wise in this age, let him become a fool that he may become wise. For the wisdom of this world is folly with God.

October 15

COLE PORTER

Cole Porter was born on a farm in Peru, Ind. He really belonged in some big city where he could mix with bright young people and dance the night away to elegant music. In fact after graduating from Yale that's exactly what he did. Porter was a composer and lyricist who best symbolized the glitter and cosmopolitan wit of urban America in the 1930s, 40s, and 50s. He wrote music for more than 40 Broadway productions and motion pictures. Among his dozens of well-known songs are "Let's Do It," "Night and Day," "I Get a Kick Out of You," "I've Got You Under My Skin," and "I Love Paris." Porter himself was crippled in a riding accident in 1937 and lived the rest of his life in pain, mostly in a wheelchair. He died in California on Oct. 15, 1964.

PROCESSIONAL: *Is 42, 10-11* Sing to the Lord a new song, his praise from the end of the earth! . . . Let the desert and the cities lift up their voice, let the inhabitants of Sela sing for joy, let them shout from the top of the mountains. *Ps 30, 11-12* Thou has turned for me my mourning into dancing; thou hast loosed my sackcloth and girded me with gladness, that my soul may praise thee and not be silent.

PETITION: What is this thing called love?/This funny thing called love?/ Just who can solve its mystery?/Why should it make a fool of me?/I saw you there one wonderful day./You took my heart and threw it away./That's why I ask the Lord in heaven above,/What is this thing called love?*

October 16

GEORGE C. MARSHALL

For 20 years George C. Marshall stood quietly and determinedly in the highest circles of power in the government, asking nothing for himself and everything from his subordinates. Seemingly cold, and with a fearsome temper, he was admired just the same by nearly everyone. Marshall was born in Uniontown, Pa. in 1880, graduated from Virginia Military Institute and entered the U.S. Army. He quickly became known as a brilliant staff officer, rising to become chief of staff during World War II. Later he was secretary of state and secretary of defense under Truman. In 1953 he was awarded the Nobel Peace Prize for his Marshall Plan to rebuild war-torn Europe. Marshall died on Oct. 16, 1959.

COMMUNION: *Amos 9, 14* I will restore the fortunes of my people Israel, and they shall build the ruined cities and inhabit them; they shall plant vineyards and drink their wine, and they shall make gardens and eat their fruit.

RECESSIONAL: *Jer 1, 10* "See I have set you this day over nations and over kindgoms, to pluck up and to break down, to destroy and to overthrow, to built and to plant."

October 17

Julia Ward Howe

Julia Ward Howe was the daughter of a socially prominent New York family. She was an unknown minor poet in 1862 when the *Atlantic Monthly* published her "Battle Hymn of the Republic"—new lyrics for an old tune which became the semi-official marching song of Union soldiers and which made Mrs. Howe famous. After the war she became an influential suffragette and a peace lobbyist. She died on Oct. 17, 1910 at the age of 91.

PROCESSIONAL: He has sounded forth the trumpet that shall never call retreat;/He is sifting out the hearts of men before His Judgement Seat;/Oh! Be swift my soul to answer Him, be jubilant my feet! Our God is marching on. *Response* Glory, glory hallelluia! Glory, glory hallelluia! Glory, glory hallelluia! His truth is marching on.*

OFFERTORY: As our gift this day we surrender our treasured belief that you will always fight for our cause, Lord God. We have felt your absence too keenly to believe that any longer. The only course left open is to reconcile ourselves with each other—knowing that when we are together you are not far distant. Then you will be on our side again.

October 18

Lee Harvey Oswald

He was like the others before him: lonely, insecure, and compelled to lash out at forces that hemmed him in. He was the product of failure, born Oct. 18, 1939, his mother desperately poor, his father dead. All his encounters were undermined by anger. Such a man needs only to be offered an object to strike. Lee Harvey Oswald found one, as did John Wilkes Booth, Charles Guiteau, Leon Czolgosz. Once again a lonely man with a gun made humanity pause and shudder.

PROCESSIONAL: *Mt 11, 12* "From the days of John the Baptist until now the kingdom of heaven has suffered violence, and the men of violence take it by force." *Ps 10, 17-18* O Lord, thou wilt hear the desire of the meek; . . . thou wilt incline thy ear to do justice to the fatherless and the oppressed, so that man who is of the earth may strike terror no more.

*From "The Battle Hymn of the Republic" by Julia Ward Howe.

PETITION: When you met him, Father, did you comfort him, did you embrace him, did you call him by name? O judge of the living and the dead, did you take Lee into your home? When our time comes shower your mercy also on us who look upon our neighbor with hatred, who conceal weapons in our words. Gaze upon us with forgiveness, as perhaps you did with Lee, who was our likeness and our brother.

October 19

EDNA ST. VINCENT MILLAY

Edna St. Vincent Millay symbolized, along with Scott Fitzgerald, the sensitivity and moral independence of young America in the 1920s. Her poetry, especially her sonnets, celebrated the loss and gains of love and signalled that modern women could speak as plainly as men about romantic experiences. She was born in Maine, and she died at her home in the New York Berkshires on Oct. 19, 1950.

RECESSIONAL: Love is not all: it is not meat nor drink/Nor slumber nor a roof against the rain;/Nor yet a floating spar to men that sink/And rise and sink and rise and sink again;/Love can not fill the thickened lung with breath,/Nor clean the blood, nor set the fractured bone;/Yet many a man is making friends with death/Even as I speak, for lack of love alone./It well may be that in a difficult hour,/Pinned down by pain and moaning for release,/Or nagged by want past resolution's power,/I might be driven to sell your love for peace,/Or trade the memory of this night for food./It well may be. I do not think I would.*

October 20

JOHN DEWEY

John Dewey, the noted American philosopher and educator, was born in Burlington, Vt.. on Oct. 20, 1859. Building on the pragmatism of William James, he was the first to suggest that learning occurs most readily through a series of personal experiences rather than through drill and memorization. This "progressive education" became the focus of controversy during Dewey's tenure at the University of Chicago and Columbia, but it remains the basis of most modern learning theories. Dewey retired from teaching in 1930 but continued to write prolifically until his death in 1946.

PETITION: God give us a thirst for the feel of things, for the heft and texture of ideas, their smell, their taste. Like your servant John, make us want to tangle with living, not watch it from afar. For then life will be ours, and we will be alive.

COMMUNION: *Sir 4, 11-12* Wisdom exalts her sons and gives help to those who seek her. Whoever loves her loves life, and those who seek her early will be filled with joy.

October 21

WILLIAM LLOYD GARRISON

William Lloyd Garrison was one of the great moral leaders in American history. Son of an alcoholic sea captain, and with little formal education, he founded a newspaper, the *Liberator*, which became the single most influential voice against the institution of slavery. His attacks upon public hypocrisy, particularly in the churches, aroused popular indignation to a pitch where Garrison, on this day in 1835, was dragged by a mob through the streets of Boston and nearly killed. In time, however, the public mood changed, and Garrison became a much-revered figure. His death in 1879 was the cause of mourning throughout the nation.

PROCESSIONAL: *2 Mac 1, 27* Gather together our scattered people, set free those who are slaves among the Gentiles, look upon those who are rejected and despised, and let the Gentiles know that thou art our God. *Ps 34, 17* When the righteous cry for help, the Lord hears, and delivers them out of all their troubles.

COMMUNION: *Ex 14, 13-14* "Fear not, stand firm, and see the salvation of the Lord, which he will work for you today . . . The Lord will fight for you, and you have only to be still."

October 22

LYMAN ABBOTT

Lyman Abbott was the principal founder of the Christian "social gospel" in the 20th century. In his 90 years he was able to experience the clerical

184

activism that grew up around abolition and the slavery issue in the 19th century and apply it to a host of social and economic problems of the modern industrial age. Abbott, a Congregationalist clergyman was born in Roxbury, Mass. in 1835 but spent most of his ministry in Terre Haute, Ind. and New York City. He was the longtime editor of *Christian Union* magazine, later called *Outlook*. Abbott died in New York on Oct. 22, 1922.

PETITION: Pull open the doors of our white churches, God. Hurl your thunderbolts at their steeples. Pull open the doors of our stone buildings and drive your people into the streets. You gave us temples for our worship, but alas we turned them into tombs. Now you compel us to acknowledge that while your memory is honored inside, your spirit walks without.

RECESSIONAL: *Mt 5, 14-16* "You are the light of the world. A city set on a hill cannot be hid. Nor do men light a lamp and put it under a bushel, but on a stand, and it gives light to all in the house. Let your light so shine before men, that they may see your good works and give glory to your Father who is in heaven."

October 23

ZANE GREY

For most people the very name of Zane Grey evokes images of cowboys riding through the purple sage, of innocent Eastern girls finding romance in the arms of swarthy but virtuous Arizona gunfighters. Grey, along with Owen Wister, pioneered that most American of literary forms: the western novel. It was a most unexpected achievement for Grey, a New York City dentist who had barely seen the West when he started to write. The stories he produced were basically myths that pictured the frontier the way people wanted to see it. History may have suffered, but Zane Grey, his millions of readers, and his publisher were enriched by the experience. Zane Grey died on Oct. 23, 1939.

PROCESSIONAL: In the hour of dusk, darkness blurs reality. See, the empty horizon fades and disappears. Now the horizon is inside you. *Response* Night is long, oh so long on the prarie. Gotta find me somebody to love.

OFFERTORY: Do you mind, Lord, that we make ourselves to be heroes? Does it bother you that we pretend to be strong, and noble, and courageous? Believe these stories we tell about ourselves, Lord God. Take us not as we are, but as we want to be.

October 24

DANIEL WEBSTER

Daniel Webster was born on a New Hampshire farm and grew up to become a member of the House and the Senate, Secretary of State under three Presidents, and the greatest orator of his age. Some said his oratory was more style than content, yet they acknowledged him to be a man of enormous influence and integrity. With Henry Clay he was a prime mover in the Compromise of 1850 which delayed the onset of the Civil War by 10 years. Webster believed in the Union; Americanism was a religion to him. He died on Oct. 24, 1852, before his dream was torn apart.

PROCESSIONAL: *Ezek 37, 22* I will make them one nation in the land, upon the mountains of Israel; and one king shall be king over them all. *Ps 106, 4-5* Remember me, O Lord, when thou showest favor to thy people; help me when thou deliverest them; that I may see the prosperity of thy chosen ones, that I may rejoice in the gladness of thy nation, that I may glory with thy heritage.

RECESSIONAL: You have brought us together, Father; it is you who make us one. Where can we be free except as members of your people? Can liberty lie in separation? Strengthened by our fellowship at your table we echo the words of your servant Daniel: "Liberty and union, now and forever, one and inseparable."

October 25

FRANK NORRIS

Frank Norris, a journalist and novelist, was a principal contributor to American naturalistic writing in the 20th century. Born in Chicago, he worked in New York, San Francisco, and in Cuba during the Spanish-American War. His novels—*McTeague, The Octopus*, and *The Pit*—vividly portrayed the cruelty and power of American society around the turn of the century and made Norris an early "muckraker" whose writings led to social and political reforms. Norris died in California on Oct. 25, 1902.

OFFERTORY: We claim this bread is simple food, born of the soil, rainwater, and sunlight. But it is also the product of price supports, the commodities market, labor unions, and grain speculators. Unseen hands have touched this wheat, bought it and sold it, made and lost money from it, before it was carried to this table. Think of us, Lord God, and all those other people too, as you add your hand to theirs.

October 26

DeWitt Clinton

DeWitt Clinton served as mayor of New York City, governor of New York State, U.S. Senator, and was a candidate for the Presidency in 1812, running against James Madison. He is remembered principally for his 15-year struggle to build the Erie Canal, linking the Hudson River with the Great Lakes, a massive engineering project completed with much fanfare on Oct. 26, 1825. The canal guaranteed that New York would be the nation's principal Atlantic seaport, and it insured that the great unsettled midwest would be joined culturally to the north rather than to the south.

COMMUNION: Body flows into body. Blood joins with blood. Our continents are brought together. Across the wasteland and the void we make commerce, O Lord.

RECESSIONAL: *Deut 11, 31-32* You are to pass over the Jordan to go in to take possession of the land which the Lord your God gives you; and when you possess it and live in it, you shall be careful to do all the statutes and the ordinances which I set before you this day.

October 27

THEODORE ROOSEVELT

Theodore Roosevelt was born Oct. 27, 1858 in New York. He was a weak, sickly boy who turned himself into a rugged outdoorsman: a hearty, back-slapping, bull-voiced social advocate and political reformer. He served as police commissioner of New York City, undersecretary of the Navy, governor of New York State, vice president under McKinley, and President for seven years between 1901 and 1908. While his administration was marked by heavy-fisted imperialism, it also demonstrated concern for the country's natural beauties and opposition to the growing power of business monopolies. Roosevelt was defeated in a new try for the presidency in 1912. He died in 1919.

PROCESSIONAL: *Is 55, 4-5* Behold, I make him a witness to the peoples, a leader and commander for the peoples. Behold, you shall call nations that you know not, and the nations that knew you not shall run to you. *1 Mac 14, 4* He sought the good of his nation; his rule was pleasing to them, as was the honor shown him, all his days.

PETITION: You, God of the big stick, speak softly as your servant Theodore tried to do. Do not bully us, we pray, or treat us like ignorant savages. We have our pride, after all. The gods of old were heavy-handed gods. Let yours be a reign of gentleness.

October 28

EMMA LAZARUS

Emma Lazarus was a poet, a civic leader, and a Zionist. Born in New York in 1849, she found her true cause when the first wave of Jews from European ghettoes reached the United States in the 1880s. By defending their heritage and aspirations she emerged as a champion of all immigrants who came to the new world in search of freedom. On Oct. 28, 1886 President Cleveland dedicated the Statue of Liberty in New York harbor. One of Emma Lazarus's poems was inscribed on its base: "Give me your tired, your poor,/Your huddled masses yearning to breathe free,/The wretched refuse of your teeming shore./Send them, the homeless, tempest-tost to me,/I lift my lamp beside the Golden Door."

PROCESSIONAL: *2 Sam 7, 10* I will appoint a place for my people Israel, and will plant them, that they may dwell in their own place, and be disturbed no more. *Ps 18, 27-28* For thou dost deliver a humble people; but the haughty eyes thou dost bring down. Yea, thou dost light my lamp; the Lord my God lightens my darkness.

PETITION: Aided by the memory of your servant Emma, may we your other pilgrim people find reason for hope in our dark journey, and, when the final shore is reached, find a light for our steps and welcoming arms to enfold us.

October 29

JOSEPH PULITZER

Born in Hungary of German and Jewish parents, Joseph Pulitzer came to the United States in 1864 to fight in the Civil War and to become a lawyer and then a newspaper editor in St. Louis. In 1883 he purchased the New York *World* and quickly made it one of the most influential and profitable newspapers in the country. Despite its cutthroat competition with Hearst's *Journal*, the *World* remained a responsible and conservative paper supporting the rights of the working class. Pulitzer died on Oct. 29, 1911. His will established annual prizes that bear his name for letters, drama, music, and journalism.

OFFERTORY: We do not offer you stale bread, Lord God, left over from yesterday. This is the bread of the world at this moment: of people being born and people dying, of people in pain and people laughing, of people trying, and falling, and getting up again. This is the bread of now. Take it and change it: If we give you news, then give us wisdom.

COMMUNION: *Ps 89, 11* The heavens are thine, the earth also is thine; the world and that all is in it, thou hast founded them.

October 30

JOHN ADAMS

John Adams was the second President of the United States. He was one of the drafters of the Declaration of Independence, served as ambassador to France with Benjamin Franklin, and was America's first vice president. He was the founder of the Federalist party, a rigid aristocrat who distrusted the populist notions of Thomas Jefferson, his bitterest enemy, and in later years his correspondent in a celebrated exchange of letters. Adams was born on this day in 1735. He died on the 4th of July in 1826, just a few hours before Jefferson died.

PETITION: Cast your gracious eyes upon your people, O Lord. Bend down your arms to embrace them, even John your unbending servant. Do not punish his stiffness; you were the one who created us in such diversity. Rather, may his name and the names of all who followed him be numbered in your elected society.

RECESSIONAL: I pray to heaven to bestow the best of blessings on this house and all that shall hereafter inhabit it. May none but honest and wise men ever rule under this roof.*

October 31

HARRY HOUDINI

Harry Houdini was born Eric Weiss, the son of a Jewish rabbi in Appleton, Wis. He began his career as a trapeze performer but soon turned to the art of escaping from manacles, jails, and locked boxes—which he did

*Prayer of John Adams engraved on the mantel of the state dining room in the White House.

with astonishing ease. Once, bound with rope and locked in a packing case that was fastened with steel tape, he was dropped into New York harbor, only to appear on the surface 59 seconds later. Houdini specialized in exposing mediums and other fake spiritualists. Before his own death on Holloween Day 1926 he promised to try making contact from beyond the grave. For 30 years his friends sat up each Oct. 31st, waiting. Houdini never made it.

PETITION: Oh God help us who are not as slippery as your friend Harry. Use some of your tricks. You of all people can appreciate that delicious moment of appearing before the astonished eyes of the multitude, free at last. Please, don't deny it to us.

NOVEMBER

November 1

STEPHEN CRANE

Born in Newark, N.J. on Nov. 1, 1871, Stephen Crane worked as a New York newspaper reporter before turning to fiction. He developed a simple prose style with minutely observed details that stood in sharp contrast to the florid manner of his day and which influenced a whole generation of American naturalistic writers. Crane's most famous stories include *The Red Badge of Courage*, "Bride Comes to Yellow Sky," and "The Open Boat."

PETITION: Survival, Lord, is what we seek. After the battle, after the flood, after the final confrontation, does it matter whether we are winners or losers? What is victory worth if we cannot pull air into our lungs? Survival, Lord, is what we seek.

OFFERTORY: There was a man with a tongue of wood/Who essayed to sing,/And in truth it was lamentable./But there was one who heard/The clip-clapper of this tongue of wood/And knew what the man/Wished to sing,/And with that the singer was content.*

November 2

DANIEL BOONE

Daniel Boone has been called the first westerner. He was the first American to step deliberately across the barrier of the Appalachians with the object of settling the wild lands beyond. In 1775 with a band of 30 woodsmen he blazed a trail from the Cumberland Gap in Tennessee 300 miles through dense forests to a site near present-day Louisville. Within 15 years 300,000 settlers found homes along this so-called Wilderness Road. Boone, who was born this day in 1734, was captured twice by indians, narrowly escaped death many times, had most of his land claims disallowed, and died as an embittered old man in Missouri in 1820.

*"There Was a Man with a Tongue of Wood" by Stephen Crane.

PROCESSIONAL: *2 Kings 19, 23-24* "I have gone up the heights of the mountains, to the far recesses of Lebanon; I felled its tallest cedars, its choicest cypresses; I entered its farthest retreat, its densest forest. I dug wells and drank foreign waters, and I dried up with the soul of my foot all the streams of Egypt. "*Ps 78, 52, 54* Then he led forth his people like sheep, and guided them in the wilderness like a flock . . . And he brought them to his holy land, to the mountain which his right hand had won.

RECESSIONAL: From this mountain we step forth into the darkness. From this clearing we go down into the shadows, hoping that the path we take leads to the final river, and a place to rest, and the truth we have been searching for.

November 3

WILLIAM CULLEN BRYANT

William Cullen Bryant was an editor who planned originally to be a lawyer and who is best remembered as a poet. He spent most of his adult life as editor of the New York *Post*, making it one of the leading journals of the land and an early champion of the Republican party. Bryant's poetry,. especially his famous *Thanatopsis*, exalted the nobility of nature in a romantic vein reminiscent of Wordsworth. He was born this day in 1794; he died in 1878.

PROCESSIONAL: Stranger, if thou hast learned a truth which needs/No school of long experience, that the world/Is full of guilt and misery, and hast seen/Enough of all its sorrows, crimes, and cares,/To tire thee of it, enter this wild wood . . .* *Ps 84, 1-2* How lovely is thy dwelling place, O Lord of hosts! My soul longs, yea, faints for the courts of the Lord; my heart and flesh sing for joy to the living God.

COMMUNION: Be resolved to flesh once more. Proclaim a new covenant with the earth and with nature—not so as to lose your being, but to find it.

November 4

WILL ROGERS

Will Rogers was born Nov. 4, 1879 in Oklahoma, when that state was still

*From "Inscription for the Entrance to a Wood" by William Cullen Bryant.

called the Indian Territory. He began his career as a cowboy, appeared in rodeos, learned some rope tricks and moved onto the vaudeville stage. If the rope tricks failed, he talked, and soon his discovered people preferred to listen than watch. He had a knack of revealing human folly that made even his victims laugh. Once he said: "I don't belong to any organized political party. I'm a Democrat." He died at the height of his fame, in a plane crash in 1935.

OFFERTORY: The words we use may be frivolous, but what they stand for is the truth. You, Lord God, are not put off by appearances. You see the real hurt and not the pratfall, the real tears and not the laughing mask. Look then upon the inner part; bind up that wound in us so deep we dare not speak of but in jest. The gifts we offer may be bread and wine, but what they stand for is ourselves.

RECESSIONAL: *Job 8, 20-21* "Behold, God will not reject a blameless man, nor take the hand of evildoers. He will yet fill your mouth with laughter, and your lips with shouting."

November 5

EUGENE V. DEBS

Born in Terra Haute, Ind. on Nov. 5, 1855, Eugene V. Debs was a colorful and controversial figure in American political life from 1894, when he directed a strike of Pullman employees in Chicago, until his death in 1926. It was Debs's dream to move trade unionism away from the bargaining table and make it a direct force in local and national elections. He was a founder of the Socialist party and its candidate for President of the United States in 1904, 1908, 1912, and 1920. During that last race he received nearly a million votes despite the fact that he was still in jail for his pacifist ideas during World War I.

PETITION: Along with compassion, Lord, give us the breadth of vision possessed by your servant Eugene. Don't let us get caught up in a kind of charity that's devoid of justice. Help us to realize that as a consequence of loving one person we must also love humanity.

COMMUNION: Where there is a lower class, I am in it. While there is a criminal element, I am of it. While there is a soul in jail, I am not free.*

*From a speech by Eugene V. Debs.

November 6

JOHN PHILIP SOUSA

John Philip Sousa was born Nov. 6, 1854 in Washington, D.C. of Portuguese-American parents. He began studying music at the age of six, and when he was 26 he was already master of the U.S. Marine Corps Band. In this capacity, and as the leader of Sousa's Band from 1892 onward, he won renown as a composer and conductor—being dubbed "the march king" by an English journal. He wrote nine comic operas and hundreds of marches, including "The Washington Post," "Semper Fidelis," and "The Stars and Stripes Forever."

RECESSIONAL: Farewell humility. Today let's strut in gaudy clothes. Let's call attention to ourselves. Let's wallow in chauvinism. There is a place for meekness, to be sure. But on this day it's good-bye moderation, hello sounding brass!

November 7

ELEANOR ROOSEVELT

Eleanor Roosevelt was born in 1884, the niece of Theodore Roosevelt. She was a shy, self-conscious woman in 1905 when she married her cousin Franklin. Partly in an effort to escape the home influence of his mother, she forced herself to accept a public life of her own, finding a common cause with the poor and persecuted. She was their champion and lobbyist during her husband's terms as governor of New York and President of the United States. After his death she served as U.S. representative to the United Nations and chairman of its Human Rights Commission. She died on Nov. 7, 1962.

PROCESSIONAL: *Jud 13, 20* "May God . . . visit you with blessings, because you did not spare your own life when our nation was brought low, but have avenged our ruin, walking in the straight path before our God." *Ps 46, 5* God is in the midst of her, she shall not be moved.

COMMUNION: It is in giving that we feel unworthy, Lord, not in taking. Feed us then with courage, as you did for our sister Eleanor, that we may overcome our reserve and learn to sustain each other.

194

November 8

FRANCIS PARKMAN

Francis Parkman was Harvard educated, of an old Puritain family, and seemed headed for a safe career in law in 1846 when he decided to go west over the Oregon Trail through land that was still wild and largely unexplored. From this journey grew an autobiographical history called *The Oregon Trail* that made Parkman famous and abruptly changed his career. Over the next 30 years, despite a debilitating illness, he produced a monumental history in eight volumes of the French and English settlements in North America. Parkman was the first of the great American historians, and he set forth the theme that was to absorb historical writing for the next century: the lure of the frontier. Parkman died on Nov. 8, 1893.

OFFERTORY: It is the past we give you, Father: not our own deeds but the deeds of those who live in our bones—heroes and scholars and rulers and teachers, explorers and strivers and saints. May you, Lord, find justice in their accomplishments, and also meaning. And in your care may this past of ours, like dark, hidden roots, nourish and sustain us in the days to come.

RECESSIONAL: *Ps 117, 11-12* I will call to mind the deeds of the Lord; yea, I will remember thy wonders of old. I will meditate on all thy work, and muse on thy mighty deeds.

November 9

SIGMUND ROMBERG

Sigmund Romberg was the most prolific and most successful composer of operettas in the history of the American theater. The 78 productions he wrote contained over 2000 songs, such as "Stout-Hearted Men," "When I Grow Too Old to Dream," "Sweetheart," and "Lover Come Back to Me." Romberg was born in Austria and came to the United States when he was 22. His most famous score was that for *The Student Prince*, produced in 1924. He died Nov. 9, 1951.

OFFERTORY: God we have concocted for ourselves a world of gingerbread people, candy soldiers, and make-believe love. It probably couldn't be helped. But won't you take at least some of this and make it into real food, quick, before we starve?

195

COMMUNION: *Deut 31, 19* Now therefore write this song, and teach it to the people of Israel; put it in their mouths, that this song may be a witness.

November 10

VACHEL LINDSAY

Vachel Lindsay was born Nov. 10, 1879 in Springfield, Ill., the home of his hero Abraham Lincoln. In truth Lindsay was a man with many heroes —Bryan, Altgeld, Gen. William Booth (founder of the Salvation Army), and others. Lindsay has a mystical vision of American history that he celebrated in his odd, heavily accented poetry and which he proclaimed, or rather chanted, from public stages across the nation. Among his best known works are *The Congo* and *Abraham Lincoln Walks at Midnight*. Lindsay died in 1931.

PETITION: Let not young souls be smothered out before/They do quaint deeds and fully flaunt their pride./It is the world's one crime that its babies grow dull,/Its poor are ox-like, limp and leaden-eyed./Not that they starve, but starve so dreamlessly,/Not that they sow, but that they seldom reap,/Not that they serve, but have no gods to serve,/Not that they die but that they die like sheep.*

November 11

GEORGE S. PATTON

George S. Patton was born Nov. 11, 1885 in California and attended VMI and West Point. Trained as a cavalry officer, he switched with relish to tank warfare in World War I and in the period between the wars. With the coming of the Second World War, Patton was ready. In North Africa, Sicily, and in Western Europe he became the hard-driving exponent of mechanized warfare, sending armored columns deep into enemy territory. Patton was a profane and colorful general who saw war in simple terms and who excelled as long as it stayed simple. He died following an automobile accident shortly after the war ended in 1945.

PROCESSIONAL: *Is 66, 15* "For behold, the Lord will come in fire, and his chariots like the storm-wind, to render his anger in fury, and his rebuke with flames of fire." *Ps 18, 37-38* I pursued my enemies and overtook them; and did not turn back till they were consumed. I thrust them through, so that they were not able to rise; they fell under my feet.

*"The Leaden-Eyed" from *Collected Poems* by Vachel Lindsay. Copyright 1914 by Macmillan Publishing Co., Inc., renewed 1942 by Elizabeth C. Lindsay. Used by permission.

PETITION: God you gave us sharp blades for carving out an empire. You gave us sharp blades, strong bodies, and an aptitude for violence. And they did great deeds, and the blades were raised in triumph. O now God teach us what to do with these blades, to which our hands are frozen.

November 12

JAMES M. CURLEY

When James Michael Curley was sprung from the federal pen in 1947 he was met by a brass band in Boston and paraded to City Hall. Despite the five-month term for mail fraud, he was still the mayor of Boston. Curley was the archetype of the colorful and mildly corrupt Irish politician who wrested control of America's eastern cities from the WASP aristocracy in the last century and held sway until the 1950s. Beginning in 1913, Curley served four terms as mayor, one term as governor of Massachusetts, and three terms in the U.S. House of Representatives. He combined courtly manners with the wiles of a cobra, once threatening to open floodgates beneath a bank that wouldn't loan money to the city. Curley was born in 1894; he died on Nov. 12, 1958.

OFFERTORY: Receive, Lord God, this bread which we have made from the wheat of our years. And if there is some chaff mixed in—if the taste and texture is less than perfect—then close your eyes and eat it anyway. It's the best we can do, and it would likely come out the same even if we had our whole lives to live over.

COMMUNION: *Is 60, 14* The sons of those who oppressed you shall come bending low to you; and all who despised you shall bow down at your feet.

November 13

LOUIS BRANDEIS

Louis Brandeis was born Nov. 13, 1856 in Louisville, Ky., went to Harvard, and became in time one of the first public-service lawyers. In 1916 President Wilson appointed him to the Supreme Court, making him the first Jew ever to sit on that bench. Brandeis served for 23 years with great distinction, frequently a companion in dissent with Justice Holmes. A civil libertarian, he was also a distinguished spokesman for American Judaism and a supporter of the Zionist movement. Brandeis died in 1941.

PROCESSIONAL: *Esther 10, 3* He was great among the Jews and popular with the multitude of his brethren, for he sought the welfare of his people and spoke peace to all his people. *Ps 75, 2-3* At the set time which I appoint I will judge with equity. When the earth totters, and all its inhabitants, it is I who keep steady its pillars.

PETITION: Inspired by your servant Louis, may each of us, Lord God, maintain a watchful eye upon your family and on their welfare. Help us bring healing to our brothers and sisters, to make them whole, and to help them to that promised land where all of us shall live in peace.

November 14

ROBERT FULTON

Robert Fulton was a self-taught inventor whose development of the steamboat opened up the great inland waterways of America. Although trained as a portrait painter, Fulton showed early talent with mechanical devices, from guns to canal locks. In 1800 he developed a working submarine with torpedoes that actually sank a ship. The journey of the *Clermont* from New York City to Albany in 1806 turned his interest decisively to surface craft. He spent his last year building boats and organizing freight and passenger lines. Fulton was born on Nov. 14, 1765. He died in 1815.

PETITION: Free us, God, from the fear of failure, the fear of folly. Help us to dare new things, as did your servant Robert—to try what others think cannot be done. Unshackled from the chains of popular wisdom, we can then explore the land from which you beckon us—upstream.

November 15

MARIANNE MOORE

Marianne Moore was born on Nov. 15, 1887 in St. Louis, went to school in Pennsylvania, and lived most of her life in Brooklyn where she sallied forth in quaint dress to cheer ardently for the Brooklyn Dodgers, and later the New York Yankees. She also wrote poetry in her own unique but disciplined style—poetry brimming with gentle ironies and unexpected commentaries on human behavior. She was the recipient of many poetry awards, including the Pulitzer Prize in 1951. She died in 1972.

COMMUNION: He/sees deep and is glad, who/accedes to mortality/and in his imprisonment, rises/upon himself as/the sea in a chasm, struggling to be/free and unable to be,/in its surrendering/finds its continuing.*

*Excerpt from "What Are Years?" from *Collected Poems* by Marianne Moore. Copyright 1941 by Marianne Moore, renewed 1969 by Marianne Moore. Reprinted by permission of Macmillan Publishing Co., Inc.

November 16

W.C. HANDY

W.C. Handy was born Nov. 16, 1873 in Florence, Ala., his parents being former slaves. He began playing the cornet as a youth despite the objections of his devout parents who disapproved of "profane" music. Working at odd jobs, Handy finally settled in Memphis where he started to put folk songs, spirituals, and jazz together in a new form of music he called "blues." In the next dozen years he wrote "Memphis Blues," "Beale Street Blues," "St. Louis Blues," and many others. Although blind and in poor health, the Father of the Blues continued to write and publish music until his death in New York in 1958.

COMMUNION: *Ps 137, 1-3* By the waters of Babylon, there we sat down and wept, when we remembered Zion. On the willows there we hung up our lyres. For there our captors required of us songs, and our tormentors, mirth, saying, "Sing us one of the songs of Zion!"

RECESSIONAL: Feelin' tomorrow lak I feel today,/Feel tomorrow lak I feel today,/I'll pack my trunk, make my getaway . . ./Oh ashes to ashes and dust to dust./I said ashes to ashes and dust to dust./If my blues don't get you, my jazzing must.*

November 17

ANNE HUTCHINSON

At first Anne Hutchinson met with her friends merely to discuss the latest sermon in 17th-century Boston. In time, however, she began to expound her own views, suggesting that the Puritain fathers were too rigid, that simple faith was more important than their insistance on works. Her suggestions gave rise to the Antinomian Controversy, America's first "heresy," which in turn became embroiled in colonial politics and which led to Hutchinson's banishment from Massachusetts this day in 1637, along with her husband and 14 children. When she was killed six years later in Rhode Island by a band of maurading indians, the Puritans considered it an act of God.

PROCESSIONAL: *Lam 1, 13* "From on high he sent fire; into my bones he made it descend; he spread a net for my feet; he turned me back; he has left me stunned, faint all the day long." *Response:* While I draw this fleet-

*From "St. Louis Blues," words and music by W.C. Handy. Copyright controlled by Handy Brothers Music Co., Inc.

ing breath,/When my eyes shall close in death,/When I rise to worlds un-known/And behold thee on thy throne,/Rock of Ages cleft for me,/let me hide myself in thee.*

OFFERTORY: *Rom 12, 1-2* I appeal to you therefore, brethren, by the mercies of God, to present your bodies as a living sacrifice, holy and acceptable to God, which is your spiritual worship. Do not be conformed to this world but be transformed by the renewal of your mind, that you may prove what is the will of God, what is good and acceptable and perfect.

November 18

HENRY WALLACE

Henry Wallace came out of Iowa to rise and fall spectacularly across the American political landscape. He was editor of his family's farm magazine in 1933 when Franklin Roosevelt appointed him Secretary of Agriculture, and rewarded him seven years later with the vice presidency. But Wallace, the plain-spoken idealist, had enemies among Democratic party regulars, and so was dumped in 1944 in favor of Harry Truman. Four years later, Wallace, having broken with Truman over cold-war policies, ran for the presidency on the Progressive ticket with the backing of a coalition of leftist groups. He lost badly. Sensing that he had been used, Wallace retired in disillusionment to his Connecticut farm where he died on Nov. 18, 1965.

OFFERTORY: We raise this offering without illusion, God. So often have our hopes been dashed that they cannot bear much expectation. Ritual has lapsed into rote: What we want to happen will not happen; the people we dream of being we will not become. Yet gestures have their own momentum. So we come to this sacred place again, bearing the gifts that didn't work last time, in the hope that our very lack of expectation may be a climate for your will.

RECESSIONAL: *Bar 4, 23-24* I sent you out with sorrow and weeping, but God will give you back to me with joy and gladness for ever. For as the neighbors of Zion have now seen your capture, so they soon will see your salvation by God, which will come to you with great glory and with the splendor of the Everlasting.

*"Rock of Ages," a traditional hymn.

200

November 19

BILLY SUNDAY

After Brigham Young, Billy Sunday was the first American to make religion "work" on a big scale. Billy was an orphan and a onetime professional baseball player who for 40 years conducted revivals and tent meetings across the land. His manner leaned heavily toward flamboyance and sensationalism, but his method was completely professional. He was the first to hire a staff of revival "specialists" to pave the way for him and offer backup services. An estimated 100 million persons heard him preach, and a million of those claimed to be converted as a result. Billy was born on Nov. 19, 1862 in Ames, Iowa; he died in 1935.

PROCESSIONAL: *Is 11, 4* With righteousness he shall judge the poor, and decide with equity for the meek of the earth; and he shall smite the earth with the rod of his mouth, and with the breath of his lips he shall slay the wicked. *Num 14, 10* Then the glory of the Lord appeared at the tent of meeting to all the people of Israel.

PETITION: Call us, Lord! Use some new voice to burn away this cynicism. Create some new fire to warm these icy places. It's been so long since we've felt the spark of your breath: we your people, stacked together like tinder. Come into our midst!

November 20

NATHANIEL CURRIER

Nathaniel Currier was the best known printmaker in this nation's history, producing more than 7,000 different lithographs acknowledged today not as great art but as colorful portrayals of life in late 19th-century America. From 1859 onward he was in business with James Ives who supervised the art staff and production, and who helped to make the name Currier & Ives known throughout the world. Currier died on Nov. 20, 1888; Ives died in 1895.

COMMUNION: Over the river and through the woods/To grandfather's house we go,/The horse knows the way to carry the sleigh/Through the white and drifted snow./Over the river and through the woods,/Trot fast my dapple gray,/Spring over the ground like a hunting hound,/For this is Thanksgiving Day.*

*Traditional Thanksgiving song, author unknown.

RECESSIONAL: *Ps 143, 5-6* I remember the days of old, I meditate on all that thou hast done; I muse on what thy hands have wrought. I stretch out my hands to thee; my soul thirsts for thee like a parched land.

November 21

WILLIAM BRADFORD

On this day in 1620, 41 adult males aboard the ship *Mayflower*, anchored off Cape Cod, signed a formal compact which was, in fact, the first step toward self-government in the American colonies. One of the men was William Bradford, from Yorkshire, who after the first terrible winter at Plymouth became the colony's governor and served in that capacity for 30 years. Bradford was a strong but diplomatic man, able to maintain generally good relations with the indians and the dissenters within the pilgrim community. It was largely through his efforts that the Plymouth colony, begun in such hope, survived and eventually prospered.

PETITION: Moved by the memory of your servant William, we your people do renew this day our solemn compact with each other, for the ordering and perservation of our body; and we pray you Lord to put your seal on this free assembly of pilgrims.

RECESSIONAL: *Ex 6, 2-4* God said to Moses, "I am the Lord. I appeared to Abraham, to Isaac, and to Jacob as God Almighty . . . I also established my covenant with them, to give them the land of Canaan, the land in which they dwelt as sojourners."

November 22

JOHN F. KENNEDY

According to Joseph Alsop, "of all the men in public life in his time, John Fitzgerald Kennedy was the most ideally formed to lead the United States of America." He had wit, style, courage, brilliance of mind, and simplicity of manner. It is probably true that Kennedy was not a great President, and yet he seemed then and seems now to be the epitome of what a President should be. When he was killed this day in 1963 some part of America's youth died with him.

PROCESSIONAL: The Minstrel Boy to the war is gone,/In the ranks of death you'll find him./His father's sword he hath girded on,/And his wild harp slung behind him.* *Ps 45, 2* You are the fairest of the sons of men; grace is poured upon your lips; therefore God has blessed you for ever.

RECESSIONAL: With a good conscience our only sure reward, with history the final judge of our deeds, let us go forth to lead the land we love, asking His blessing and His help, but knowing that here on earth God's work must truly be our own.**

November 23

BILLY THE KID

Billy the Kid was not nice. He killed at least 21 persons and apparently enjoyed it. He also rustled cattle, robbed and looted, gambled, and probably cheated at the card table. Some people have suggested that Billy, alias William H. Bonney, might have been mentally incompetent. He was competent all right; he just wasn't nice. Billy was born on Nov. 23, 1859. He was shot and killed in 1881 by Sheriff Pat Garrett after a chase lasting several months.

OFFERTORY: The ghost dismounts his spectre horse./He stoops and sifts the sand between his fingers./He cups it in his hand, and croons:/"Receive this gift, dark father,/This sand of Alamagordo,/Where death and life and half-life meet./Together we did sow the seed,/And here upon this desert place, it bloomed."

COMMUNION: *Ps 55, 23* But thou, O God, wilt cast them down into the lowest pit; men of blood and treachery shall not live out half their days. But I will trust in thee.

November 24

JUNÍPERO SERRA

Junípero Serra was born in Majorca, Spain, on Nov. 24, 1713. Entering the Franciscan order he was a university professor in Spain before being assigned at the relatively old age of 36 to the American missions. Serra spent several years in Mexico, ministering to the poor and the indians. In

*"The Minstrel Boy," an old Irish ballad.
**From John F. Kennedy's Inaugural Address, 1961.

1769, by then almost 60 years old, he undertook a series of journeys through Arizona and California establishing new missions and strenuously defending the rights of indians. Among the missions he personally founded are those at San Diego, San Luis Obisbo, San Francisco, Santa Clara, and (in 1776) San Juan Capistrano. He died in Carmel, Calif. in 1784.

PETITION: You, Lord God, gave us strong leaders to serve the needy and not the other way around. Inspired by the example of your son Junípero, may we grow in solicitude toward our weak and helpless brothers. Success in this is measured not by the degree of their alleviation but by our generosity.

RECESSIONAL: *Mt 20, 26-28* Whoever would be great among you must be your servant, and whoever would be first among you must be your slave; even as the Son of man came not to be served but to serve, and to give his life as a ransom for many.

November 25

UPTON SINCLAIR

Upton Sinclair was born in 1878 in Baltimore and was a professional writer by the age of 15. He became famous in 1906 through his novel *The Jungle* which portrayed conditions in the Chicago meatpacking plants and which led to the passage of federal food-inspection laws. Sinclair's novels —nearly 20 of them—were focused on political problems of his day and reflected their author's ardent socialism. Moving to California, he ran six times for public office, nearly winning a gubernatorial campaign in 1934. Sinclair won the Pulitzer Prize in 1942; he died on Nov. 25, 1968.

OFFERTORY: Receive this gift of America—as a promise clean and noble but in the making tarnished, spoiled, and put to venal uses. We offer it to you today with no illusion, but with a hope that after all you may prefer reality to dreams, and that in your hands it might become if not pure once more at least a place wherein your people still can live, and strive, and hear your word, and answer it.

COMMUNION: *Esther 10, 9* And my nation, this is Israel, who cried out to God and were saved. The Lord has saved his people; the Lord has delivered us from all these evils.

November 26

Albert B. Fall

Albert B. Fall seemed to be the very model of the modern politician. Born Nov. 26, 1861, he served two terms in the U.S. Senate before he was named Secretary of the Interior by Harding. But then Fall ran into trouble. When oil companies expressed interest in properties held by the Navy in Wyoming, Fall obligingly had the land (called the Teapot Dome) transferred to his department, then leased it to the oil companies in return for a $100,000 kickback. News of the deal was soon whispered around Washington. Although the rest of Harding's inner circle escaped punishment, Fall was caught, convicted, and served a year in jail. After all, someone had to take the blame.

OFFERTORY: For all our faults, Lord God, we offer you one scapegoat, a victim, a fall guy. We pray that you will be satisfied with this token, leaving the rest in our hands. You, after all, have become used to this arrangement, and so have we. The mystery is this: Why does the loaf we keep for ourselves leave us hungry, while the crust we give to you feed the multitude?

RECESSIONAL: *Mic 3, 9-12* Hear this, you heads of the house of Jacob and rulers of the house of Israel, who abhor justice and pervert all equity, who build Zion with blood and Jerusalem with wrong. Its heads give judgement for a bribe, its priests teach for hire, its prophets divine for money; yet they lean upon the Lord and say, "Is not the Lord in the midst of us? No evil shall come upon us." Therefore because of you Zion shall be plowed as a field; Jerusalem shall become a heap of ruins, and the mountain of the house a wooded height.

November 27

Eugene O'Neill

Eugene O'Neill wrote 12 major dramas that rank him among the world's greatest playwrights; four won Pulitzer Prizes. In addition, he is the only American dramatist to have been awarded the Nobel Prize for literature. O'Neill was a dark, brooding spirit, the product of a tortured family life laid bare in his last works. While they may be tragic, his dramas are ultimately pleas against despair, documents of human nobility in the face of defeat. O'Neill's wounded people cling to the need for faith even as its consolations are stolen from them. O'Neill died on this day in 1953—crippled, embittered with his public, and with his greatest plays still unproduced.

OFFERTORY: What is it we are looking for? We know it is something we lost: perhaps an inheritance thrown away, its value left unrealized. Trapped and powerless, we have no gift worth giving—except this determination to live out our days, taking small graces as they come, but knowing that the central thing, whatever once we had, is gone now. Gone.

COMMUNION: *Lam 5, 20-21* Why dost thou forget us for ever, why dost thou so long forsake us? Restore to us thyself, O Lord, that we may be restored! Renew our days as of old!

November 28

WASHINGTON IRVING

Washington Irving was a man-about-town in early 18th-century New York. Only vaguely interested in law, Irving enjoyed both observing and being a part of the cosmopolitan social set. He wrote a satyrical history of the city, but it was not until he visited England that he was inspired to try a more ambitious project, a book of fantastic tales containing such stories as "The Legend of Sleepy Hollow" and "Rip Van Winkle." In future years he produced biographies and travel books. None of them met with great success, but Irving's reputation as America's first man of letters was firmly established. He died at his Hudson Valley home on Nov. 28, 1859.

PETITION: Come Lord, shed your light in all our scary corners; sweep away the goblins in our minds. We find ourselves more frightening than even you. Too long have we been spooked by booming thunder, floating heads, and other nighttime fears. Come, point your light at them so we can laugh, and sleep untroubled, sleep in peace, and undisturbed.

RECESSIONAL: Inside your house we find protection from the shadows, Lord. Your table is a feast of light.

November 29

LOUISA MAY ALCOTT

Louisa May Alcott grew up in the heady atmosphere of the Massachusetts enlightenment, being tutored by her father Bronson, an educator and philosopher, and sometimes by their neighbor Thoreau. She was attracted to writing from youth but found only modest success before *Little Women* appeared in 1868. It was a story illuminated by the light and happiness of her own childhood, and it had the pleasant effect of shoring up the family's shaky financial status. Louisa wrote other books, supported genteel liberal causes, and never married. She was born on her father's 33rd birthday (Nov. 29, 1832), and she died just two days after he did in 1888.

OFFERTORY: Shower blessings on your children, Father, who have no thing to give that you would value in return, except their love. In this exchange all families are born and live.

COMMUNION: *Job 42, 15* And in all the land there were no women so fair as Job's daughters; and their father gave them inheritance among their brothers.

November 30

MARK TWAIN

He was born Samuel Langhorne Clemens on Nov. 30, 1895 in Hannibal, Mo., and although he became the toast of two continents, although he moved to the east and lived in a mansion, his imagination always returned to that small, dusty town where he grew up. Clemens became an intimate of the rich and a friend of Presidents. He became a businessman, a publisher, a public speaker, a civil libertarian, and a humorist with a strain of dark pessimism. But alone in his study he was a different, a truer person: he was back in Hannibal again. And he used that name he heard first as a boy growing up by the Mississippi: Mark Twain.

PROCESSIONAL: *Esther 10, 5-6* "I remember the dream that I had concerning these matters, and none of them has failed to be fulfilled. The tiny spring which became a river, and there was light and the sun and abundant water." *Ps 103, 2, 5* Bless the Lord, O my soul, and forget not all his benefits . . . who satisfies you with good as long as you live so that your youth is renewed like the eagle's.

RECSSIONAL: Knowledge bore us along like a lazy river, revealing wonders to our eyes. We had traded in our innocence as the price of the journey. At last we came to the end of knowledge. The river divulged its final secret, its ultimate revelation; it told us innocence is best. Restore to us, God, that which time tears from our hands. Our home is over Jordan.

DECEMBER

December 1

ALFRED T. MAHAN

Admiral Alfred Mahan had that combination of brilliance and arrogance that is typical of ideologists from emerging superpowers. Born in 1840 of a military family (his father taught at West Point), Mahan graduated from the U.S. Naval Academy and later became its president. In 1890 he published *The Influence of Sea Power Upon History*, extolling the importance of naval might and setting in motion the naval arms race that preceded World War I. Mahan had contempt for diplomatic solutions; strength, he said, and genius were sufficient to protect a nation. He died on Dec. 1, 1914, the year when strength and genius failed.

PETITION: Send humility, Lord God, especially to the mighty, lest they come to think that possession of power is license to use it. For in your design strength and sorrow have been made brothers, and the one who reaches for domination can lose hold of all his beginnings.

COMMUNION: *Rev 8, 8-9* Something like a great mountain, burning with fire, was thrown into the sea; and a third of the sea became blood, a third of the living creatures in the sea died, and a third of the ships were destroyed.

December 2

JOHN BROWN

As time went on and his business failures mounted, John Brown began to have visions. Mainly he dreamed of an armed insurrection of slaves in which thousands of blacks rallied to the banner of freedom which he, Brown, would hold aloft. Emerson thought him a good, sensible person, but many others believed he has lost touch with reality. Brown went to Kansas with five of his sons in 1855 to kill slaveholders. In October of 1859 he occupied the federal arsenal at Harper's Ferry, Va. expecting the slaves to support him. None did. He was captured, tried, found guilty, and on Dec. 2, 1859 he was hanged.

PROCESSIONAL: *Is 30, 27* Behold, the name of the Lord comes from far, burning with his anger, and in thick rising smoke; his lips are full of indignation, and his tongue is like a devouring fire. *Response* John Brown's body lies a mould'rin' in the grave,/John Brown's body lies a mould'rin' in the grave,/John Brown's body lies a mould'rin' in the grave,/But his soul goes marching on.

RECESSIONAL: The souls of the wrathful are silent; they sink without a murmur into your arms, Lord God. But the fires that they started burn still, and in your wisdom you do not stamp them out.

December 3

GILBERT STUART

Gilbert Stuart was the most celebrated portrait artist of his day, and he painted the most celebrated people: Jefferson, John Adams, John Quincy Adams, Madison, and John Jacob Astor. He was born Dec. 3, 1755 in Rhode Island and studied art in London and Paris. Eventually he established his studio in Boston. Stuart is best known for his portraits of George Washington, three of which were done from life, and one of which was snatched by Dolly Madison from the wall of the White House just before the British burned the place.

OFFERTORY: God, Father, as we give bread and wine not just for your sake, so do we honor our fathers and founders not just for their sakes. The praise we give them comes back to us as nourishment. We are a people with a past; in confessing this, we become a people with a future.

COMMUNION: *Wis 8, 10-11* I shall have glory among the multitudes and honor in the presence of the elders . . . I shall be found keen in judgment, and in the sight of rulers I shall be admired.

December 4

LILLIAN RUSSELL

Lillian Russell was the queen of the American operetta stage in the late 19th century, famed for her bustle, her beauty, and for her ability to make headlines as much as for her soprano voice. She was born Dec. 4, 1861 in Clinton, Iowa, went to a convent school, sang in the choir, studied violin, voice, and acting. In New York she became a leading lady in Offenbach and Gilbert & Sullivan operas. In later years she starred in vaudeville and straight comedy, although after 1912 her appearances were confined to the lecture stage. She died in Pittsburgh in 1922.

PETITION: Grant, O Lord, that we too, like your daughter Lillian, might put our education to some useful service. And in your kingdom grant to those of lesser talents which are exploited to their limits a greater place of honor than to those who have ability but not desire.

December 5

WALT DISNEY

Walt Disney was born Dec. 5, 1901 in Chicago. After service in World War I he moved to Kansas City where he worked as a commercial artist and experimented with animated films. He met with little success until 1926 when he made a talking cartoon starring a mouse named Mickey. In 1938 he made a full-length cartoon feature, *Snow White and the Seven Dwarfs*, that made him famous throughout the world. While technically brilliant, the Disney trademark was escapism, not art. During three decades scarred by war and turmoil, Disney and the Disney studios created songs, books, movies, and ultimately entire cities of exquisite, sweet make-believe.

PROCESSIONAL: *Sir 47, 8-9* He sang praise with all his heart, and he loved his Maker. He placed singers before the altar, to make sweet melody with their voices. *Response* Zip-A-Dee-Doo-Dah, Zip-a-dee-ay,/My, oh my, what a wonderful day!/Plenty of sunshine, headin' my way,/Zip-A-Dee-Doo-Dah, Zip-a-dee-ay!*

OFFERTORY: Be not dismayed, Lord God, if we persist in covering our gifts with sugar. Since when is it a crime to crave the sweetness and the light? You were the first to paint a picture of a "land of milk and honey," so don't blame us. Our only prayer is that you nourish us with real life in all its rawness, and real tears, and real love. This way it will be possible to have our cake, but never eat it.

December 6

LEADBELLY

Huddie Ledbetter knew little besides trouble until he was 45. Things weren't easy for a part-indian, part-negro growing up in Shreveport, La.,

---

*"Zip-A-Dee-Doo-Dah, My Oh My, What a Wonderful Day!" from Walt Disney's motion picture *Song of The South*, words by Ray Gilbert, music by Allie Wrubel. Copyright 1945 by Walt Disney Music Company. Used by permission.

and Ledbetter (or "Leadbelly" as he liked to call himself) spent as much time in jail as out. The only thing he seemed to do well was sing and play his 12-string guitar. In 1934 he was discovered by Alan and John Lomax, archivists of American folk music, who introduced him to concert stages across the United States and in Europe. He was a natural, untrained artist who had a way of turning simple melodies and lyrics into poetry. Leadbelly died on Dec. 6, 1951, just at the dawning of the folk-music revolution he helped inspire.

COMMUNION: *Ps 98, 4-5* Make a joyful noise to the Lord, all the earth; break forth into joyous song and sing praises! Sing praises to the Lord with the lyre, with the lyre and the sound of melody!

RECESSIONAL: You caused me to weep, you caused me to mourn,/You caused me to leave my home./But the very last words I heard you say/Was "Please sing me one more song."*

December 7

THOMAS B. REED

Thomas B. Reed was a huge man, better than six feet tall and nearly 300 pounds. He ruled the House of Representatives like a great Buddha, iron-handed, imperturbable, with a wit that was both celebrated and feared. To the opposition he was "Czar Reed," especially after 1890 when he instituted rules that ended stalling tactics by the House minority and made Reed's office the second most powerful in the land. Asked whether he thought the Republicans would nominate him for President in 1892, Reed said: "They might do worse, and I think they will." They did. Disillusioned with the rising tide of American imperialism, Reed abruptly resigned from Congress in 1898, and he died four years later on December 7th.

PETITION: Bring order to our midst, Father: order in our habits, order in our heads. Order is a power game; rules are given by the highest player to fix the lines of his domain. So our request is this: bring freedom to your people, yes; but if you are indeed a king, then order too.

COMMUNION: *Ps 74, 16-17* Thine is the day, thine also the night; thou hast established the luminaries and the sun. Thou hast fixed all the bounds of the earth.

*From "Goodnight Irene," words and music by Huddie Ledbetter & John A. Lomax. TRO © copyright 1936 (renewed 1964) and 1950 Ludlow Music, Inc., New York, N.Y. Used by permission.

December 8

ELI WHITNEY

Eli Whitney has been described as the great "Yankee mechanic"—a man who not only invented things but who devised new methods to manufacture them. He was of solid New England stock, born Dec. 8, 1765 in Massachusetts and educated at Yale. In 1794 he built a "gin" for separating cotton lint from its seeds, a job previously done by hand. The machine worked so well that cotton became a high-profit crop; slaves were imported from Africa to tend the fields, and the stage was set for the American Civil War. Before that happened however, Whitney, disgusted with people who infringed on his patents, ceased with the manufacture of cotton gins and started making guns.

PROCESSIONAL: *Mt 13, 26* When the plants came up and bore grain, then the weeds appeared also. *Joel 3, 14-15* Multitudes, multitudes, in the valley of decision! For the day of the Lord is near in the valley of decision. The sun and the moon are darkened, and the stars withdraw their shining.

RECESSIONAL: Progress is our expectation and our hope. And our fear. Today we have put something together, and now we venture forth to see if it will work. Lord, bless these new discoveries of ours, and bless us too— in case the road we think takes us to salvation does in fact lead to our destruction.

December 9

LOUELLA PARSONS

Louella Parsons was the queen of the Hollywood gossip columnists for more than 40 years, recording the deeds of the gods and goddesses of the silver screen for millions of avid readers. She got into the gossip business in 1922 after a stint as a scriptwriter in Chicago; at her apogee as movie editor of INS she was appearing in 407 daily newspapers. Louella's style was gushing and sometimes witless, but she was a bulldog in pursuit of a story, and her influence inside the film industry was enormous. She was born in 1881, and she died on Dec. 9, 1972.

PETITION: Mention our names, Lord God, in your accounting. There are many roles we still can play if you but call us. O Lord, we wait on tenterhooks for you to speak our names.

COMMUNION: *Sir 43, 9* The glory of the stars is the beauty of heaven, a gleaming array in the heights of the Lord.

December 10

EMILY DICKINSON

On Dec. 10, 1830 a daughter was born to a prominent attorney in Amherst, Mass. The young lady grew up and lived in that family house for her whole life, becoming in her later years a recluse, dressed wholly in white, who wrote odd, mystical poems she stitched together in packets. Unread then, they became after her death the record of a Puritan soul struggling with passion.

PROCESSIONAL: *Song 3, 1-2* Upon my bed by night I sought him whom my soul loves; I sought him, but found him not; I called him, but he gave no answer. "I will rise now and go about the city, in the streets and in the squares; I will seek him whom my soul loves." I sought him, but found him not. *Ps 88, 13-14, 18* But I, O Lord, cry to thee; in the morning my prayer comes before thee. O Lord, why dost thou cast me off? Why dost thou hide thy face from me? Thou hast caused lover and friend to shun me.

COMMUNION: To make a prairie it takes a clover and one bee,—/One clover, and a bee,/And revery./The revery alone will do/If bees are few.*

December 11

FIORELLO LA GUARDIA

For eleven colorful years between 1934 and 1945 Fiorello La Guardia was the mayor of New York City. He was a stubby little man with a high-pitched voice who had been born in Greenwich Village of an Italian father and a Jewish mother on Dec. 11, 1882. La Guardia first astonished New Yorkers in 1916 when, as a liberal Republican, he defeated the Tammany Hall candidate in a race for Congress. He proved himself to be such a good fighter that eventually all the parties supported him, and he was elected mayor on a fusion ticket. He improved city services, sided with the unions, and fought corruption and political bossism.

PETITION: Save us, your elected people, God; but just as much, save the city that we live in. Who can even think of paradise while surrounded by litter, noise, and fear? Peddlers hawk knickknacks in your temple; our votes and even our voices have been stolen. Come, invade these precincts. Hang a star above our roofs where we dumb oxen, we poor asses wait in darkness.

*"To make a prairie it takes a clover and one bee" by Emily Dickinson.

COMMUNION: *Is 26, 1-2* "We have a strong city; he sets up salvation as walls and bulwarks. Open the gates, that the righteous nation which keeps faith may enter in."

December 12

COLIN KELLY

On Dec. 12, 1941 Capt. Colin P. Kelly Jr., piloting a B-17 Flying Fortress from Clark Field, Luzon, dropped three bombs on what appeared to be a warship, later claimed to be the Japanese battleship *Haruna*. Witnesses said the target disappeared in smoke. Enroute to its base, the B-17 was shot down and Kelly was killed. Posthumously awarded a D.S.C., he was praised and wept over as the first American hero of World War II. Later records show he missed the ship, if indeed he ever saw one.

PROCESSIONAL: Off we go into the wild blue yonder,/Climbing high, into the sun. *Is 29, 5-7* And in an instant, suddenly, you will be visited by the Lord of hosts with thunder and with earthquake and with great noise, with whirlwind and tempest, and the flame of a devouring fire. And the multitude of all the nations that fight against Ariel . . . shall be like a dream, a vision of the night.

OFFERTORY: It is not sacrifice we shrink from, God, nor the possibility of death, but the fear that, when forced to spend ourselves, we will do so frivolously. All our gifts are made in darkness, and we stand mute, waiting for a signal of acceptance.

December 13

SAMUEL GOMPERS

Samuel Gompers was born in London in 1850. Emigrating to New York, he rose to become a leading member of the Cigarmakers' International Union. In 1886 he became president of the American Federation of Labor, and for the next 38 years until his death he was the single most powerful figure in the American labor movement, leading it finally to a place of respectability and influence. Generally conservative, Gompers opposed all forms of socialism and promoted craft unions at the expense of industrial unions. He died on Dec. 13, 1924.

COMMUNION: *Deut 24, 14-15* "You shall not oppress a hired servant who is poor and needy . . . you shall give him his hire on the day he earns it, before the sun goes down (for he is poor, and sets his heart upon it); lest he cry against you to the Lord, and it be sin in you."

RECESSIONAL: Strengthened by the union we find at your table, we your people, God, are ever more determined to see the good things of this world apportioned equally. You have fed us with your being; henceforth we will not be content with scraps from the banquet of life.

December 14

WALTER LIPPMANN

Walter Lippmann, the most prestigious political journalist of his day, perhaps of his century, was the only child of a comfortable German-Jewish New York family. The well-ordered, intellectual atmosphere of his youth was carried into his profession, as for 60 years he commented on wars, economic depression, and political crises with Olympian detachment. Presidents and dictators listened to his words, and weighed them. Lippmann stood as a great defender of Western democracy. While he lived long enough to be greatly honored, he also lived to see the world of his youth destroyed and the light of democracy flicker and fade in many nations. He died on Dec. 14, 1974.

PROCESSIONAL: *Ex 19, 10-11* "Go to the people and consecrate them today and tomorrow, and let them wash their garments, and be ready by the third day; for on the third day the Lord will come down upon Mount Sinai in the sight of all the people. *Ps 105, 21-22* He made him lord of his house and ruler of all his possessions, to instruct his princes at his pleasure, and to teach his elders wisdom.

PETITION: Protect your nation in uncertain times, Lord God. Shelter your people in their years of crises so that they will not be struck and scattered. Their habits may change, their rulers may change, even the shape of their lives may change. But keep your people intact. Renew that spirit that first brought them together that they may persevere from generation to generation.

December 15

SITTING BULL

Sitting Bull was a leader of the Dakota Sioux during the Indian Wars of the 1860s and 1870s, although in truth he was more of a medicine man than a fighting chief. He participated in the defeat of Custer in 1876 and subsequently fled to Canada. Making peace with the whites, he toured with Buffalo Bill's Wild West Show for several years before retiring to a reservation. On Dec. 15, 1890 a group of soldiers attempted to arrest him. His followers resisted, and in the melee Sitting Bull was shot dead.

OFFERTORY: O our Mother the Earth, O our Father the Sky,/Your children are we, with tired backs/We bring you gifts you love./Then weave for us a garment of brightness;/May the warp by the white light of morning,/May the weft be the red light of evening,/May the fringes be the falling rain,/May the border be the standing rainbow./Thus weave for us a garment of brightness,/That we may walk fittingly where birds sing,/That we may walk fittingly where grass is green,/O our Mother the Earth, O our Father the Sky.*

December 16

SAMUEL ADAMS

Sam Adams was probably the one true rabble-rouser of the American revolution. A distant cousin of the aristocratic Adamses of Quincy, Sam deliberately affected unkempt manners and dress to ingratiate himself with the working classes of colonial Boston. It was Adams who masterminded the Boston Tea Party on Dec. 16, 1773, Adams who first voiced the need for a Continental Congress, and Adams whose presence with John Hancock in Lexington drew British troops into a fatal encounter that led to armed warfare. After the war, with nothing to agitate against, Adams slipped into obscurity. He died in 1803.

PETITION: No more will we endure these insults, God! We've had enough! If it was your idea that we be treated like children this way, you can find yourself another people! On the other hand, if our old docility secretly displeased you, if our new-found courage makes you proud—well then, we implore you, be our brother still. And our cause.

COMMUNION: *Neh 2, 19-20* They derided us and despised us and said, "What is this thing that you are doing? Are you rebelling against the king?" Then I replied to them, "The God of heaven will make us prosper, and we his servants will arise and build."

*"Song of the Sky Loom" (Tewa Indians).

December 17

WILBUR AND ORVILLE WRIGHT

On the 17th of December in 1903 a spidery contraption of struts and fabric, powered by a 12-horsepower motor, lifted from a wooden track laid upon the sand at Kitty Hawk, N.C. It was mankind's first powered flight, and while it was hardly noticed at the time, it eventually made heroes of the reticent young brothers who owned a bicycle repair shop in Dayton, O. Wilbur Wright, the older brother who piloted that first flight, died in 1912; Orville died in 1948.

OFFERTORY: From the hands of your sons Wilbur and Orville we received the gift of flight. But we took their gift and armed it with guns and bombs and napalm and used it against our brothers. Now, Father, we lay a gift of bread and wine before your throne of justice. Use it as you will, but not for our destruction, we beg you. From your inaccessible height look down on us with mercy.

COMMUNION: *Ps 104, 1, 3-4* Lord my God, thou art very great! . . . who makest the clouds thy chariot, who ridest on the wings of the wind, who makest the winds thy messengers, fire and flame thy ministers.

December 18

ISAAC HECKER

Isaac Hecker was a visionary, a mystic who sought to reconcile opposites. Fleeing from the confines of bourgeois life in New York City where he was born Dec. 18, 1819, he sat at the feet of Emerson and Thoreau before deciding that the Roman Church and its priesthood had a clearer call for him. Once in the church Hecker was attacked for his American spirit, just as he was derided outside for his allegiance to Rome. For 40 years until his death in 1888 he carried on a prodigious work of public relations on both fronts, writing, speaking, advising bishops, founding a native community of priests. Some said he was naive, but Hecker had a way of making naïveté a weapon rather than a weakness. Most visionaries do.

PROCESSIONAL: *Jud 16, 14* Let all thy creatures serve thee, for thou didst speak, and they were made. Thou didst send forth thy Spirit, and it formed them. *Ps 89, 19-20* Of old thou didst speak in a vision to thy faithful one, and say: "I have set the crown upon one who is mighty, I have exalted one chosen from the people. I have found David, my servant; with my holy oil I have anointed him."

RECESSIONAL: No utopia can satisfy my soul. No make-believe communion. From here the way leads into darkness, to the mountain, and to
death. On that day the gates of the garden will be opened, and there at last
will I enjoy the vision of the fruitland and the brook.

December 19

HENRY CLAY FRICK

Henry Clay Frick's manner was as hard as his name. He was an ironfisted
man, cold and unbending. Frick was born Dec. 19, 1849 in the coal region
of Pennsylvania. Smart and aggressive, he first became the coal czar; then
he was operating boss for Andrew Carnegie at U.S. Steel. During the
Homestead strike in 1892 he got armed detectives to battle with the
strikers, convinced the authorities to proclaim martial law, and then got
scabs to run the plants. When it came to ruthlessness he had no match.
When Frick died his will bequeathed a park for the people of Pittsburgh
and an art museum for the people of New York. His relatives wondered
why the people weren't more grateful.

PETITION: Put away your thundering, Lord God, and quit your pushing!
There's a little bit of Frick in you at times! We won't be driven to salvation, so lead us there instead. And if encounter is your wish, then let it be
communion and not a confrontation.

COMMUNION: *Ps 147, 17-18* He casts forth his ice like morsels; who can
stand before his cold? He sends forth his word, and melts them; he makes
his wind blow, and the waters flow.

December 20

NORMAN THOMAS

There was something faintly ridiculous about Norman Thomas—all those
times running for President on the Socialist ticket and, of course, always
losing. Yet no one laughed. The truth is, everyone liked him—no, admired
him. He was a total gentleman, firmly wed to his convictions, and, if
called to account, a brilliant speaker and a formidable debater. Ohio
born, he had been a Presbyterian minister working among the poor before
he turned to politics. When he died on Dec. 20, 1968 his achievements
were manifest: leader of the Socialist party, a founder of the American
Civil Liberties Union, the moving force behind such ideas as minimum

218

wage, the five-day week, and low-cost housing. Whatever he was, he was not ridiculous, or a failure.

PROCESSIONAL: *Job 29, 14-16* I put on righteousness, and it clothed me; my justice was like a robe and a turban. I was eyes to the blind, and feet to the lame. I was a father to the poor, and I searched out the cause of him whom I did not know. *Mt 5, 6* "Blessed are those who hunger and thirst for righteousness, for they shall be satisfied."

COMMUNION: You shall be food for those who are forgotten; your presence shall nourish the oppressed.

December 21

F. SCOTT FITZGERALD

F. Scott Fitzgerald grew up in St. Paul, Minn. from whence his middle-class parents managed to send him to an eastern boarding school and Princeton. That sense of being in the social elite but not of it dominated his life and his art—the five novels and 150 short stories that memorialized the Roaring Twenties and the pitiful crash that followed. Fitzgerald's life paralleled the age. It was marked by brilliance, drunkeness, nervous collapse, his wife's madness, and failure. Throughout it all, said John Cheever, Fitzgerald's writing preserved an "angelic austerity of spirit" that succeeded in making his era live for all time. Fitzgerald died of a heart attack on Dec. 21, 1940.

PETITION: Look with mercy on your servant Scott, O Lord, whose life was one-way downhill, whose art was one-way up. The first course was sheer momentum, no blame in that; the other sheer struggle. Measure men, as meteors, not by the power that propels them, but by the light they leave behind.

RECESSIONAL: *Eccles 9, 7-9* Go, eat your bread with enjoyment, and drink your wine with a merry heart; for God has already approved what you do. Let your garments be always white; let not oil be lacking on your head. Enjoy life with the wife whom you love, all the days of your vain life which he has given you under the sun, because that is your portion in life . . .

December 22

MOTHER CABRINI

Francesca Cabrini was the last of 13 children born to middle-class parents in Lombardy, Italy around 1850. An honor student, Francesca wished to enter a convent but was refused because of frail health. So she started her own convent. Sent to the United States in 1889, she began a monumental service to Italian immigrants and other urban poor, establishing schools, orphanages, and hospitals in the U.S., South America, and Europe. Altogether she crossed the ocean 30 times and founded 67 houses staffed by 1500 sisters. Mother Cabrini died in Chicago on Dec. 22, 1917 of malaria. In 1946 she became the first American citizen to be canonized a saint.

PROCESSIONAL: *Is 25, 4* Thou hast been a stronghold to the poor, a stronghold to the needy in his distress, a shelter from the storm and a shade from the heat. *Ps 73, 25-26* Whom have I in heaven but thee? And there is nothing upon earth that I desire besides thee. My flesh and my heart may fail, but God is the strength of my heart and my portion for ever.

COMMUNION: *Mt 11, 28-29* "Come to me, all who labor and are heavy laden, and I will give you rest. Take my yoke upon you, and learn from me; for I am gentle and lowly in heart, and you will find rest for your souls."

December 23

JOSEPH SMITH

Joseph Smith was born in Vermont on Dec. 23, 1805 and grew up near Palmyra, N.Y. When he was 22 he said he discovered some golden plates inscribed in a strange language as a vision had promised he would. Translated they became *The Book of Mormon*, and Smith became the first leader of the Church of Jesus Christ of the Latter Day Saints. Attracting a band of followers, he taught them and protected them through many trials and persecutions until 1844 when a mob of anti-Mormon bigots in Carthage, Ill. pulled him from a jail and killed him.

OFFERTORY: An offering of dreams: We give you a world where people work for the common good, a world where sharing is the norm, where self-control is not just for computors. Take these visions, Father; see what you can do with them, since we cannot. We, your earthbound people, dabble in what might be, while you, transcendent Lord, deal with what is.

RECESSIONAL: *Ex 34, 27* And the Lord said to Moses, "Write these words; in accordance with these words I have made a covenant with you and with Israel."

December 24

CLEMENT CLARK MOORE

Clement Clark Moore was a scholar of classics in New York City. On the afternoon of Dec. 24, 1822, while shopping for his family's Christmas turkey, he composed a poem in his head that he later wrote down and gave as a present to his children. It began, " 'Twas the night before Christmas, when all through the house not a creature was stirring, not even a mouse . . ." The poem was later published in a newspaper and became immensely popular, causing such embarrassment to Moore that for 15 years he denied he had written it.

PROCESSIONAL: With visions in our heads we await your coming, O Lord. The city made dumb by snow will awake to the sound of bells. *Response* In thy dark streets shineth the everlasting light. The hopes and fears of all the years are met in thee tonight.

COMMUNION: *Ex 16, 6-7* "At evening you shall know that it was the Lord who brought you out of the land of Egypt, and in the morning you shall see the glory of the Lord."

December 25

CLARA BARTON

Clarissa Harlowe Barton was born on Christmas Day 1821 in Oxford, Mass. Even as a youth she had her own mind, was something of a tomboy and an achiever. She was a teacher at age 15, and founded her own school. The Civil War found her employed at the U.S. Patent Office where she secured medicine and supplies for soldiers. Unsatisfied with this, she was soon taking medicine onto the battlefield and ministering to the wounded. After the war she lobbied for U.S. participation in the Geneva Convention which created the International Red Cross. When in 1882 the American Red Cross was formally established, Clara Barton was its first president, and she served in that capacity 30 years until her death in 1912.

PROCESSIONAL: *Is 61, 1* The Spirit of the Lord God is upon me, because the Lord has annointed me to bring good tidings to the afflicted; he has sent me to bind up the brokenhearted, to proclaim liberty to the captives, and the opening of the prison to those who are bound. *Ps 61, 8* So will I ever sing praises to thy name, as I pay my vows day after day.

RECESSIONAL: The poor of the earth cry out, and you have come to them.

The suffering and the sick cry out, and you have come to them. The helpless and the homeless cry out, and you have come to them. Your presence consoles them, and is their glory.

December 26

JACK BENNY

Jack Benny was once described as the world's finest comedian—a comedian being a person who says things funny, as opposed to a comic who says funny things. Benny took ordinary human traits and made them funny by enlarging them to ridiculous proportions. Vanity and stinginess were his special targets. When a make-believe mugger once accosted him and demanded "your money or your life," Benny replied: "I'm thinking it over." Benny grew up in Waukegan, Ill., skipping school to play his violin in a vaudeville theater. For more than 40 years he appeared on radio and television as a hot-tempered skinflint. In truth he was shy, generous, and loved by his friends. Jack Benny died on Dec. 26, 1974.

PETITION: Don't tear away our disguises, God. Don't strip us of those small pretensions, those vanities, those little lies that fool no one but which we must keep nonetheless. You see, we must maintain a front. People expect it of us, and we need it for defensive reasons. You in your wisdom, God, will not deny us these consolations. In heaven all your people will be 39.

COMMUNION: *Prov 22, 1-2* A good name is to be chosen rather than great riches, and favor is better than silver or gold. The rich and the poor meet together; the Lord is the maker of them all.

December 27

JEROME KERN

On this day in 1927 a new musical opened on Broadway. It was called *Show Boat*, and it was recognized almost immediately as a classic of the American stage, heaping laurels on its already-famous composer, Jerome Kern. In all Kern wrote music for 26 stage plays and numerous other revues and motion pictures. Songs such as *Smoke Gets In Your Eyes*, *The Way You Look Tonight*, *Ol' Man River* and *All The Things You Are* brought a new level of sophistication to popular music and strongly influenced followers like Gershwin and Richard Rodgers. Kern, an affable,

222

pixieish man, was born in New York City in 1885 and died there in 1945.

PROCESSIONAL: They asked me how I knew/My true love was true,/I of course replied "Something here inside/Cannot be denied."* *Ps 21, 2-4* Thou hast given him his heart's desire, and hast not withheld the request of his lips. For thou dost meet him with goodly blessings; thou dost set a crown of fine gold upon his head. He asked life of thee; thou gavest it to him, length of days for ever and ever.

December 28

WOODROW WILSON

Woodrow Wilson will forever be the symbol of American strength and American innocence. He was a man of absolute principle. Much admired and much scorned, he was eventually broken by his refusal to compromise issues he believed to be just. As president of Princeton, governor of New Jersey, and President of the United States, Wilson held himself above ordinary politicians and their methods. But at Versailles and in the U.S. Senate the politicians had their revenge, and the man who fought "to make the world safe for democracy" became democracy's victim. Wilson was born on this day in 1856; he died in 1924.

PROCESSIONAL: *Wis 8, 14-15* I shall govern peoples, and nations will be subject to me; dread monarchs will be afraid of me when they hear of me; among the people I shall show myself capable, and courageous in war. *Ps 55, 16, 18* But I call upon God; and the Lord will save me. He will deliver my soul in safety from the battle that I wage; for many are arrayed against me.

PETITION: Bestow upon us, Lord God, something more than moral rectitude. Give us craftiness as well, and flexibility, and humor. Give us all those human qualities which in their absence make rectitude seem like mere rigidity. And to your servant Woodrow, give him peace at last.

December 29

CHARLES GOODYEAR

Charles Goodyear was born Dec. 29, 1800 in New Haven, Conn. He died

*"Smoke Gets In Your Eyes" from *Roberta*, music by Jerome Kern and lyrics by Otto Harbach, ©1933 by T.B. Harms Co. Copyright renewed. Reprinted by permission.

in 1860, long before the automobile made his name known around the world. In 1839 by accident he dropped some India rubber mixed with sulphur on his stove and thereby discovered the process of vulcanization which keeps rubber firm at high temperatures. The discovery made possible the development of the pneumatic tire and other rubber products for industrial and commercial use. Goodyear realized little from his discovery; he spent the rest of his life defending patents for his process, and he died leaving his family $200,000 in debt.

OFFERTORY: Who will really know, Lord God, whether these gifts will be accepted, whether you will smile or whether you will turn away? We assume your pleasure, as we do your presence, on faith. Time alone will prove the truth of our inventions and our prayers. Only our children, looking back, will be able to say that you were with your people on this day, or you were not.

COMMUNION: *Ex 13, 21-22* And the Lord went before them by day in a pillar of cloud to lead them along the way, and by night in a pillar of fire to give them light, that they might travel by day and by night; the pillar of cloud by day and the pilar of fire by night did not depart from before the people.

December 30

AL SMITH

Al Smith was too poor to be called lace-curtain Irish. He was born in the shadow of the Brooklyn Bridge on Dec. 30, 1873, his father a junkman who died when Al was a boy. He described himself later as a graduate of the Fulton Fish Market. He started as a ward heeler for Tammany Hall, served in the state assembly, and was elected governor in 1922. Reformers feared the worst, but Smith served four terms with great distinction, and in 1928 he received the Democratic party's nomination for U.S. President. His Catholicism and his support of prohibition repeal cost him the election, won by Herbert Hoover in a landslide. Smith died in 1944.

PETITION: Receive Al Smith your servant, God, along with all the rest of those we turned away because they did not meet our preconceptions. It seems your kingdom is so much easier to gain entrance to than ours.

RECESSIONAL: *2 Cor 4, 8-9* We are afflicted in every way, but not crushed; perplexed, but not driven to despair; persecuted, but not forsaken; struck down, but not destroyed.

December 31

ROBERTO CLEMENTE

There were some ballplayers as good as Roberto Clemente. Not many, but some. A few surpassed his .318 lifetime batting average, his 3000 career base hits, his 12 All-Star selections. A few players could match his rifle arm, a few his wicked batting stroke. But in the eyes of his native Puerto Ricans Clemente was something more: he was a proud and compassionate hero who brought playgrounds to the children and glory to their parents. On Dec. 31, 1972 Clemente chartered a cargo plane to carry relief supplies to earthquake-devastated Nicaragua. The plane crashed into the sea, and Roberto Clemente was killed.

OFFERTORY: Our storehouse of gifts is not inexhaustible, O Lord. Nor is our youth, our strength, and our quickness. Over the years of our days we have clung to them, hoarded them. But in the end they are all run out, and you sequester what is left our bodies and ourselves. (Surely you remember how it ends.) Still in all, there is faith in this last giving: every force demands a counter-force, every going-away impells a coming-back, and every end foreshadows a beginning.

COMMUNION: *Jn 15, 13* Greater love has no man than this, that a man lay down his life for his friends.

INDEX

A

B

Bradstreet, Anne	September 16
Brady, Matthew	January 15
Brandeis, Louis D.	November 13
Brown, John	December 2
Bryan, William Jennings	March 19
Bryant, William Cullen	November 3
Bunche, Ralph	August 7
Burbank, Luther	March 7
Burnham, Daniel	September 4
Burr, Aaron	September 1
Byrd, Richard E.	March 11

C

Cabrini, Frances Xavier	December 22
Cahan, Abraham	August 31
Calhoun, John C.	March 18
Capone, Al	January 25
Carnegie, Andrew	August 11
Carrel, Alexis	June 28
Carroll, John	January 8
Carson, Kit	May 23
Carson, Rachel	April 14
Cather, Willa	April 24
Catlin, George	July 26
Chambers, Whittaker	April 1
Choate, Rufus	October 1
Clark, George Rogers	February 24
Clay, Henry	June 29
Clemente, Roberto	December 31
Clinton, DeWitt	October 26
Cobb, Ty	July 17
Cody, "Buffalo Bill"	February 26
Cohan, George M.	July 3
Columbus, Christopher	October 12
Colt, Samuel	July 19
Coolidge, Calvin	January 5
Cooper, Gary	May 7
Cooper, James Fenimore	September 15
Coxey, Jacob	April 16
Crane, Stephen	November 1
Crockett, Davy	August 17
Cummings, E.E.	October 14
Curley, James M.	November 12
Currier, Nathaniel	November 20
Custer, George A.	June 25

D

Darrow, Clarence	March 13
Davis, Jefferson	June 3
Debs, Eugene V.	November 5
Decatur, Stephen	February 16
De Forest, Lee	June 30
deMille, Cecil B.	August 12
Dewey, George	May 1
Dewey, John	October 20
Dickenson, Emily	December 10
Dillinger, John	July 22
Disney, Walt	December 5
Dole, Sanford	July 7
Dooley, Tom	January 18
Douglas, Stephen A.	April 23
Douglass, Frederick	February 20
Downing, Andrew J.	July 28
DuBois, W.E.B.	February 23
Duke, James B.	October 10
Dulles, John Foster	February 25
Duncan, Isadora	September 14
Dunne, Finley Peter	July 10
DuPont de Nemours, E.I.	June 24

E

Eakins, Thomas	July 25
Earhart, Amelia	July 2
Eastman, George	March 14
Eddy, Mary Baker	July 16
Edison, Thomas A.	February 11
Edwards, Jonathan	March 22
Eisenhower, Dwight D.	June 6
Eliot, Charles W.	March 20
Ellington, Duke	April 29
Emerson, Ralph Waldo	May 25
Ericsson, John	March 9

F

Fall, Albert B.	November 26
Farmer, Fannie	March 23
Faulkner, William	September 25

Fermi, Enrico	August 6
Field, Marshall	January 16
Fitzgerald, F. Scott	December 21
Ford, Henry	July 30
Foster, Stephen	January 13
Franklin, Benjamin	January 17
Frémont, John C.	July 13
Freneau, Philip	January 2
French, Daniel Chester	April 20
Frick, Henry Clay	December 19
Frost, Robert	January 29
Fulton, Robert	November 14

G

Garfield, James A.	September 19
Garrison, William Lloyd	October 21
Garvey, Marcus	June 10
George, Henry	September 2
Geronimo	February 17
Gershwin, George	September 26
Gibbons, James	July 23
Goddard, Robert H.	October 5
Goethals, George Washington	August 15
Gompers, Samuel	December 13
Goodyear, Charles	December 29
Gould, Jay	September 24
Grant, Ulysses S.	April 27
Greeley, Horace	February 3
Grey, Zane	October 23
Griffith, D.W.	January 22
Guthrie, Woody	July 14

H

Hale, Nathan	September 22
Halsey, William F.	August 16
Hamilton, Alexander	July 12
Hancock, John	January 23
Handy, W.C.	November 16
Harriman, Edward H.	September 9
Harte, Bret	May 5
Hawthorne, Nathaniel	July 4
Haywood, Bill	February 4

Hearst, William Randolph	August 14
Hecker, Isaac	December 18
Hemingway, Ernest	July 21
Henry, O.	September 11
Henry, Patrick	May 29
Holland, John Philip	February 29
Holley, Alexander	July 20
Holliday, Billie	April 7
Holmes, Oliver Wendell	March 6
Homer, Winslow	September 29
Hoover, Herbert	August 10
Hoover, J. Edgar	May 3
Hopper, Edward	May 15
Houdini, Harry	October 31
Houston, Sam	March 2
Howe, Julia Ward	October 17
Hughes, Charles Evans	April 11
Hughes, Langston	May 22
Hull, Cordell	October 2
Hutchinson, Anne	November 17

I

Irving, Washington	November 28
Ives, Charles	May 19

J

Jackson, Andrew	March 15
Jackson, "Stonewall"	January 21
James, Jesse	September 5
James, William	August 26
Jay, John	May 17
Jefferson, Thomas	April 13
Jogues, Isaac	January 10
Johnson, Jack	March 31
Johnson, Lyndon B.	August 27
Jolson, Al	May 26
Jones, Bobby	March 17
Jones, John Paul	September 28
Joseph, Chief	September 21

K

Kauffman, George S	June 2
Keller, Helen	June 27
Kelly, Colin	December 12
Kennedy, John F.	November 22
Kennedy, Robert F.	June 5
Kern, Jerome	December 27
Key, Francis Scott	January 11
King, Martin Luther	April 4

L

La Follette, Robert M.	June 18
La Guardia, Fiorello	December 11
Langley, Samuel P.	August 22
Lawrence, Ernest O.	August 8
Lawrence, James	June 4
Lazarus, Emma	October 28
Leadbelly	December 6
Lee, Robert E.	January 19
Lewis, Meriwether	August 18
Lewis, Sinclair	February 7
Lincoln, Abraham	February 12
Lindbergh, Charles	May 20
Lindsay, Vachel	November 10
Lippmann, Walter	December 14
Lombardi, Vince	June 11
London, Jack	January 12
Long, Huey	August 30
Longfellow, Henry Wadsworth	February 27
Lowell, Amy	February 9
Luce, Henry	February 28

M

MacArthur, Douglas	January 26
Mack, Connie	February 8
Madison, James	March 16
Mahan, Alfred T.	December 1
Malcolm X	February 21
Mann, Horace	August 2
Marquette, Jacques	May 18
Marshall, George C.	October 16

Marshall, John	January 20
Masters, Edgar Lee	August 23
Mather, Cotton	February 13
Maury, Matthew	February 1
McCarthy, Joseph	May 2
McCormack, Cyrus	May 13
McGuffey, William	May 4
McKay, Donald	September 20
McKim, Charles F.	August 24
McPherson, Aimee Semple	October 9
Mellon, Andrew	March 24
Melville, Herman	August 1
Mencken, H.L.	September 12
Merganthaler, Ottmar	May 11
Merton, Thomas	January 31
Millay, Edna St. Vincent	October 19
Miller, Glen	March 1
Mitchell, Billy	February 19
Monroe, James	April 28
Monroe, Marilyn	August 5
Moore, Clement Clark	December 24
Moore, Marianne	November 15
Morgan, J.P.	April 17
Morphy, Paul	June 22
Morse, Samuel F.B.	April 2
Morton, William	August 9
Mott, Lucretia	January 3
Muir, John	April 21
Murrow, Edward R.	April 25

N

Nast, Thomas	September 27
Nation, Carry	June 9
Neibuhr, Reinhold	June 21
Norris, Frank	October 25

O

Oakley, Annie	August 13
Ochs, Adolf S.	September 18
Olmsted, Frederick Law	August 28
O'Neill, Eugene	November 27
Oppenheimer, J. Robert	April 22
Oswald, Lee Harvey	October 18

P

Paine, Thomas	June 8
Parker, Charlie	August 29
Parkman, Francis	November 8
Parrington, Vernon L.	June 16
Parsons, Louella	December 9
Patton, George S.	November 11
Peary, Robert E.	April 6
Penn, William	June 23
Perry, Oliver Hazard	September 10
Pershing, John J.	July 15
Philip, "King"	June 20
Pinkerton, Allan	August 25
Poe, Edgar Allan	October 7
Polk, James K.	June 15
Pollack, Jackson	January 28
Porter, Cole	October 15
Pulaski, Casimir	October 11
Pulitzer, Joseph	October 29
Pyle, Ernie	April 18

Q

R

Ransom, John Crowe	April 30
Reed, Thomas B.	December 7
Reed, Walter	September 13
Remington, Frederic	October 4
Reuther, Walter	May 9
Revere, Paul	January 1
Rockefeller, John D.	July 8
Rockne, Knute	March 4
Roebling, John and Washington	May 24
Rogers, Will	November 4
Romberg, Sigmund	November 9
Roosevelt, Eleanor	November 7
Roosevelt, Franklin Delano	April 12
Roosevelt, Theodore	October 27
Rosenberg, Julius and Ethel	June 19
Ross, Betsy	January 30
Rush, Benjamin	April 19
Russell, Lillian	December 4
Ruth, Babe	February 6

S

Sacco and Vanzetti	April 15
Saint-Gaudens, Augustus	August 3
Sandburg, Carl	January 6
Sanger, Margaret	September 6
Scott, Winfield	June 13
Serra, Junípero	November 24
Seton, Elizabeth	January 4
Sherman, William Tecumseh	February 14
Sinclair, Upton	November 25
Sitting Bull	December 15
Smith, Al	December 30
Smith, Joseph	December 23
Sousa, John Philip	November 6
Stein, Gertrude	July 27
Stevenson, Adlai	February 5
Stowe, Harriet Beecher	July 1
Stuart, Gilbert	December 3
Stuart, J.E.B.	May 12
Stuyvesant, Peter	September 8
Sullivan, Ed	October 13
Sullivan, John L.	February 2
Sullivan, Louis	September 3
Sunday, Billy	November 19
Sutter, John	January 24

T

Taft, Robert A.	July 31
Taft, William Howard	March 8
Tarkington, Booth	July 29
Tesla, Nikola	January 7
Thomas, Norman	December 20
Thoreau, Henry David	May 6
Thorpe, Jim	March 28
Tilden, Bill	February 10
Tillich, Paul	August 20
Truman, Harry S	May 8
Tubman, Harriet	March 10
Turner, Nat	August 21
Twain, Mark	November 30
Tweed, "Boss"	April 3

U

Unknown Soldier   May 30

V

Van Buren, Martin   July 24
Vanderbilt, Cornelius   May 27

W

Wallace, Henry A.   November 18
Warren, Earl   July 9
Warren, Joseph   June 17
Washington, Booker T.   April 5
Washington, George   February 22
Webster, Daniel   October 24
Webster, Noah   May 28
Westinghouse, George   October 6
Whitman, Walt   May 31
Whitney, Eli   December 8
Whittier, John Greenleaf   September 7
Williams, Roger   March 30
Willkie, Wendell   February 18
Wilson, Woodrow   December 28
Wise, Isaac Meyer   March 26
Wolfe, Thomas   October 3
Woodhull, Victoria   September 23
Woolworth, F.W.   April 8
Wright, Frank Lloyd   April 9
Wright, Wilbur and Orville   December 17
Wrigley, William   September 30

Y

York, Alvin C.   October 8
Young, Brigham   June 1

Z

Zaharias, Babe Didrickson   June 26
Zenger, Peter   August 4
Ziegfeld, Flo   March 21